Tourism research

Issues in Tourism series

Edited by Brian Goodall, *University of Reading* and Gregory Ashworth, *University of Groningen*, The Netherlands. The Advisory Board includes K.H. Din, *University of Kedangsaan*, Malaysia; C.R. Goeldner, *University of Colorado*, USA; J. Jafari, *University of Wisconsin*, USA; and D.G. Pearce, *University of Canterbury*, New Zealand

The growing significance of tourism as an economic activity is reflected in the increased recognition it has been given at national and local levels. There has been a rapid development of specialist educational and training facilities for academics and professionals, including wide-spread research activity, and the discipline could now be said to have 'come of age'. The books in this series provide rigorous, focused discussions of key topics in current international debates on tourism. They tackle the social, economic and environmental consequences of the rapid developments, taking account of what has happened so far and looking ahead to future prospects. The series caters for all those wanting to understand what is happening at the forefront of the field and how it will filter through to general tourism practice.

Forthcoming titles in the series

Tourism and Heritage Attractions
Richard Prentice

The Economics of Tourism
Thea Sinclair and Mike Stabler

Tourism for the Environment
Colin Hunter and Howard Green

Tourism research

Critiques and challenges

Edited by
Douglas G. Pearce
and Richard W. Butler

London and New York
in Association with the International Academy for the
Study of Tourism

First published in 1993
by Routledge
11 New Fetter Lane, London EC4P 4EE

Simultaneously published in the USA and Canada
by Routledge
a division of Routledge, Chapman and Hall Inc.
29 West 35th Street, New York, NY 10001

Typeset in Baskerville by LaserScript Limited, Mitcham, Surrey
Printed and bound in Great Britain by
Biddles Ltd, Guildford and King's Lynn

British Library Cataloguing in Publication Data
A catalogue record for this book is available from the British Library.

ISBN 0–415–08319–2
Library of Congress Cataloging in Publication Data has been applied for.

Contents

Plates

Figures

Tables

Contributors

Richard Butler	Department of Geography, University of Western Ontario, London, Ontario
Erik Cohen	Department of Sociology and Anthropology, The Hebrew University of Jerusalem, Jerusalem
Graham Dann	Department of Government and Sociology, University of the West Indies, Bridgetown, Barbados
Donald Hawkins	International Institute of Tourism Studies, The George Washington University, Washington, DC
Marie-Françoise Lanfant	Unité de Recherche en Sociologie du Tourisme International, Centre National de la Recherche Scientifique, Paris
Douglas Pearce	Department of Geography, University of Canterbury, Christchurch, New Zealand
Philip Pearce	Department of Tourism, James Cook University of North Queensland, Townsville
John Pigram	Department of Geography and Planning, University of New England, Armidale, New South Wales
Krzysztof Przeclawski	University of Warsaw, Warsaw
Brent Ritchie	World Tourism Education and Research Centre, University of Calgary, Calgary

Chapter 1

Introduction

Douglas G. Pearce

Introductory chapters or review papers dealing with tourism frequently allude to its comparative recency as a field of study. Pioneer papers can be traced to the 1930s or even earlier but it has only been since the late 1960s that a significant and substantial body of literature on tourism has started to emerge. A lot of this literature is seen to be fragmented and lacking a firm sense of direction. Much tourism research has been methodologically unsophisticated and not supported by a strong theoretical base (Dann, Nash and Pearce 1988). Such characteristics are explained, if not excused, by the infancy of the field but this temporal dimension alone is an inadequate explanation. A related and equally important factor has been the often uncritical manner in which much tourism research has been undertaken. The emphasis has been on the results with very little attention being paid to the way in which the research has been carried out. Review papers, both disciplinary and thematic, frequently outline what we know rather than how we came to know it. Concepts and techniques are often adopted by researchers from their parent disciplines and applied with little or no modification or explicit rationale to tourism problems. The tourism literature has never been rent by widespread ongoing debates about theoretical or methodological issues. The rejoinder sections of the mainstream tourism journals are scarcely hotbeds of critical dialogue and dissent – at best the occasional article will move someone to comment critically on it, the original author will respond and there the matter is left to rest.

Certainly there are important exceptions to these general observations, particularly in some technical areas. There has never been universal agreement on the definition of the term tourism, for example (see Przeclawski in Chapter 2). Many of the limitations and deficiencies in the use of some international tourism statistics were recognized early on. The use and abuse of economic multipliers in assessing the impact of tourism stimulated debate and provoked a continuing series of technical discussions from quite an early stage (see Bryden and Faber 1971, Archer 1977). Other economic issues have also generated critical technical appraisals, such as calculating the balance of payments contributions of international tourism (see Gray 1970, Baretje 1982, White and Walker 1982) or estimating visitor expenditure (see Pearce 1981, Sheldon 1990). The continuing dialogue amongst anthropologists resulting from different theoretical perspectives on tourism (Nash 1981, 1984, Graburn 1983, Lett 1989) is a somewhat exceptional example of sustained disciplinary debate in this field.

All too often, however, concepts, techniques and broader methodologies have been employed with little or no discussion or justification for their use nor any appraisal of their limitations. This is not to say they have necessarily been used wrongly or inappropriately but simply that their use has been taken for granted or accepted uncritically. As Pearce notes in Chapter 3, for example, a comparative approach has been adopted by a number of tourism researchers without any explicit elaboration or reference to the wider issues debated elsewhere. In the absence of fuller and more open discussion and debate it is difficult to build solid foundations for tourism research.

Towards the end of the 1980s this situation appeared to be changing. Books devoted specifically to tourism research were published and methodological issues started to be addressed more systematically. Two important handbooks appeared: Ritchie and Goeldner's (1987) volume covered a wide range of applied research issues while Smith's (1989) set out a large number of analytical techniques in a step-by-step fashion. Pearce's (1987) geographical analysis of tourism incorporated an examination of conceptual, data and technical issues with wide-ranging empirical examples. Calls for a more critical appraisal of tourism research were made in the influential special issue of the *Annals of Tourism Research* (15, 1, 1988) on 'Methodological Issues in Tourism Research'. This included not only the excellent overview paper by Dann, Nash and Pearce (1988) which outlined general trends and issues but also critical state-of-the-art reviews of more specific themes. The launch of *Progress in Tourism Recreation and Hospitality Management* the following year added a useful forum for continuing critical review.

Recent individual papers also illustrate this trend and highlight some of the issues. Reid and Andereck undertook a systematic review of statistical analyses used in tourism research, arguing:

Periodic monitoring of statistical techniques used in research efforts allows appraisal of their contributions to a field and assessment of their value to practitioners . . . By examining the techniques used, one can gauge the methodological sophistication of current tourism research efforts and assess the popularity of various techniques employed.

(Reid and Andereck 1989: 21)

From their review of articles in three major tourism journals they concluded:

Much research either ignores or fails to clearly report useful descriptive statistics. Inclusion of relevant descriptive statistics often provides greater understanding of an article's salience and content for those uncomfortable with other statistical methods employed. In addition, the statistical tests used also need to be *clearly identified and justified*. For example, many readers may be aware that ANOVA is used, but others might profit by a brief description of the statistical method and *reasons why its use is appropriate in a particular context. A short technique description also forces researcher accountability and allows readers to evaluate the appropriateness of statistical tests used* [emphasis added].

(Reid and Andereck 1989: 24)

Weber (1991: 7) contends that 'The identification and the systemization of errors within the domain of tourism demand research . . . could make a positive contribution to the advancement of tourism research.' Her own approach combined a ten-year review of journal articles with a survey of tourism research institutions. Having identified common problems such as the reliability and availability of statistical data, Weber then focuses on problems and errors associated with the research process itself. Here she raises questions of the inappropriate definition of goals and variables as well as other more commonly identified problems with questionnaire design and survey implementation. Weber notes, however, that 'Aside from the sample errors, which can be partially detected and quantified, there is no direct and simple method of estimating the magnitude of other errors.'

Crouch (1991) addresses the question of the review process itself. After stressing the need for building a solid foundation through the integration and synthesis of a body of work as it develops, Crouch argues (p. 67): 'An approach is required which ensures that the best use is made of this research and that future research is founded on a reasonably complete understanding of the past research.' He then underlines the limitations of the traditional narrative review, particularly in dealing with a rapidly expanding field of study, and advocates the use of meta-analysis which involves a more structured and quantitative approach. These examples of an increasingly considered and critical approach to tourism research essentially reflect changes within the field of study. These changes have been driven in the main by academic researchers and testify to a growing maturity in the field of tourism research. At the same time, more critical appraisals of tourism research are resulting from external forces. In particular, the pressure of tightening budgets has led to calls for greater accountability of publicly-funded tourist organizations whose activities as a consequence have come under much closer scrutiny (Pearce, 1992). As organizations are asked to justify their expenditure on marketing campaigns or visitor servicing, the issue of the credibility of research results is coming to the fore, be it in conversion studies or the measurement of the economic impacts of visitor expenditure. In the United States, the Department of Commerce went so far as to convene a task force on accountability research in 1988 (Wynegar 1989). The results of the task force's work appeared in a series of succinct and timely articles in the *Journal of Travel Research* which emphasized marketing issues and provided a very useful and insightful review of economic impact studies (Davidson and Wiethaupt 1989, Burke and Lindblom 1989, Burke and Gitelson 1990, Siegel and Ziff-Levine 1990, Perdue and Pitegoff 1990, Fleming and Toepper 1990).

This volume derives primarily from the first trend, that towards an increasingly critical appraisal of tourism research by academic practitioners, but the issues raised also have practical and policy implications as the latter chapters in particular stress. The chapters of this book are revised and enlarged versions of papers originally presented at the second meeting of the International Academy for the Study of Tourism held in Calgary in July 1991.[1] The Academy was established in 1988 as a limited membership, multidisciplinary body 'to further the scholarly research and professional investigation of tourism, to encourage the application of the findings, and to advance the international diffusion and exchange of tourism knowledge'. At the Academy's first seminar in Zakopane in 1989, members addressed the topic of alternative tourism (Smith and Eadington, in press). In Calgary they explored the theme of 'Methodological and conceptual issues in tourism research'.

The chapters which follow highlight a number of important concerns, provide a series of comprehensive, international critiques from the viewpoint of several disciplines, and identify significant challenges confronting researchers and users of tourism research, both now and in the future. While varying in scope, scale and theme and reflecting the diverse disciplinary and geographical structure of the Academy's membership, these chapters are linked by the common purpose of developing a more thorough and critical approach to tourism research and its application and outlining directions which might be followed in the future. Several authors also draw attention to the research implications of the globalization of tourism issues and the need for appropriate institutional structures and frameworks to support tourism research.

Przeclawski (Chapter 2) addresses the issue of the need for an interdisciplinary approach to the study of tourism given its very complex nature but then takes this further by examining the influence which different philosophical backgrounds may have on research and the implications of this for fostering such an approach. Douglas Pearce (Chapter 3) considers the rationale of a particular method – the comparative approach – and its applications in tourism research before reviewing systematically the range of methodological questions which arise. This is followed by Cohen's detailed critique of touristic images (Chapter 4) in which further aspects of comparative research are raised along with other theoretical and methodological issues. Lanfant (Chapter 5) then traces from a personal perspective the development of the study of international tourism within her discipline – sociology – and outlines the challenges which research on that topic presents to sociologists. Subsequent chapters focus on more specific topics or themes. Dann (Chapter 6) draws attention to limitations in the use of two very common variables employed in tourism research – nationality and country of residence – and raises a number of previously neglected theoretical considerations. Philip Pearce (Chapter 7) outlines a blueprint for a theory of tourist motivation which he then uses to examine and evaluate specific theories in this important field. Butler (Chapter 8) then provides an in-depth critique of the assessment and monitoring of the impacts which the development of tourism generates, focusing in particular on methodological aspects of pre- and post-assessment techniques. The last three chapters in this volume are concerned with the research challenges presented in the field of tourism policy. In Chapter 9 Pigram's specific focus on bridging the policy implementation gap in rural tourism complements Hawkins' concern with more global policy issues. Hawkins (Chapter 10) describes the research process involved in the identification of nineteen major policy issues then raises a number of research questions associated with each of these, thereby demonstrating the continuing interaction between research and policy.

In the final chapter Ritchie develops a number of these global issues in the context of the different roles of research in tourism management and policy making and then proposes a Global Tourism Network as one means of implementing the research agenda he outlines.

A common theme running through these chapters is the need for tourism researchers to be more explicit in what they do. We should not take for granted the methods, concepts or data that we use but rather examine these critically, exploring, appraising, setting out and justifying underlying assumptions, theoretical considerations, technical factors and limitations in use. Building stronger foundations in tourism research requires more open discussion on these matters. In addition to stimulating further debate on the specific topics examined – for not all readers will agree on the points raised and conclusions drawn – it is hoped that these chapters, through the examples they provide, will also encourage others to explore similar issues in other related areas so as to advance tourism research. This is the general challenge arising from these critiques.

NOTE

1   Chapter 11 is an invited contribution from the Calgary meeting's host, Brent Ritchie, which complements and rounds out some of the issues and themes presented in earlier chapters.

ACKNOWLEDGEMENTS

The editors wish to acknowledge the support they have received from their respective departments during the editing of this volume. In particular, thanks go to Linda Harrison and Anna Moloney of the Geography Department, University of Canterbury, for typing the manuscript and also to Alastair Dyer for graphic assistance.

REFERENCES

Archer, B. H. (1977) *Tourism Multipliers: the State of the Art*, Bangor Occasional Papers No. 11, Bangor: University of Wales Press.
Baretje, R. (1982) 'Tourism's external account and the balance of payments', *Annals of Tourism Research* 9, 1: 57–67.

Bryden, J. M. and Faber, M. (1971) 'Multiplying the tourist multiplier', *Social and Economic Studies* 20, 1: 61–82.

Burke, J. F. and Gitelson, R. (1990) 'Conversion studies: assumptions, accuracy and abuse', *Journal of Travel Research* 28, 3: 46–51.

Burke, J. F. and Lindblom, L. A. (1989) 'Strategies for evaluating direct response tourism marketing', *Journal of Travel Research* 28, 2: 33–7.

Crouch, G. I. (1991) 'Building foundations in tourism research', in R. D. Bratton, F. M. Go and J. R. B. Ritchie (eds) *Conference Proceedings, New Horizons in Tourism and Hospitality Education, Training and Research*, Calgary: University of Calgary: 67–75.

Dann, G., Nash, D. and Pearce, P. (1988) 'Methodology in tourism research', *Annals of Tourism Research* 15, 1: 1–28.

Davidson, T. L. and Wiethaupt, W. B. (1989) 'Accountability marketing research: an increasingly vital tool for travel marketers', *Journal of Travel Research* 27, 4: 42–4.

Fleming, W. R. and Toepper, L. (1990) 'Economic impact studies: relating the positive and negative impacts to tourism development', *Journal of Travel Research* 29, 1: 35–42.

Graburn, N. H. H. (1983) 'The anthropology of tourism', *Annals of Tourism Research* 10, 1: 9–33.

Gray, H. P. (1970) *International Travel – International Trade*, Lexington: DC: Heath.

Lett, J. (1989) 'Epilogue', in V. L. Smith (ed.) *Hosts and Guests: the Anthropology of Tourism*, 2nd edn, Philadelphia: University of Pennsylvania Press: 275–9.

Nash, D. (1981) 'Tourism as an anthropological subject', *Current Anthropology* 22, 5: 461–8.

Nash, D. (1984) 'The ritualization of tourism: comment on Graburn's "The Anthropology of Tourism"', *Annals of Tourism Research* 11, 3: 503–22.

Pearce, D. G. (1981) 'Estimating visitor expenditure, a review and New Zealand case study', *International Journal of Tourism Management* 2, 4: 240–52.

——(1987) *Tourism Today: a Geographical Analysis*, Harlow: Longman and New York: Wiley.

——(1992) *Tourist Organizations*, Harlow: Longman and New York: Wiley.

Perdue, R. R. and Pitegoff, B. E. (1990) 'Methods of accountability research for destination marketing', *Journal of Travel Research* 28, 4: 45–9.

Reid, L. J. and Andereck, K. L. (1989) 'Statistical analyses use in tourism research', *Journal of Travel Research* 28, 2: 21–4.

Ritchie, J. R. B. and Goeldner, C. R. (eds) (1987) *Travel Tourism and Hospitality Research: a Handbook for Managers and Researchers*, New York: Wiley.

Sheldon, P. J. (1990) 'A review of tourism expenditure research', *Progress in Tourism, Recreation and Hospitality Management* 3: 28–49.

Siegel, W. and Ziff-Levine, W. (1990) Evaluating tourism advertising campaigns: conversion vs advertising tracking studies, *Journal of Travel Research* 28, 3: 51–5.

Smith, S. L. J. (1989) *Tourism Analysis: a Handbook*, Harlow: Longman and New York: Wiley.

Smith, V. L. and Eadington, W. (eds) (in press) *Tourism Alternatives: Potentials* and *Problems in the Development of Tourism*, Philadelphia: University of Pennsylvania Press.

Weber, S. (1991) 'Problem areas and sources of errors in tourism demand research', *Tourist Review* 46, 3: 2–8.

White, K. J. and Walker, M. B. (1982) 'Trouble in the travel account', *Annals of Tourism Research* 9, 1: 37–56.

Wynegar, D. (1989) 'US Department of Commerce Task Force on Accountability Research', *Journal of Travel Research* 27, 4: 41–2.

Chapter 2

Tourism as the subject of interdisciplinary research

Krzysztof Przeclawski

The aim of this chapter is to discuss the role of interdisciplinary research in tourism and to examine the significance of differing philosophical backgrounds in such research. The chapter begins by noting that tourism is a very complex phenomenon which has been studied by various disciplines. However, tourism should also be the subject of interdisciplinary research. After establishing the differences between multidisciplinary and interdisciplinary research, consideration is given to the ways in which differing philosophical backgrounds influence the way research is undertaken.

TOURISM AS A VERY COMPLEX PHENOMENON

There have been many different attempts to answer the question of what tourism is. Unfortunately no definition has so far gained widespread acceptance. Some would even suggest that such a definition would be impossible to formulate, if indeed it were really needed. In general, tourism has been defined by experts dealing with various fields of knowledge and these definitions reflect their point of view. An economist, a town planner or a sociologist will each perceive tourism in a different way.

According to Hunziker, in what is regarded now as one of the classic definitions:

> Tourism is the sum of the relations and phenomena which result from travelling and visiting an area by non-residents providing that it does not entail resettlement or paid work.

> (Hunziker 1951)

Nettekoven defined mass tourism as:

the sum of the social and economic phenomena stemming from a voluntary and temporary change of place of residence taken up by strangers to satisfy their non-material needs while making use of installations meant for a large number of people.

(Nettekoven 1972)

This author has suggested the following definition:

Tourism, in its broad sense, is the sum of the phenomena pertaining to spatial mobility, connected with a voluntary, temporary change of place, the rhythm of life and its environment and involving personal contact with the visited environment (natural, cultural or social).

McIntosh and Goeldner write:

tourism may be defined as the sum of the phenomena and relationships arising from the interaction of tourists, business suppliers, host governments and host communities in the process of attracting tourists and other visitors,

(McIntosh and Goeldner 1986)

whereas a tourist is 'a person who travels from place to place for nonwork reasons'.

Boyer (1972) saw tourism as a leisure time activity that takes for granted a change of place and one in which 'Motion, moving around are the elements which make the tourist'. Valene Smith (1989) is of similar opinion. Although she admits that it is difficult to define tourism, Smith classified it among leisure-time activities: 'in general a tourist is a temporarily leisured person who voluntarily visits a place away from home for the purpose of experiencing a change'.

Having quoted many different definitions of tourism, Stephen Smith noted:

There are many difficulties in defining the words tourist, trip, tourism, visitor, and similar terms. These difficulties become especially apparent when one begins to compare the definitions used by various governments. Progress has been made towards consensus of international definitions, but there is still much variation in domestic tourism terminology. Tourism analysis may emphasize either the traveller or the trip, depending on the particular problem being studied.

(Smith 1989)

As these definitions show, there is a general consensus that tourism involves travelling and a temporary visit to a place away from home and that this change of place is voluntary. But differences in the views of individual authors continue to exist, for example, in terms of purpose of visit. To be able to answer the question of what tourism is, consideration must be given to what sort of phenomenon it is, as there have been many misunderstandings in this respect.

The treatment of tourism exclusively as a form of leisure is too limiting. The nature of tourism should also be sought, for instance, in our attitude to space – it should be treated as an element of the wider process of our spatial mobility. In this sense, tourism could simply be regarded as the process of the change of place in space by an individual or a group of people, a temporary change of the place of sojourn. Many of tourism's spatial characteristics have been analysed and reviewed by Pearce (1987) and Mitchell and Murphy (1991). Tourism also has various economic, psychological, social, cultural and other attributes.

As an economic phenomenon, tourism develops according to economic forces, especially those of supply and demand. Tourism has become a business and the term 'tourist market' is commonly used (Eadington and Redman 1991).

Tourism is also a psychological phenomenon. A tourist trip is preceded by a specific need (or needs) which generates a motive for travel and establishes a purpose for the trip. An image of the trip is created in the mind, comparisons with which are made while travelling (Pearce and Stringer 1991). The question of tourist motivations is explored in detail by Philip Pearce in Chapter 6.

Tourism is a social phenomenon too, as tourists assume a social role during the course of a trip. Social contacts, occasional or frequent, are experienced with such people as fellow travellers, trip organizers, guides and the local population. Social ties may develop as a result. Moreover, other factors, such as travel motivation and choice of destination, may be dependent on social images and stereotypes attributed to tourism as well as on variables such as age, sex and education (Dann and Cohen 1991).

At the same time, tourism is a cultural phenomenon, a function and manifestation of culture. But tourism also involves a transmission of culture and is in a sense an encounter, a 'shock' or 'clash' of cultures. As such, tourism can be a factor in cultural change (V. Smith 1989). Furthermore, as all contemporary cultural phenomena are very complex and we can speak of different cultures or subcultures, so we can also speak of different forms of tourism which are functions of different subcultures or cultural trends. Cultural change then may depend on the form of tourism concerned, which in turn is influenced by the character of the relevant cultures.

Tourism typologies have been based on a variety of dominant features (Pearce, in press). These include features such as:

1   type of tourists
2   duration of the trip
3   group size
4   organizer of the trip
5   types of tourist destination
6   types of accommodation
7   modes of transport

This author sees the most important typology as one which is based on the behaviour of the tourist (Przeclawski 1986). From this perspective the following forms of tourism might be distinguished:

(a)   cognitive tourism, that is discovering nature, past cultures contemporary culture, other people, oneself
(b)   tourism for recreation and entertainment
(c)   tourism for health treatment
(d)   'creative tourism' – one's own creative work or work for the benefit of the population visited
(e)   educational tourism
(f)   professional tourism – business, congresses, conferences
(g)   pilgrimage tourism
(h)   tourism for family reasons
(i)   sex tourism
(j)   profit-making tourism

TOURISM AS A SUBJECT FOR MANY DISCIPLINES

Because tourism is a very complex phenomenon, many disciplines have developed an interest in it. Without being exhaustive, these include: psychology, pedagogics, sociology, anthropology, economics, marketing, law, geography, architecture, physical planning, history, philosophy, ecology, political science, biology and medicine. It is neither possible nor necessary to describe here the specific field of interest of each of these disciplines, many of which are reviewed in a recent special issue of the *Annals of Tourism Research* (Farrell and Runyan, 18, 1, 1991). It should be noted though that some, such as economics, have been dealing with tourism for a comparatively long time while others, such as sociology, are relatively 'young' (Graburn and Jafari 1991). Each of these disciplines provides a partial rather than a holistic point of view. If, for example, marketing authors say 'tourism is a service' (Calantone and Mazanec 1991) they are right, because it is. But they are only partially right because tourism is more than a service. If economists observe that tourism is an 'industry' (Eadington and Redman 1991) that is also true but once more only partly so, because tourism is more than an industry, and so on. To obtain a more holistic, comprehensive understanding of tourism a more integrative approach is needed.

MULTIDISCIPLINARY AND INTERDISCIPLINARY RESEARCH

As well as being the subject of many separate disciplines, tourism can also be the subject of multidisciplinary and interdisciplinary research. While both these terms are often used, the essential difference between the two is frequently not made clear.

In multidisciplinary research each of the disciplines involved uses its own concepts and methods. Only the general subject of the research is the same. The philosophical background of the researchers and their points of view about mankind and society may be quite different. Thus, the results obtained can only be interpreted on the level of each separate discipline. The complex comparison, the synthetic point of view is practically impossible, or may be only very superficial.

In interdisciplinary research one wants to examine a given problem simultaneously from different sides to take into consideration different aspects of the subject at the same time. Interdisciplinary research should be much more unified, much more concentrated, than multidisciplinary research. Ideally, the leader or director of the interdisciplinary research project or programme should formulate the research problem and the theoretical basis for it. Then he or she should organize a team composed of representatives from different scientific disciplines to undertake the necessary research. In carrying out this research it will usually be necessary for the various researchers to use the same or a similar sample and to undertake the investigation in the same locality or in localities selected according to the same criteria. Only this kind of research design and procedure will enable a holistic, synthesized understanding of the problem to be obtained.

Nevertheless, some real difficulties may still arise. The participants in the research programme may examine the same questions, they may verify the same hypotheses related to the same research subject but the subject could be perceived by them in different ways and the research questions could have different meanings for each of them because of their different ways of understanding mankind, society and tourism. In interdisciplinary research, therefore, something more is needed, notably some 'meta-language' which could express this holistic view. This 'meta-language' should be based on a shared perspective on people, society and tourism.

INTERDISCIPLINARY RESEARCH AND PHILOSOPHICAL BACKGROUNDS

To obtain interesting results and provide some real interpretation of interdisciplinary research, the representatives of the different scientific disciplines participating should share a common or similar philosophical point of view. This sharing is needed as a close inter-relationship exists between the philosophical background of researchers and their ways of formulating scientific questions and hypotheses.

Imagine, for example, that we want to examine one of the problems connected with youth, perhaps the causes of juvenile delinquency. We decide that an interdisciplinary approach is indispensable, so sociologists are asked about social causes of juvenile delinquency, psychologists about the psychological causes and so on. But let us assume that the philosophical background of the sociologists, of the psychologists and so on is quite different. Maybe the sociologists are rather oriented towards the so called 'humanistic sociology', maybe social interactionism. The psychologists, on the other hand, may be oriented towards Skinner's behaviourism (Skinner 1978). The results of the research would be very difficult to compare.

For tourism researchers, philosophical concepts of 'mankind', 'society', 'tourism' and so on play a very important role in formulating the research problems and in the interpretation of the research results. It is obvious that we should try to be as objective as we can in our scientific research. But we should recognize that total objectivity of the researcher is practically impossible to achieve because of this variation in the basic concepts of mankind, of the essence of society and so on. In interdisciplinary research those from particular scientific disciplines will use – as they do in multidisciplinary research – their own scientific language, their own concepts and methods. But in interdisciplinary research the researchers coming from particular disciplines should also have the same (or a very similar) understanding of what mankind is, what society is, what tourism is. In other words they should adhere to the same philosophical school of thought.

After this attempt at clarifying the basic difference between multi-disciplinary and interdisciplinary research, the issue of different philosophical backgrounds in tourism research will now be explored, showing how different ways of perceiving tourism result in different ways of formulating research problems.

As an example, two different philosophical attitudes can be taken: on the one hand, a materialistic one such as Skinner's behaviourism or even Marxism; on the other, the Christian personalistic one, for instance Teilhard de Chardin's point of view (Teilhard de Chardin 1985). These two philosophical attitudes give different answers to the fundamental questions: what is a human being, what factors influence human behaviour and what is a social group?

From the materialistic point of view, human beings are purely material, physical beings and are mortal. Religion is a cultural phenomenon created by men, as is the image of God and eternal life. The whole world is composed of only one – materialistic – element. There is no place in this philosophy for such concepts as soul, spirit, God. Human life and social group activity depend on the same laws and regularities as the rest of Nature: the laws of evolution, conflict and the unity of opposites. God, who created the world and human beings, does not exist – it is human beings who created God (Larousse 1984).

For Skinner the most important law is the reaction to stimuli. For Marx, the struggle of the opposites. Man is first of all determined by historical and social factors (Skinner 1978). So human beings, determined by biological and social factors, are very much involved in supply and demand. Man is first of all a consumer of goods. In his leisure time he probably would be rather oriented towards pleasure (rest, play, sex, drugs, etc.).

From the point of view of Christian philosophy, on the other hand, human beings, are composed of body and soul. Man is a corporeal and spiritual unity; the human being is a person, a rational and free subject of action for whom life does not end with death. This human being is able to make choices, to take decisions, to love, to strive for perfection. The human being is 'auto-determined'. According to Teilhard de Chardin, further evolution depends on the efforts of man. The social group means a system of relations of free persons. Social groups, nations and finally the whole of mankind could and should constantly seek deeper understanding of themselves and greater cooperation (Teilhard de Chardin 1955).

Let us imagine now two different tourists. One of them adopts (perhaps unconsciously) the materialistic point of view, the other one, the personalistic. Would it be too superficial to assume that the first tourist will look on tourism as being related primarily to pleasure? Convinced that we have only one life he or she wants to take advantage of it. Could we suggest that tourists taking part in sex tourism or using drugs belong to that category? On the other hand, could we suggest that the second type of tourist, the one with the personalistic philosophy, would be more interested in getting to know the world, by looking for spiritual and transcendental values and also would be happy to meet other people while travelling? This may be an over-simplification – maybe a 'hippy' of the 1960s would fall into both of those categories – but I am still convinced that a profound difference exists between somebody who looks at life as a preparation for the real 'life after life' and somebody who believes that death means the irreversible end.

Such considerations apply not only to tourists but also to members of 'intermediary groups' or 'brokers'. If they belong to the first category, are they looking at tourism above all as a source of income and profit? Tourism for them is big business. International corporations know precisely the force of their power related, for instance, to the local population. Brokers belonging to the second category, on the other hand, would like to perceive their task as a service. The same could be said about the local population – the inhabitants of places visited by tourists. They may look on tourists only or primarily as a source of income or they may look on them as guests. In this second case they could of course also be conscious of the dangers related to social relations and to the impact tourism may have on the values of the visited community, even if the community does gain economically from it.

Thus it can be said that theoretically the values and behaviour of tourists, brokers and hosts are interrelated. Reality is always more complex. A 'Skinner type' tourist may be served by a 'Teilhard de Chardin' broker; in the host community there are different types of inhabitants, and so on. But we have to be conscious of those differences in our perception of the world and in our behaviour. It must also be said that our analysis cannot be static, it should be dynamic. Points of view may change, even the philosophy of life may be changed. Social life is a permanent exchange of interactions. But what about the researcher? It could be taken for granted that an experienced investigator – irrespective of his or her own point of view – knows very well that people have different value systems and that their behaviour depends on it, and can therefore understand different motivations for their behaviour.

But unfortunately the full objectivity of the investigator in practice is very difficult to attain. Rather, a materialistic philosophy of life will influence the researcher to look on people as being motivated first of all by materialistic values. A personalistic philosophy, on the contrary, will lead to the belief that human behaviour is determined by spiritual and transcendental values. As a result, the understanding of tourism could be very different.

In the first case tourism is above all an industry or market. From the point of view of the tourist, tourism means consumption. From the point of view of the broker and of the local population, tourism is a source of income. In the second, tourism is essentially a form of man's behaviour. Tourism can be a means of getting to know the world, of meeting people, of constructing a 'noosphere' (a sphere of the mind), of seeking perfection, of meeting with God. Tourism is simply a contemporary way of living. It is a means of achieving different goals and different kinds of values. Thus two different points of view can result in two different conceptions of tourism.

Consequently we can reiterate that the formulation of research questions and hypotheses and the interpretation of research results depend on these differences in our understanding of mankind, society and tourism. These differences are also influencing the continuing discussion between those who believe that the only scientific methods are quantitative ones and those who believe that the social sciences must be aware of their methodological specificity and therefore that the 'qualitative' methods are not only justified but very much needed. When undertaking research we must be aware of the philosophical assumptions of the investigation. The results of the particular disciplines will then be more complex. This is the only way to attempt to build some 'scientific schools' and develop elements of the theory of tourism.

One additional remark is needed before conclusions are drawn. A distinction must be made between philosophy and ideology. Philosophy is based on human reason in analysing the real world. The philosopher has a particular image of the world while the idealist indulges in wishful thinking, based on a view of the world as it should be. Here only the philosophical point of view has been taken into consideration.

CONCLUSIONS

An investigator inclined to the materialistic way of thinking should take into account that leaving aside the human spirit makes a true analysis of the market impossible. Market analysis without humanistic analysis will be false. Marketing based only on economic categories of costs and profits leads nowhere. Such analysis will sooner or later be proved one-sided, because it does not take spiritual needs into account. On the other hand, the humanistic investigator who wants to avoid being onesided, should remember that *'primum edere deinde philophare'*. The existence and the rules of the market cannot be forgotten.

The contemporary world needs dialogue. Dialogue provides for better mutual knowledge and understanding, for the possibility of coexistence and cooperation and agreement as to the basic principles of individual points of view. Knowledge and understanding are the preconditions of the dialogue. The discussion can be productive when the participants in it not only know their own views but also are aware of the views of the other side. Knowledge fosters greater tolerance to dissimilarity. This in turn is instrumental to coexistence, to development without mutual interference, without 'converting' one another. Tolerance also strengthens respect for views different from our own. A general conclusion is that although we start from different points, in practice we still share a great number of common values. It may turn out that there is a wide sphere where cooperation in the implementation of common values is possible.

This chapter has dealt with philosophical differences between researchers. We also have to be aware that other differences exist which also influence the researcher's view of mankind and society. For example, a religious as well as philosophical dialogue may be needed. Tourism can also play a significant role in the dialogue between religions. Through travel tourists meet with symbols of the professed religions or encounter tourist attractions which are elements of cultures originating in religious inspiration and tradition. Tourists may visit churches, mosques and synagogues and take part in services, pilgrimages and prayers, admire the beauty and architecture of sacred buildings, sculptures and paintings or listen to sacred music. The knowledge of other religions obtained through these works of art and symbols forms one of the crucial platforms for the dialogue between religions and is an indispensable foundation for their coexistence and cooperation.

Jean Delumeau wrote that at the time of the Renaissance, the national identity of European peoples was strengthening, while the process of unification of Western culture was carried out (Delumeau 1967). It seems to me that this observation is also relevant today in relation to the whole globe. Thus the process of 'touristification' can be treated as a manifestation of the materialization of Teilhard's concept of 'unity in multitude' at which the world aims.

REFERENCES

Boyer, M. (1972) *Le Tourisme*, Paris: Editions du Seuil.
Calantone, R. J. and Mazanec, J. A. (1991) 'Marketing management and tourism', *Annals of Tourism Research* 18, 1: 101–19.
Dann, G. and Cohen, E. (1991) 'Sociology and tourism', *Annals of Tourism Research* 18, 1: 155–69.
Delumeau, J. (1967) *La Civilisation de la Renaissance*, Paris.
Eadington, W. R. and Redman, M. (1991) 'Economics and tourism', *Annals of Tourism Research* 18, 1: 41–56.
Farrell, B. H. and Runyan, D. (1991) 'Ecology and tourism', *Annals of Tourism Research* 18, 1: 26–40.
Graburn, N. M. H. and Jafari, J. (1991) 'Introduction: tourism social science', *Annals of Tourism Research* 18, 1: 1–11.
Hunziker, W. (1951) *Le Tourisme Social*, Berne: Alliance Internationale du Tourisme.
Larousse (1984) 'Marxisme et matérilisme dialectique', in *Dictionnaire de la Philosophie*, Paris: Larousse: 168–9.
McIntosh, R. W. and Goeldner, C. R. (1986) *Tourism: Principles, Practices and Philosophies*, New York: Wiley.
Mitchell, L. S. and Murphy, P. E. (1991) 'Geography and tourism', *Annals of Tourism Research* 18, 1: 57–70.
Nettekoven, L. (1972) *Massentourismus in Tunesien*, Starnberg: Studienkreis für Tourismus.
Pearce, D. G. (1987) *Tourism Today: a Geographical Analysis*, Harlow: Longman and New York: Wiley.
——(in press) 'Alternative tourism: concepts, classifications and questions', in V. L. Smith and W. R. Eadington (eds) *Alternative Tourism: Potentials and Problems in the Development of Tourism*, Philadelphia: University of Pennsylvania Press.
Pearce, P. L. and Stringer, P. F. (1991) 'Psychology and tourism', *Annals of Tourism Research* 18, 1: 136–54.
Przeclawski, K. (1973) *Turystyka i Wychowanie* (Tourism and Education), Warsaw: Nasza Ksiegarnia.
——(1986) *Humanistic Foundations of Tourism*, Warsaw: Institute of Tourism.
Skinner, B. F. (1978) *Poza Wolnoscia i Godnoscia* (Beyond Freedom and Dignity), Warsaw: Piw.
Smith, S. L. J. (1989) *Tourism Analysis: a Handbook*, Harlow: Longman and New York, Wiley.
Smith, V. (1989) *Hosts and Guests: the Anthropology of Tourism*, 2nd edn, Philadelphia: University of Pennsylvania Press.
Teilhard de Chardin, P. (1955) *Le Phénomène Humain*, Paris: Seuil.
——(1985) *Zarys Wszechswiata Personalistycznego* (Outline of the Personalistic Universe), Warsaw: Pax.

Chapter 3

Comparative studies in tourism research

Douglas G. Pearce

The comparative approach has yet to emerge as a distinctive, readily recognizable methodology in tourism research despite its application to a wide variety of problems during the last two decades. Long debates have occurred over the use of multipliers and other technical matters and broad disciplinary reviews have appeared in the special issues of the *Annals of Tourism Research* and elsewhere, but within the tourism literature there has been little or no discussion on the merits or otherwise of comparative studies such as is to be found in sociology, political science or planning (see Przeworski and Teune 1970, Lijphart 1975, Masser 1981). When a comparative approach has been adopted by tourism researchers there has generally been little elaboration on its use, with at best only passing mention of methodological issues or fleeting reference to other work. Studies have not built upon each other and no cohesive body of work using a comparative perspective is to be found. This chapter seeks to redress this situation by stimulating broader discussion of comparative approaches to tourism research. The chapter begins by addressing the question, what is a comparative approach? Applications of comparative studies in tourism research are then reviewed and a range of methodological issues considered before conclusions are drawn. A number of related issues are also examined by Cohen in Chapter 4 with regard to the more specific theme of touristic images.

A COMPARATIVE APPROACH

The question of what constitutes a comparative approach in tourism research has essentially been taken for granted for no definition nor much discussion is evident in the literature. In general, the term is used in papers dealing with the analysis of a problem in two or more places, usually, but not exclusively, in a cross-national context (see Thompson 1971, Chenery 1979, Loukissas 1982, Kemper 1979, Moller 1983, Pearce 1983, 1987a, Hall 1990). Without being explicit, these writers are using the term in a similar manner to Warwick and Osherson (1973: 8) to refer to 'social scientific analyses involving more than one social system or in the same social system at more than one point in time'. To this extent, segmentation studies of residents or visitors in any one community or place are not considered to be comparative, even though differences between segments or groups may be analysed (see Belisle and Hoy 1980). Warwick and Osherson also note (p. 7) that 'Comparison in its broadest sense is the process of discovering similarities and differences among phenomena'. This involves more than the mere juxtaposition of case studies, for to be comparative the analysis must at the very least draw out and attempt to account for similarities and differences. Collections of national or regional case studies which fail to do this are therefore not comparative (see Pye and Lin 1983, Williams and Shaw 1988), even though the different case studies focus on the same or similar themes, a point recognized by Richter (1989: 17) in her study of tourism politics in a number of Asian countries.

Writers in other fields emphasize the need to develop this comparative element and underline the contribution that comparative studies may make to deriving generalizations and building and testing theories:

the role of comparative research in the process of theory-building and theory-testing consists of replacing proper names of social systems by the relevant variables

(Przeworski and Teune 1970: 30)

All theory aims at generality in the relationships postulated between variables. Cross cultural comparison is essential, for there is no other way to determine the generality of findings than to test them in all relevant cultural settings

(Warwick and Osherson 1973: 3)

the comparative method allows us to go beyond description (what? when? how?) towards the more fundamental goal of explanation (why?)

(Hayne and Harrop 1982: 7)

Explanation or generalization through comparative research is usually sought via one of two paths: a positive approach in which similarities are identified in independent variables associated with a common outcome, or a negative one whereby independent variables associated with divergent outcomes are identified (Warwick and Osherson 1973: 52). Lijphart (1971, 1975) sees the comparative method (which he distinguishes from the comparative perspective) as 'one of the basic methods – the others being experimental, statistical and case study methods – of establishing general empirical proportions' and one that is commonly used in 'many variables, small N' cases. A common way of minimizing problems in these circumstances is adopting 'control through common features' or the 'most similar systems' approach. This contrasts with the 'most different systems' strategy where 'the principal task . . . is to progressively eliminate variables that do not explain the differences in dependent variables and to identify those with some explanatory power' (Masser 1981: 7). The logic and merits of these two strategies are discussed further by Lijphart (1975), Meckstroth (1975) and Masser (1981).

Comparative research might thus be distinguished not only by the interrelated analysis and interpretation of phenomena in two or more contexts but also by the purposes for which it is undertaken. Masser (1981) identifies two major sets of reasons in his review of the case for comparative studies: one relates to the practical value of such studies and the transfer of experience which might result, the second concerns the extent to which comparisons stimulate the development of theory. Here Masser cites Feldman on comparative public policy:

> The introduction of comparison into the analysis of public policy promises to explore the range of choice available to societies whose perception of choice may be bound by institutions, economic, social structure, and culture. It promises insight into the role of institutions by exploring parallel institutions operating in other systems. And it promises embracing theory for politics, as well as policy, beyond the boundaries erected by the details of systems because comparison helps establish norms for judgment and helps distinguish the essential from the trivial.
>
> (Feldman 1978: 87)

Both sets of factors also apply to research in tourism, with comparative studies having been undertaken for each of these reasons.

APPLICATIONS IN TOURISM RESEARCH

Some of the earliest applications of comparative studies in tourism were for purely pragmatic purposes, namely to benefit from other countries' experiences to help solve specific practical problems. This was

Thompson's explicit rationale in comparing recreation and tourism in the Colorado Rockies and the Swiss Alps:

> without complete and accurate data for the study of the recreational system, truly definitive evaluation of the proper direction of future development is extremely difficult. On what basis, then, can one construct a rational plan for the future? One possibility is to derive alternatives from the study of similar use of recreational resources in an area where successful methods have been developed. Such an area should be one with fundamental similarities to Colorado and one where relatively comprehensive statistical data are available for analysis.
>
> (Thompson 1971: 7)

Thompson concludes her comparative study with a list of twenty-five recommendations regarding the future development of tourism and recreation in the Rockies.

Similarly, Chenery (1979) sought solutions in continental Europe to the tourism planning issues being faced by London in the early 1970s, his aim being (p. 8): 'to establish the pressures being placed on other European capitals by tourism and to discover how the authorities concerned react to them in the planning policies they adopt.' The most comprehensive research programme yet on tourism and the environment, that coordinated by the OECD in the 1970s (OECD 1981a, 1981b), involved a comparative analysis of some twenty case studies from twelve member states. Three basic questions were raised at the outset:

1   Under what circumstances does the development of a tourist industry result in a deterioration of environmental quality in the host country?
2   To what extent does a deterioration of environmental quality in a particular area result in a decrease in the number of tourists visiting that area?
3   Is it possible to design a tourist development policy that has no negative impact and, if so, what would be the costs of such a policy?

Although analysis of the case studies was not without its problems, a number of generalizations with practical implications and applications could be made (Pearce 1980). Environmental deterioration, for instance, was shown to occur most commonly under the following circumstances: a rapid and largely uncontrolled growth of the tourist industry, especially where characterized by marked seasonal peaks, in areas with little or no planning, few controls and financial or technical inability to provide adequate infrastructure.

In the latter two examples there was a reasonably tight comparative framework. In other cases a more general, often impressionistic, comparison of conditions in other countries' tourist industries has been offered as a means of presenting solutions to both specific and general problems. Owen (1990), for example, asks the question 'can UK resorts learn from European experience?' while Sharpe (1990) suggests American hoteliers might look to Japan for directions in the 1990s. Sharpe notes (p. 98): 'I don't advocate copying the Japanese approach to business. But I think we could profit greatly from looking at some of the concepts underlying Japan's business behaviour that might have an application to the way westerners run hotels'.

Looking to the experience of others may prove particularly attractive before embarking on new directions of our own. Thus parallels are being drawn between the US experience with deregulation in the 1980s and likely changes in the structure of the European airline industry in the 1990s (Wheatcroft 1988).

Care has obviously to be taken in this and other cases regarding the transferability of the experience from one context to another. Truly comparative studies are needed, not just the simple transfer of results from one place to another or the adoption of ideas or concepts without further consideration. Archer's (1982) compilation of multiplier values, for example, shows that although there is some consistency in multipliers for like areas, values do vary from place to place depending on structural and other factors. Similarly, what works well, or badly, in one time or place, will not necessarily perform the same later or elsewhere. This point is well made by Hall with regard to the applicability to the Third World of the Albanian and Korean models of Stalinist approaches to tourist development:

> while the specific conceptual approaches to tourism development may have much to commend themselves for relatively poorly endowed societies wishing to exploit a comparative advantage, it is difficult to imagine the conditions of Albania and North Korea being sufficiently replicated elsewhere for such a model to hold long-term validity.
>
> (Hall 1990: 52)

Indeed, it might be argued that there has already been much questionable transfer of tourist development to and among Third World countries. Conversely, mistakes made in one place are not necessarily avoided elsewhere at a later date, leading to the conclusion that lessons that might be learnt have not been.

Transferability is related in part to the extent to which findings or experiences can be generalized. It is in terms of generalization that comparative research has also had some modest input on a more theoretical level. According to Leichter:

The process of theory building may be viewed as involving four stages:
1 problem selection
2 systematic observation (entailing the classification of variables)
3 generalization
4 explanation

(Leichter 1979: 11)

While comparative studies in tourism have so far generated or tested little theory in themselves, some have provided, through clarification of issues and the classifications produced, a basis for further research, while others have moved from description along the path to explanation.

Comparative studies can contribute to problem selection by requiring a more explicit and specific elaboration and identification of the factors and issues to be discussed, particularly in contrast to case studies which are often general and descriptive. Nelson (1978a), for example, offered a general set of guidelines for papers to be presented at an international conference on national parks, one which highlighted the following factors: ecology, strategies and institutional arrangements, perceptions, attitudes and values and technology. A comparative study in a centennial collection of papers on national parks in New Zealand makes the point that a different perspective emerges from a comparison with European parks than, as is more frequently the case, with North American ones (Pearce and Richez 1987). The European comparison emphasizes the early establishment of the national park system in New Zealand and leads to an explanation in terms of broader Old World–New World conditions and pressures and patterns of use. A comparison of tourist development in Languedoc–Roussillon with the Baltic coast of Germany (Moller 1983) and Cancun (Pearce 1983), if it does not give rise to a theory of tourist development at least leads to a specification of development factors to be taken into account, notably site and situation factors, development processes, objectives, demand characteristics and resulting impacts.

Many of the earliest comparative studies produced interesting classifications or typologies of tourist development (see Barbaza 1970,

Peck and Lepie 1977). Though none has been widely adopted and the typology literature is fragmented, lacks cohesion and is without much sense of common direction, as has been argued elsewhere, 'a better, systematic basis for discriminating between different forms of tourism would not only provide a firmer foundation for exploring further aspects of alternative tourism but also go a long way to establishing some common ground on which a more theoretical and unified approach to the study of tourism might be developed' (Pearce 1992).

Much of this writer's recent work on the geography of tourism has been concerned (Pearce 1987b: 127) 'to identify basic patterns through comparative studies and to explain these so as to develop a more general understanding of the processes at work'. The use of localization curves to compare the spatial structure of tourism in eight European countries, for example, led to the observation that international tourism was usually more concentrated geographically than domestic tourism. The general pattern found was then explained in terms of a set of interrelated supply and demand factors. Likewise, the systematic comparison of the geography of tourism on small islands resulted in the conclusion (Pearce 1987b: 164) that 'the combination of smallness and insularity produces spatial structures which are more evident there than in most mainland countries and destinations'. Again, the identification of common patterns leads to the search for general explanations. These are found in the specific characteristics of small islands, raising the question of whether other, more conceptual models developed from a limited number of examples from the Caribbean and the South Pacific (Hills and Lundgren 1977, Britton 1982) do have wider applicability to other developing countries.

In the now voluminous impact literature considerable debate has occurred over the costs and benefits which tourism generates (Pearce 1989). Reviews can bring some order to this disparate body of research but much of the debate appears to have arisen from the use of a range of techniques applied to different problems associated with a variety of types of tourism in different contexts. Comparative studies can serve a very useful purpose in the search for generalizations in this field by providing a sounder basis for comparing like with like and by establishing more clearly the role of contextual and causal factors. This case is well made and illustrated by Loukissas whose research:

uses a comparative analysis approach to explore differences in tourism development and industry impact among the Greek Islands. Examination of a group of culturally and physically homogeneous entities permits an analysis of how different local conditions and tourism characteristics result in varied patterns of development.

(Loukissas 1982: 525)

Similarly, Kemper concludes from his 'controlled comparison' of tourist development in Taos and Patzcuaro:

If a sufficient number of such structural charts were assembled for a variety of tourist regions, one might be able to say, with more certainty than at present, precisely what are the crucial components of 'successful' and 'marginal' tourism.

(Kemper 1979: 107)

An ambitious cross-national study into the role of tourism as a factor of change carried out under the aegis of the Vienna Centre (Bystrza-nowksi 1989) was also set up on similar grounds:

The basic concept was to have the empirical studies carried out in several countries on the same basis and according to the same pattern i.e. common aims, common problem areas, the same working hypotheses, in localities with the same strictly defined criteria. . . .
The authors were convinced that the cross-national study, following such a common pattern, would create a data base for comparative analysis.

(Przeclawski and Travis 1989: 11)

As it transpired, the final studies were less uniform than intended but a number of generalizations could still be made. Positive perceptions of the impact of tourism, for example, were associated with economic factors while social aspects were seen to be less influenced by tourism.

Other local area studies have compared communities with different levels or types of tourist development (see Rothman 1978, England, Gibbons and Johnson 1980, Murphy 1983, Haukeland 1984, Garland and West 1985). The results of these different studies suggest that the relationship between the level of development and attitudes towards tourism is clearly not unidirectional as implied in Doxey's (1975) irridex, for no consistent firming of support for nor strengthening of opposition to tourism is found as development increases. Here, too, comparative studies have provided a useful means of testing a concept which has gained some currency but which has often been accepted uncritically. The scope for comparative research in assessing the economic impact of tourism in developing countries is also strongly evidenced by studies in the Caribbean and the South Pacific (Seward and Spinrad 1982, Britton 1990).

Longitudinal studies which provide comparisons over time not space, that is, which compare the same communities at different dates, also have the potential to offer insights into the social and economic impacts which tourist development may have.

Indeed, where it is possible to determine conditions before and after the development of tourism, links between the growth of tourism and associated impacts might be established more directly and fully than comparisons between places having differing levels of development and impact and, especially, 'one-off' studies in any given place. Comparative studies of this nature have been undertaken by Préau (1983) and Swindin (1985) in the French Alps. Both combine contemporary fieldwork with the use of communal records and other archival data to establish earlier conditions, with Préau examining changes in Courchevel between 1948 and 1973 and Swindin developments in Les Contamines Montjoie between 1962 and 1982. Direct participation in business activities resulting from the development of tourism, for example, was shown to be a function of the capacity to invest or a history of local commercial enterprise.

In addition to testing theories, comparative studies might also be used to demonstrate the application and utility of new analytical techniques, for example those dealing with tourist travel patterns. Thus Pearce and Elliott (1983) illustrate the potential of the Trip Index by reference to visits to an isolated national park and to a major urban area while Leiper (1989) shows the possibilities of the Main Destination Ratio by comparing ratios derived for travellers from Australia, New Zealand and Japan. Once their utility has been demonstrated, these new techniques may in turn form the means for undertaking other comparative studies (Uysal and McDonald 1989).

METHODOLOGICAL ISSUES

Three broad approaches to comparative research in tourism can be distinguished in the studies just reviewed:

1 comparative case studies
2 element by element comparisons
3 quantitative and graphical analyses.

Although Cohen (1979) argues that all case studies are implicitly part of the comparative study, even if they involve only a single case, comparative case studies here are seen as those that have been designed specifically as part of the comparative process, that is they are set up, analysed and interpreted as part of a more general research design with common findings subsequently being produced and interrelated. Good examples of this are found in the applied research of Chenery (1979) and the OECD tourism and environment programme discussed above. Chenery defines the problem in terms of planning issues in London then explores these by means of case studies from Paris, Amsterdam, Copenhagen, Munich, Vienna and Rome, each of which follows a common outline. Comparisons with London are made in each case with more general conclusions being drawn in the final chapter. In the OECD programme, guidelines were prepared by the secretariat which directed attention to the general characteristics of the area, the economic dimensions of the tourist industry and to the legal and institutional context (Pearce 1980). A more detailed framework for examining environmental impacts was also provided, one which identified a number of tourist-generated stressor activities, the associated stresses, subsequent environmental responses and societal reactions to these. Case studies usually provide the empirical detail with the comparative issues being drawn out and pulled together in a final integrative section or chapter (see Seward and Spinrad 1982) or occasionally in an introductory chapter or volume (see Nelson 1978b, Bystrzanowksi 1989).

In the second set of studies, on the other hand, the comparison occurs throughout as each element or variable from the examples in question is in turn examined and compared. This element by element comparison is the approach most commonly used in the studies cited earlier (see Kemper 1979, Moller 1983, Pearce 1983, Hall 1990, Owen 1990). Where there is only a two-way comparison, as in these cases, a large number of variables can be handled sequentially although there are clear limits to generalization. Kemper, for example, compares in turn the characteristics of Taos and Patzcuaro, tourism in each area and then the role of the public and private sectors at different levels. The element by element approach is not limited to two-way comparisons – Britton (1990) covers five South Pacific states and Pearce (1987b) draws heavily on seven island destinations – but questions of manageability do arise as the number of examples grows.

Where the scope of the problem warrants and the nature of the data allows, quantitative techniques may be used to increase the number of cases examined. Loukissas (1982) derived a fourfold typology of thirty-eight Greek islands based on two independent variables – community size and tourist density – and then analysed three sets of dependent variables: location of tourism development, differences in characteristics of tourism development and differences in impacts. Standard social survey methods have been used in the comparative community studies cited earlier (see England, Gibbons and Johnson 1980 and Murphy 1983). Several graphical techniques have been used by this writer to examine the spatial structure of tourism, notably the localization curves mentioned above (Pearce 1987b) and time-series graphs and mapped histograms to compare Mediterranean charters (Pearce 1987a).

Whatever the approach adopted, a number of general issues arise. First, as Heckser (1957: 69) pointed out in his seminal study: 'comparison is not sensible unless it is based on a clearly understood problem which is brought up for solution', a point equally relevant to other approaches! Good examples of a clear problem statement or use of an effective conceptual framework include *inter alia* the studies by Nelson (1978a), Chenery (1979), Kemper (1979), Loukissas (1982) and Hall (1990), while some of the difficulties involved are outlined by Przeclawski and Travis (1989). This writer concluded his examination of the national and regional structure of tourism in Europe by noting:

> Without this comparison, the definition of specific objectives and questions at the outset (prompted in part by existing models) and the use of a common method or framework of analysis, it would not have been possible to distinguish general patterns and trends from situations peculiar to a particular country or region.
>
> (Pearce 1987b: 150)

At the same time, as noted earlier, developing a comparative approach can itself aid in problem selection and formulation, with the need to compare leading to a refinement of our powers of description (Heckser 1957), for example, in the element by element studies.

Second, there is the question of conceptual equivalence and equivalence of measurement (Warwick and Osherson 1973), especially in cross-cultural studies. Do the concepts and terms used mean the same thing in each study area? This point is well made by Andreani *et al.* (1977: 86) with regard to social tourism in Italy and Yugoslavia: 'the use of the expression "social tourism", is becoming more widespread; while at the same time it tends to cover an even more complex diversity of facts. Everything points to the conclusion that by extending the field of our research territorially, we should certainly not have gained in clarity'. Similarly, the 1989 meeting of the International Academy for the Study of Tourism highlighted the diversity in the concept of alternative tourism (Smith and Eadington 1992). If the IUCN definition of national parks is used then some countries such as the United Kingdom do not have national parks even if they possess reserved areas labelled as such by their own authorities (Pearce and Richez 1987). Later in this volume, Dann (Chapter 6) explores limitations in the use of nationality and country of residence variables in comparative and other research. These studies all suggest that as much care must be taken with the use of such apparently straightforward terms as with the compilation of tourism statistics, where difficulties of cross-national comparability of definitions and measurements have long been recognized (Pearce 1987b).

Problems of equivalence and other practical difficulties which emerged during the course of the Vienna Centre project (Przeclawski and Travis 1989, Przeclawski 1989) included:

1 selection of localities not always following the original criteria
2 differences in the number of localities chosen
3 failure to carry out the necessary desk research in some cases
4 use of telephone interviews in the USA compared with personal interviews elsewhere
5 differences in the populations sampled – not all studies included samples of both residents and tourists as specified
6 variations in the degree of interviewer training
7 variations in the questionnaires used and difficulties in translating master questionnaires into several languages. Subsequent observed differences in the degree of host/guest contact, for example, are inconclusive as the term 'tourist' was never defined for the respondents.

Third, particular attention in comparative studies must be given to contextual factors. If one of the basic purposes of comparative studies is to test theories in, or to generalize from, a range of contexts then it follows that the contextual factors – the independent variables in such studies – need to be clearly and explicitly identified and described. The same is true of the more pragmatic studies – the extent to which experiences can be transferred successfully will depend in large part on the similarity of salient conditions between countries or cases. Britton (1990) stresses the economic and historic contexts of his five South Pacific countries, Kemper (1979) provides a good descriptive background to tourism in Taos and Patzcuaro while Loukissas (1982) quantifies the key characteristics of his Greek islands.

Constraints other than those alluded to already (e.g. conceptual equivalence and data comparability) must also be recognized. Finance and logistics clearly present a major obstacle, especially in cross-national studies. Where the organizational framework exists, comparative studies might be undertaken by national researchers in each country and their efforts pooled, as in the OECD tourism and environmental programme and in the Vienna Centre study of cultural change. Other international bodies, such as the International Academy for the Study of Tourism, might also play a greater role in fostering such research. Particularly clear problem statements and conceptual frameworks are needed for such joint efforts to succeed. At the same time, the merits of international comparisons should not be over-emphasized at the expense of possibly more feasible regional or local studies which might also contribute to theory building or yield practical benefits. Indeed, by holding certain national institutional and cultural factors constant, local or regional comparative studies may offer even more scope for exploring variations in other elements as Loukissas (1982) demonstrated in Greece. The community impact and attitude studies discussed above have also shown the value of comparative research at the less logistically demanding local level (see Murphy 1983, Garland and West 1985). In Chapter 11 Ritchie proposes a Global Tourism Research Network which might facilitate the incorporation of local studies into a comparative international programme.

CONCLUSIONS

Comparative studies offer tourism researchers a way forward in a field still largely dominated by descriptive, ideographic work. The disparate studies reviewed here signal the potential which comparative research has for developing generalizations and explanations, for testing theories and techniques. They have also demonstrated the practical possibilities and constraints of transferring experiences and learning from others, something that will undoubtedly become more significant with the increasing globalization of the world economy and the tourist industry. There is, however, still much scope for the refinement of comparative approaches in their application to tourism. Such refinement is unlikely to occur without broader debate and to be debated the approach must first be recognized. It is hoped, therefore, that the synthesis given by this chapter has focused attention on a valuable but neglected approach and provided the foundation for future research to take advantage of the potential it offers.

REFERENCES

Andreani, A. *et al.* (1977) 'Social tourism – an "empty box"'? The case in Italy and Yugoslavia', in *Social Needs and their Realization in Tourism*, Berne: Editions AIEST: 77–89.

Archer, B. H. (1982) 'The value of multipliers and their policy implications', *Tourism Management* 1, 1: 236–41.

Barbaza, Y. (1970) 'Trois types d'intervention du tourisme dans l'organisation de l'espace littoral', *Annales de Géographie*, 434: 446–69.

Belisle, F. J. and Hoy, D. R. (1980) 'The perceived impact of tourism by residents: a case study in Santa Marta, Columbia', *Annals of Tourism Research* 7, 1: 83–101.

Britton, S. G. (1982) 'The political economy of tourism in the Third World', *Annals of Tourism Research* 9, 3: 331–58.

——(1990) 'The economic role and organization of island tourist industries', in C. Kissling, (ed.) *Destination South Pacific: Perspectives on Island Tourism*, Aix-en-Provence: Centre des Hautes Etudes Touristiques: 51–71.

Bystrzanowksi, J. (ed.) (1989) *Tourism as a Factor of Change: a Sociocultural Study*, Vienna: European Coordination Centre for Research and Documentation in Social Sciences.

Chenery, R. (1979) *A Comparative Study of Planning Considerations and Constraints Affecting Tourism Projects in the Principal European Capitals*, London: British Travel Educational Trust.

Cohen, E. (1979) 'Rethinking the sociology of tourism', *Annals of Tourism Research*, 6, 1: 18–35.

Doxey, G.V. (1975) 'A causation theory of visitor–resident irritants: methodology and research inferences, *The Impact of Tourism*. Sixth Annual Conference Proceedings, San Diego: Travel Research Association: 195–8.

England, J. L., Gibbons, W. E. and Johnson, B. L. (1980) 'The impact of ski resorts on subjective well-being', *Leisure Sciences* 3, 4: 311–48.

Feldman, E. J. (1978) 'Comparative public policy: field or method?' *Comparative Politics* 10: 287–305.

Garland, B. R. and West, S. J. (1985) 'The social impact of tourism in New Zealand', *Massey Journal of Asian and Pacific Business* 1, 1: 34–9.

Hall, D. R. (1990) 'Stalinism and tourism: a study of Albania and North Korea', *Annals of Tourism Research* 17, 1: 36–54.

Haukeland, J. V. (1984) 'Sociocultural impacts of tourism in Scandinavia: studies of three host communities', *Tourism Management* 5, 3: 207–14.

Hayne, R. and Harrop, M. (1982) *Comparative Government: An Introduction*, Macmillan.

Heckser, G. (1957) *The Study of Comparative Government and Politics*, London: George Allen & Unwin.

Hills, T. L. and Lundgren, T. (1977) 'The impact of tourism in the Caribbean: a methodological study', *Annals of Tourism Research* 4, 5: 248–67.

Kemper, R. V. (1979) 'Tourism in Taos and Patzcuaro: a comparison of two approaches to regional development', *Annals of Tourism Research* 6, 1: 91–110.

Leichter, H. M. (1979) *A Comparative Approach to Policy Analysis: Health Care Policy in Four Nations*, Cambridge: Cambridge University Press.

Leiper, N. (1989) 'Main destination ratios: analyses of tourist flows, *Annals of Tourism Research* 16, 4: 530–41.

Lijphart, A. (1971) 'Comparative politics and the comparative method', *American Political Science Review* 65: 682–93.

——(1975) 'The comparable-cases strategy in comparative research', *Comparative Political Studies* 8, 2: 158–77.

Loukissas, P. J. (1982) 'Tourism's regional development impacts: a comparative analysis of the Greek Islands', *Annals of Tourism Research* 9, 4: 523–54.

Masser, I. (1981) *Comparative planning studies: a critical review.* TRP33, Sheffield: University of Sheffield.

Meckstroth, T. W. (1975) ' "Most Different Systems" and "Most Similar Systems": A Study in the Logic of Comparative Inquiry', *Comparative Political Studies* 8, 2: 132–57.

Moller, H. - G. (1983) 'Etude comparée des centres touristiques du Languedoc-Roussillon et de la côte de la Baltique en République Féderale Allemande', *Norois* 120: 545–51.

Murphy, P. E. (1983) 'Perceptions and attitudes of decision-making groups in tourism centres', *Journal of Travel Research* 21, 3: 8–12.

Nelson, J. G. (1978a) 'A general guide for participants in international comparative studies of national parks and related reserves', in J. G. Nelson, R. D. Needham and D. L. Mann, (eds) *International Experience with National Parks and Related Reserves*, Waterloo: Department of Geography, University of Waterloo, 29–33.

——(1978b) 'International Experience with National Parks and Related Reserves', in J. G. Nelson, R. D. Needham and D. L. Mann, (eds) *International Experience with National Parks and Related Reserves*, Waterloo: Department of Geography, University of Waterloo, 1–27.

OECD (1981a) *The Impact of Tourism on the Environment*, Paris: Organization for Economic Cooperation and Development.

——1981b *Case Studies of the Impact on the Environment.* Paris: Organization for Economic Cooperation and Development.

Owen, C. (1990) 'Better days at the seaside. Can UK resorts learn from European experience?' *Tourism Management* 11, 3: 190–4.

Pearce, D. G. (1980) 'Tourism and the environment: frameworks for research and development', in D. G. Pearce (ed.) *Tourism in the South Pacific. The Contribution of Research to Development and Planning*, New Zealand MAB Report no. 6, Christchurch: Department of Geography, University of Canterbury: 115–24.

——(1983) 'The development and impact of large-scale tourism projects: Languedoc-Roussillon and Cancun (Mexico) compared', in C. C. Kissling *et al.* (eds), *Papers 7th Australian/New Zealand Regional Science Association*, Canberra: 59–71.

——(1987a) 'Mediterranean charters: a comparative geographic perspective', *Tourism Management* 8, 4: 291–305.

——(1987b) *Tourism Today: a Geographical Analysis*, Harlow: Longman and New York: Wiley.

——(1989) *Tourist Development*, 2nd edn, Harlow: Longman and New York: Wiley.

——(in press) 'Alternative tourism: concepts, classifications and questions', in V. L. Smith and W. R. Eadington, (eds) *Alternative Tourism: Potentials and Problems in the Development of Tourism*, Philadelphia: University of Pennsylvania Press.

Pearce, D. G. and Elliot, J. M. C. (1983) 'The Trip Index', *Journal of Travel Research* 22, 1: 6–9.

Pearce, D. G. and Richez, G. (1987) 'Antipodean Contrasts: National Parks in New Zealand and Europe', *New Zealand Geographer* 43, 2: 53–9.

Peck, J. G. and A. S. Lepie (1977) 'Tourism and Development in Three North Carolina Coastal Towns', in V. Smith, (ed.) *Hosts and Guests: The Anthropology of Tourism*, Philadelphia: University of Pennsylvania Press, 159–72.

Préau, P. (1983) 'Le changement social dans une commune touristique de montagne: Saint-Bon-Tarentaise (Savoie)', *Revue de Géographie Alpine* 71, 4: 407–29 and 72, 2–4: 411–437.

Przeclawski, K. (1989) 'Tourism as a factor of change: conclusions', in J. Bystrzanowski (ed.) *Tourism as a Factor of Change: a Sociocultural Study*, 95–100.

Przeclawski, K. and Travis A. (1989) 'Tourism as a factor of change: introduction', in J. Bystrzanowski (ed.) *Tourism as a Factor of Change: a Sociocultural Study*, 7–16.

Przeworski, A. and Teune, H. (1970) *The Logic of Comparative Social Inquiry*. New York: Wiley-Interscience.

Pye, E. A. and T. -B. Lin (eds) (1983) *Tourism in Asia: The Economic Impact*, Singapore: Singapore University Press.

Richter, L. K. (1989) *The Politics of Tourism in Asia*, Honolulu: University of Hawaii Press.

Rothman, R. A. (1978) 'Residents and transients: community reaction to seasonal visitors', *Journal of Travel Research* 16, 3: 8–13.

Seward, A. B. and Spinrad, B.K. (eds) (1982) *Tourism in the Caribbean: The Economic Impact*, Ottawa: International Development Research Centre.

Sharpe, J. L. (1990) 'Directions for the 90s: lessons from Japan', *Cornell Hotel and Restaurant Administration Quarterly* 31, 1: 98–103.

Swindin, B. (1985) *Tourism and Socio-Economic Structure in France: the Effects of the Development of Tourism on the Socio-Economic Structure of a Mountain Village in France 1962–1982*, Gloucester: Gloucestershire Papers in Local and Rural Planning no. 28, Gloucestershire College of Arts and Technology.

Thompson, P. T. (1971) *The Use of Mountain Recreational Resources: a Comparison of Recreation and Tourism in the Colorado Rockies and the Swiss Alps*, Boulder: Graduate School of Business Administration, University of Colorado.

Uysal, M. and McDonald, C. D. (1989) 'Visitor segmentation by Trip Index', *Journal of Travel Research* 27, 3: 38–42.

Warwick, D. P. and Osherson, S. (1973) *Comparative Research Methods*, Englewood Cliffs: Prentice Hall.

Wheatcroft, S. (1988) 'European Air Transport in the 1990s', *Tourism Management* 9, 3: 187–98.

Williams, A. M. and Shaw, G. (eds) (1988) *Tourism and Economic Development: Western European Experiences*, London: Belhaven Press.

Chapter 4

The study of touristic images of native people
Mitigating the stereotype of a stereotype

Erik Cohen

Colorful posters of Andean peasants in ponchos posed next to llamas at Macchu Picchu still adorned the walls of travel agencies across the United States. But a different kind of image of the highlands also began to reach this country: pictures of mass graves, wreckage from explosions, soldiers in black ski masks and farm families mourning their dead.

(Starn 1991: 83)

The stark contrast between the touristic image of the Andean 'Indio' and the reality of the Peruvian Andes in the wake of the Shining Path uprising, so powerfully stated by Starn, exemplifies an incongruity often found all over the Third and Fourth Worlds (Graburn 1976): ethnographically idealized pictures of colourful natives, intended to titillate the prospective visitors' quest for the authenticity of the life and culture of others, versus a socio-political reality of poverty, squalor, strife and death in which these others are often involved in contemporary reality.

This incongruity is found, at varying levels of intensity, in each of the three case studies of the touristic image of native people in which the author is presently involved: the West Coast Indians of Canada, the hill tribe people of northern Thailand and the Arabs of Israel and the occupied territories. Images of proud Indians and of their rich cultural heritage stand against the struggle of Indian bands to reclaim their ancestral lands and to reconstruct their culture; images of colourfully dressed hill tribe girls stand against a reality of progressive pauperization and de-culturation of many of the hill tribe people; and, at perhaps the most extreme, images of old Arabs, peacefully tending their sheep on the 'Shepherds' Field' in Bethlehem, stand in stark contrast to terrorism, death, and the suppression of the Palestinian uprising, the *intifada*, in the occupied territories. Such images are so blatantly staged, and the contrast between them and reality so obvious, that there seems to be little place for a detailed comparative study of the nature of touristic images of native people.

In fact, we are not lacking more or less general and all-embracing answers to the question of their nature. The literature of tourism is replete with 'images of the touristic image' of native people and there is a wide consensus among researchers and commentators on the nature of this image. Natives are said to be presented, for touristic purposes, anachronistically or 'allochronically' (Fabian 1983), ahistorically or atemporally, as idealized and exotic, isolated and authentically living others, torn out of their wider contemporary socio-economic and socio-historical context (Albers and James 1988: 154). The touristic establishment is said to be constructing a spurious 'tourist space' in which natives (and non-natives) stage their own image, and thus confirm the tourists' belief that the contrived images which the establishment has created in the first place, are borne out by the reality of the destination (Boorstin 1964, MacCannell 1973, Crocombe 1973: 94; Cohen 1982: 21).

Such conclusions, while certainly enjoying considerable empirical support (see Blundell 1989), are nevertheless unsatisfactory or at least insufficient. By 'essentializing' the image of the native (Clifford 1988: 258), they create a stereotype of the stereotype which is not only overly generalized, but also, in a sense, flat and not analytical enough. The stereotype precludes a more contextualized, concrete and detailed study of the touristic images of natives in all their manifold variety, within a broad and theoretically informed comparative framework. This should be the point of departure for a programme of research on touristic images of native people, to which the present paper is a methodological prolegomenon. Though it focuses on the problems and methods of study, rather than on empirical data, its principal points will be illustrated by examples taken from the above-mentioned comparative study of the visual images of native people in a wide variety of media.

However, we have to ask at the outset 'Who are the natives?' For the purposes of this discussion, the 'natives' are all the indigenous minority groups of a country, which are generally believed to enjoy a significant degree of separate ethnic, cultural or social identity. Whether this identity 'marks' them as sights or attractions of ethnic or cultural tourism (Keyes and van den Berghe 1984) or as 'totems' (Graburn, n.d., Blundell, forthcoming) of a destination country are matters to be investigated. It is not argued here that all native people are *eo ipso* touristically equally attractive – nor that the investigation of the touristic image of native people should concentrate only on those native groups which are most established as touristic attractions. Rather, the degree of touristic 'markedness' of any group of native people is a question which research should face.

THEORETICAL FRAMEWORK

While sociologists and anthropologists of tourism over the last two decades have proposed sophisticated and discriminating theoretical frameworks and methodologies for the study of tourists and touristic institutions (Dann, Nash and Pearce 1988), the study of touristic images has failed, as yet, to benefit much from these developments. Even if such images are frequently described – and criticized – there are few attempts at theoretically refined or methodologically systematic approaches to their study; a notable exception is the work of Albers and James (1983, 1988, 1990).

In the study of images, two distinct directions of research can be distinguished:

1 An *extrinsic* direction, which focuses upon the relationship between an image and 'reality', as defined by the reseacher by other means. The researcher is interested in the image only insofar as it reflects, misrepresents, distorts or falsifies this reality, but not in the image as a subject of study by itself. This is the older approach, characteristic of researchers with a culture-critical orientation (see Boorstin 1964: 77–117).

2 An *intrinsic* direction, which focuses upon such imminent characteristics of the image itself as style, motifs, content, structure and, especially, messages encoded in the image. This more recent approach is characteristic of researchers of a cultural-anthropological or semiotic orientation (see Jules-Rosette 1984).

These two directions can, of course, be combined, but, in fact, rarely have been – at least in the study of touristic images. The approach developed here will be based on an intrinsic analysis of visual touristic images of native people, but will also strive to locate that analysis within the context of the production and use of these images, under various socio-historical circumstances and prevailing socio-political relationships between the native people and the majority population. In order to clarify the basic elements in the study of touristic images and the theoretically or empirically significant relationships between them, a 'mapping sentence' is proposed (Figure 4.1).

WHO (1) { native / non-native local / foreigner } represents WHOM (2) { native groups / majority members / foreigners } for WHOM (3) { natives / non-native locals / foreigners } HOW (4) { mode of presentation }

in what MEDIUM (5) { printed medium / advertisements / souvenir / art / event } under which SOCIO-HISTORICAL CIRCUMSTANCES (6) { cultural survival / progressive acculturation / total assimilation } of the native

people, and under which prevailing SOCIO-POLITICAL RELATIONSHIPS (7) { equality / subjugation / strife } between them and the majority population.

Figure 4.1 Basic mapping sentence for the study of touristic images of native people

Intrinsically oriented studies of touristic images focused intensely on element (4) (*how*) and (5) (in what *medium*). *Extrinsically* oriented studies focused on the relationship between a less thoroughly analysed element (4) and elements (6) (Socio-historical *circumstances*) and (7) (Socio-political *relationships* between native people and the majority population). Elements (1) (*who* represents), (2) (*whom*) and (3) (for *whom*) and their interrelations have been but rarely examined systematically. This is an area deserving much closer study. To exemplify a possible systematic approach, the relationship between any two, or all three, of these elements will be examined by the help of matrices as in Figure 4.2.

Who is Represented

		NATIVES	MAJORITY	FOREIGNERS
Who Represents	NATIVE	Natives by native	Majority by native	Foreigners by native
	MEMBER OF MAJORITY	Natives by member of majority	Majority by member of majority	Foreigners by member of majority
	FOREIGNER	Natives by foreigner	Majority by foreigner	Foreigners by foreigner

Figure 4.2 A matrix of who represents whom

The material of the author's study indicates that native people relatively rarely represent themselves, at least not in the major mass media, but are frequently represented by others. They even more rarely, if at all, represent others, that is, members of the majority population or foreigners, at least as long as they are a relatively undeveloped, marginal minority (but see Evans-Pritchard 1989). The difference between the natives' self-representation and their presentation by others in the tourist media has rarely been looked into, even though some important differences have been noted (see Albers and James 1988: 155).

Turning now to the theoretical and methodological problems in the intrinsic study of touristic images as represented in the diverse media (elements (4) and (5)), the intrinsic study of touristic images can be undertaken from a more positivistic perspective or from a more interpretative one. The most common method used by representatives of the former perspective is content analysis while representatives of the latter most commonly use some form of semiotic analysis (Albers and James 1988, 145–50). Studies conducted by content analytical methods of ethnic imagery have concentrated on such 'generic categories' as the number, gender and age of subjects, their dress, the manner of their presentation and the nature of their surroundings (Albers and James 1983: 128 ff., 1988: 145). These kinds of data are much more susceptible to quantification than are the results of semiotic analyses.

One possible pitfall in the study of touristic images by content analytic methods, particularly the less rigorous ones, is their potential for tautology: since the researcher is interested primarily in ethnically 'marked' images, he or she may disregard as irrelevant touristic materials in which native people emerge in an 'unmarked' manner. Hence, the discovery of an apparently undifferentiated stereotype may be, at least in part, a consequence of the method, which led the researcher to exclude non-stereotypical materials from consideration. To prevent this contingency, all media conveying even partly touristic images, whether oriented or accessible to local or to foreign touristic audiences, should be included in the study. In the author's own project, five broad categories of media are included: printed media (e.g. post cards, articles, brochures), advertisements, souvenirs (e.g. dolls and craft products), art featuring images of native people or their paraphernalia, and events with native or pseudo-native participants. The inclusiveness of the materials collected makes it possible to gauge the extent of 'markedness' of a particular group of native people – thus turning 'markedness' from a parameter of investigation into a variable.

The positivistic study of touristic images of native people by the method of content analysis renders some sociologically interesting results, especially when diachronically applied, as Albers and James (1983, 1988: 153–4) have shown. However, to bring the study of images into a closer relationship with prevalent theoretical approaches in the study of tourism, content analysis has to be coupled with or supplemented by interpretative methods. Indeed, one of the tasks of a research programme for the study of touristic images is to synchronize this study with the sociological study of the tourists themselves. This is particularly necessary in view of the prevailing tendency in the extant studies of touristic images to stress the emergence of a sole, ubiquitous touristic image of native peoples – a tendency, as it were, to create a stereotype of the stereotype.

When engaging on a quest for an approach which will link the study of touristic images with that of tourism proper, and break up the stereotype of the stereotype, one should note that there exists no single kind of tourist, but that tourists differ very much among themselves. Various researchers have sought to express some of these differences in theoretically relevant typologies of tourists (see Cohen 1972, Smith 1977: 8–11). One could attempt to create a theoretically relevant typology of touristic images of native people on parallel lines. Various typologies of touristic images of native people could be constructed from different theoretical perspectives. For the typology proposed below, three points of departure were chosen: one of them from semiology, the other two from the sociology of tourism.

Linguists have distinguished between 'the use of words as signs and/or symbols' and semiologists have found that this distinction has 'direct applicability to the study of photographs which contain the qualities of a sign (metanym) and those of a symbol (metaphor)' (Albers and James 1988: 140–1). Albers and James have made innovative use of this distinction between metanyms and metaphors in the study of one type of media conveying visual touristic images: post cards. It can, however, be effectively widened to the study of images in all kinds of media, including not only photographs and other printed media, but also souvenirs, the creative arts and touristic events.

Turning now to the points of departure from the sociology of tourism, one of the bases for a typology of tourists is the differential admixture of exposure to strangeness vs preservation of familiarity characteristic of various types of tourist roles (Cohen 1972). By analogy, touristic images could be similarly classified by the degree of strangeness vs familiarity of the represented sight which they seek to impress upon prospective viewers. In the sociological literature on tourism, a contrast is found between authors like MacCannell (1973, 1976), who conceive of tourists as serious seekers of authenticity, and others who, basing their approach on the processual theory of V. Turner (1969), see them as 'ludic' (i.e. playful) pilgrims (Moore 1980, cf Cohen 1988). In fact, both kinds of tourists are empirically observable (Cohen 1979a, 1985a). By analogy, a distinction between serious and ludic representations of native people in touristic images could be made. Combining these three points of departure, a typology of touristic images can be constructed (Figure 4.3).

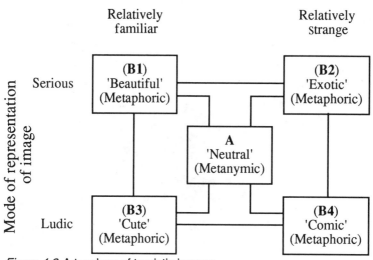

Figure 4.3 A typology of touristic images

Five types of visual touristic images of natives have been distinguished in Figure 4.3. These fall into two categories:

Metanymic ('neutral') images, in the middle of the diagram, are common in most journalistic and scientific representations (Albers and James 1988: 141). Metanymic representations appear to be infrequent in touristic images owing to the symbolic functions of such images. This perception, however, may be based on too narrow a conception of the media presenting touristic images.

Metaphoric images, these are further subdivided into four major types, placed in the four corners of the chart. They correspond to the combinations between the two dichotomized sociological variables which have served as our points of departure for the construction of the typology:

1 *Beautiful* images structured so as to elicit a *serious* appreciation on the part of viewers, according to aesthetic criteria *familiar* to them.
2 *Exotic* images structured so as to elicit a *serious* sense of astonishment or shock in the viewer, which, owing to the relative *strangeness* of the represented image, goes beyond the purely aesthetic.

Plate 4.1 Principal types of touristic images, illustrated by post cards depicting Akha hill tribe women.*

Centre: Type A ('Neutral' – metanymic). Produced by 'Hibou' (No. 28) in Thailand. Photo: Na Nelio.
Caption: 'Originated in the Tibetan highlands, Akha tribes live North of the Kok River. Their villages are located on a high plateau which makes them picturesque.'
Upper left: Type B/1 ('Beautiful' – metaphoric). Produced by 'Pioggia Ltd' (PG009) in Bangkok. Artist: Samai Sricone.
Caption: 'The hill young girl of Chiangmai.'
Upper right: Type B/2 ('Exotic' – metaphoric). Produced by 'Editions Hansjorg Mayer, Stuttgart, London' (purchased in Chiang Mai). Originally published in Lewis & Lewis, 1984.' Unnumbered, photographer not indicated.
Caption: 'Loimi-Akha women singing during first rice planting ceremony.'
Lower left: Type B/3 ('Cute' – metaphoric). Musical card produced by Kats [in Thailand] (No. N210310). (Artist not indicated.)
Caption: 'Thoughts of you are like a cool breeze on a hot day . . .'
Lower right: Type B/4 ('Comic' – metaphoric). Produced by 'Jareuk Publications', 1989, [Chiang Mai]. Artist: Wallop Manyum.
Caption: 'Akha.'
* All objects from author's collection.

3 *Cute* images structured so as to elicit a *ludic* sense of enjoyment in the viewer, by the relatively *familiar* traits of sweetness or prettiness of the represented image.

4 *Comic* images structured so as to elicit a *ludic* sense of merriment in the viewer, by the relatively *unfamiliar* traits of exaggeration or incongruence of the represented image.

The basic assumption underlying this typology is that the touristic images have been prepared for prospective viewers who are not knowledgeable about the native culture and do not share native criteria of beauty or humour. Such individuals should therefore be employed as judges for the classification of a body of materials into the proposed categories. The data of the author's study have not yet been so classified and quantified; however the categories of metanymic and metaphoric representation are illustrated in Plate 4.1 by examples derived from the materials of the study, chosen by the author himself. All the examples are taken from post cards depicting women of a single tribe, the Akha: their arrangement corresponds to that of the categories in Figure 4.3.

The lines connecting the categories in Figure 4.3 indicate that these categories represent only discrete polar cases in continua of two kinds: between metanymic and metaphoric representations and between the metaphoric representations themselves. One should note that not all images will fall clearly into any of the proposed categories; some may fall between neighbouring metaphoric categories, and others between them and the metanymic one (cf Albers and James 1988: 140–2). It should also be noted that the procedure of classification can be carried out in a different manner: instead of using judges to classify the images, one could ask a sample of tourists at the destination to do the classification according to the categories in Figure 4.3, and thus determine empirically how the images are perceived by prospective customers in terms of theoretically relevant variables. Such a procedure would also make it possible to test the hypothesis that there is a correlation between types of tourists and the types of touristic images of native people preferred by them.

A further step of analysis relating to the proposed typology would consist of examining the authenticity of the images. This problem is particularly relevant to the study of the 'neutral' metanymic images – since the apparently objective representation of native people harbours an often unexpected potential for an insidious and covert 'staging of authenticity' (MacCannell 1973, Cohen 1979b: 26–8), or for the introduction of ideological or other biases under the guise of neutrality

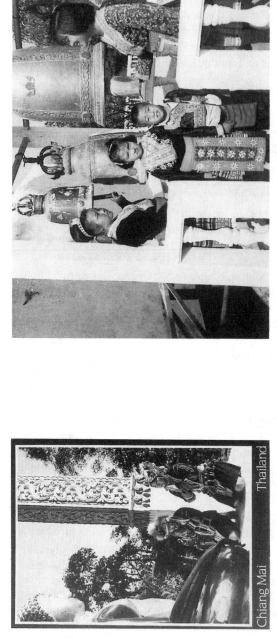

Plate 4.2 Two post cards of hill tribe people in Buddhist temples; the implicit message of such apparently neutral representations is to show that the hill tribes, formerly 'animists', now adhere to Buddhism (and are hence becoming part of the Thai nation; cf. Keyes, 1971).

(4.2a) Left: Akha women worshipping a Buddha image. Produced by 'Art Media', [Bangkok] (No. 2, 56). Photographer not indicated.

Caption: Unrelated to activity.

(4.2b) Right: Hmong (Meo) children ringing temple bells. Produced by 'Phornthip Phatana', [Bangkok] (No. C 38).

Caption: 'The children of Thai mountain folk of Meo are playing the big bell on the Doi Sutepat [Suthep] of Chiang Mai, Northern Thailand' (in English and Japanese).

(Plate 4.2). The problem is also pertinent to metaphoric images, particularly those corresponding to a serious attitude on the part of the observer: the 'beautiful' and the 'exotic' representations of native people. However, while covert staging is also a possibility here, much of the staging tends to be overt (Cohen 1979b: 26–7), in the sense that it is relatively easy to detect, or even openly admitted by the producer. Finally, those images which correspond to a ludic attitude on the part of the observer, the 'cute' and the 'comic', will usually be staged, sometimes covertly, but mostly overtly; but their staging will not be of particular salience to the observers, as long as they approach them with a ludic attitude (cf Cohen 1979a: 183–6, 1985a).

The problem of authenticity of the different types of images can also be approached from two perspectives: it can be established from the perspective of the researcher or of independent judges, using 'ethically' defined criteria of authenticity; or from the perspective of the tourists themselves, for whom the authenticity of an image depends upon some, for them, salient traits, chosen in accordance with their own 'emic' conception of authenticity (cf Cohen 1988).

The distinction between different types of touristic images of native people, whether those which are proposed here or any others, becomes theoretically and empirically more significant if it is seen in relation to the wider social context within which these images are produced: in terms of our mapping sentence, the socio-historical circumstances (element 6) of the native people and the prevailing socio-political relationships (element 7) between them and the majority population. These relations, in turn, have to be examined in a comparative context.

ELEMENTS OF COMPARISON

The first step in developing a programme for the comparative study of touristic images of native people is to determine the principal directions or aspects of comparison. On the basis of the author's study, eight principal aspects of comparison can be suggested:

1 The touristic images of natives and of non-natives (members of the majority and foreigners) in a given destination.
2 The touristic images of natives produced by different categories of producers – such as the natives themselves, the majority population and foreigners.
3 The expressly touristic and the non-touristic (political, ethnographic, etc.) images of natives.

4 The historical and the contemporary touristic images of natives.

5 The touristic images of natives produced by the various media of representation, such as the printed mass-media, advertisements, souvenirs, the arts and touristic events.

6 The touristic images of various groups of natives in a given destination.

7 The touristic images of natives of different destinations.

8 The touristic images of natives and the realities of their socio-historical conditions and their present socio-political relations with the majority population, as derived from relevant social scientific studies.

Each of these elements will be briefly taken up in the following paragraphs and as far as possible illustrated by materials from the author's study.

Touristic images of natives and non-natives (majority and foreigners)

This aspect relates to element (2) in Figure 4.1 and to the horizontal dimension of Figure 4.2. Although it is the most obvious comparison to be made, no study appears yet to have looked systematically into the question of the differences between the touristic images of native people, of the majority population and of foreigners, especially of the tourists, in a given destination. But without such a comparison, one cannot really claim with certainty that certain traits of the touristic image of the natives are characteristic or unique to them, since it is not yet known whether the image of the general population, or of specific other groups, is not characterized by similar traits. A great number of specific questions of comparison could be raised regarding this issue, but only the most important ones will be noted here.

In terms of a purely positivistic approach, the first question would relate to the relative frequency of the images of natives vs non-natives in the different media. The author's study indicates that, at least in one major medium, post cards, the native groups tend to be over-represented in all three case studies; this is especially the case in Western Canada, where the Indians are practically the only people represented on post cards (or on dolls), to the almost complete exclusion of members of the majority – with the exception of some representations of Mounties.

More detailed comparisons of the main variables used in content analysis should reveal differences between the touristic images of native people and those of the majority in terms of demographic and cultural traits such as sex and age distribution, costume and activities. The author's study shows that, while the sex and age distribution of the majority populations – of Jews on Israeli post cards and of Thais on those from Thailand – is very similar, that of the native groups is not: on post cards of Arabs, males and older people are over-represented; in those of the hill tribes – women and children (Cohen forthcoming). Such quantitative findings, in turn, create the background for an interpretative study of the post cards. This should depart from a comparison of the relative 'markedness' of the native vs the non-native groups on the post cards, and then turn to more detailed semiotic analyses of the modes of their respective representations, in terms of the concepts and typologies developed for that purpose, and exemplified in the foregoing section.

Here an insight of a semiotic nature from the author's study should be mentioned. Natives, as well as local members of the majority, are generally represented in the printed media, such as post cards and brochures, as part of the environment and of the ambience of the destination. Tourists, however, when shown in a local environment, seem not so much to constitute part of it, but rather vicariously substitute for the observer of the image – the prospective tourist; tourists depicted in the environment of the destination are there to tell the observer, as it were, 'If you were here, you would see that view or enjoy this activity'. Insofar as they appear on the post cards as substitutes for the observer, they are often turned with their back to the camera, rather than looking into it. Producers of such pictures thus appear not so much to strive to represent an image of the tourists to the observer, as to induce the observer to identify with the tourist in the picture.

Touristic images of natives – produced by the natives themselves and by non-natives (members of the majority and foreigners)

This aspect relates to element 1 in Figure 4.1 and to the first column of Figure 4.2. It complements the preceding one and, like it, appears not to have been systematically examined in the literature. In the first case the focus was on the differences between the images of different groups; here the focus is on the differences between the images of the same group, produced by different kinds of producers. The theoretically interesting question here is whether native people represent themselves in the same manner as others represent them – i.e. reproduce the touristic image imposed upon them from the outside – or strive to develop a 'counter-image', aiming to represent themselves in a manner which contrasts, and – from their point of view – corrects their touristic image, as articulated by external producers (cf Albers and James 1988: 155). The lines of such an inquiry would very much parallel those spelled out on pages 48–9.

The author's own study does not render uniform results in this respect. The hill tribes do not represent themselves in mass media or on souvenirs, all of which are produced by non-natives. The tourist art products on which their self-representations do appear – mainly those of Hmong refugees from Laos (Cohen 1990, 58 ff., see also MacDowell 1989) – are either nostalgic reconstructions of traditional tribal life, and

Plate 4.3 Hmong embroidery showing scenes from the end of the war in Laos (which brought persecution, flight, and eventually internment of Hmong refugees in camps in Thailand).
Caption: '1975 Communist entered; people have been arrested; men have been catch [sic(!)] to kill.' Signed 'by Mai Vang'.

in that respect resemble their image in the mass media, or representations of war, suffering and flight, and as such bear a message which the touristic mass media do not (Plate 4.3). When tribals participate in touristic events, they usually present themselves in festive attire, similar to their representation in the mass media, but richer and more accurate than the images on souvenirs, such as dolls and figurines, produced by others. The events themselves, such as excursions to photograph the Padaung refugee women on the Burmese border, called 'long-neck Karen' or 'giraffe women' in the advertisements (Mirante 1990), or the recently inaugurated 'hill tribe beauty contests' (Girardet 1991), are mostly organized by non-tribals.

Canadian Indians, like Indians all over North America, participated in the past in the reproduction of their own touristic image (Blundell 1989: 53–4). However, more recently, among West Coast Indians, as elsewhere in Canada and the United States, a counter-tendency has emerged, intended to render a different, more 'authentic', more accurate and realistic, or at least more differentiated image of themselves than that produced by non-natives. This tendency can be observed in some of the Indian dolls produced by natives, as well as in performances and museums initiated and organized by them (cf Blundell 1989: 54–6). However, reality often fails to bear out the ideology, and even the products and performances intended to convey a counter-image of the Indians tend in some instances to be highly stylized and simplified or to constitute mere replicas of what are presently perceived to be traditional tribal costumes and customs.

The Israeli and Palestinian Arabs represent themselves for touristic purposes along lines very similar to those along which they are represented by others (cf Albers and James 1988: 154) even though, as we shall see below, their non-touristic self-representation is of a very different character. The differences between the three societies with respect to the manner in which natives represent themselves in comparison to their representation by others, is related to their differential positions in their respective societies, to be discussed below.

Touristic and non-touristic images

The modern touristic establishment and a variety of other agents working in its periphery, produce a wide range of touristic images of native people explicitly intended for the attention, purchase or use by tourists. Major examples are post cards, brochures, posters, and a variety of souvenirs, art products and events featuring native people. However, touristic images are neither born nor exist in a vacuum. They are formed, at least partly, under the influence of other kinds of images of these people, deriving from various other perspectives: ethnographic, religious, cultural, political. These touristic images exist contemporan-

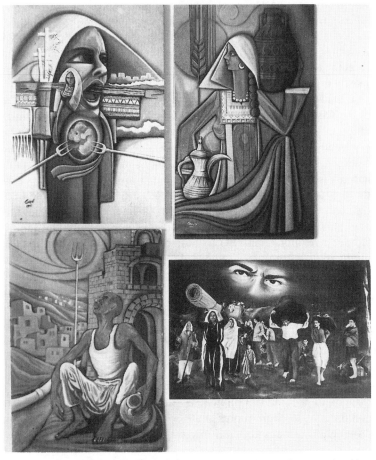

Plate 4.4 Four post cards of paintings by Palestinian painters, related to the resistance to the Israeli occupation.
(4.4a) Upper left: Kamel Mougani: 'Shatella'. Producer not indicated.
(4.4b) Upper right: Kamel Mougani: 'From Heritage'. Producer not indicated.
(4.4c) Lower left: Kamel Mougani: Untitled. Produced by 'Iben Rushd', Jerusalem.
(4.4d) Lower right: Isam Hillis: 'Fate'. Produced by 'Iben Rushd'.

eously side by side with other kinds of images, some of which have been explicitly produced with the intention to countervail them. The comparison between touristic and other images can hence serve to clarify two complementary problems.

First, which were the historical influences which helped to formulate the contemporary images of native people? Thus, contemporary touristic images of the Arabs of the Holy Land reflect the impact of biblical and Western 'Orientalist' (Said 1979, Behdad 1990) images of these people, formulated primarily in the course of the nineteenth century (cf Nir 1985). In contrast, the hill tribes of Thailand historically had no religious or cultural saliency in the West; their touristic image was hence influenced by general – and often misplaced – ideas about 'primitive' peoples, and probably to some extent by their image as it transpires from the work of ethnographers (see Bernatzik 1947, Young 1962, Seidenfaden 1967); and even that is of relatively recent origin.

Second, what are the differences between the contemporaneous touristic and non-touristic (such as anthropological, political, etc.) images of native people? There exists a stark contrast between the image of the Arabs presented by the photo post cards intended for tourists and the post cards reproducing paintings of contemporary Palestinian painters, printed for nationalistic purposes, primarily for the local Palestinian public, within the context of the Palestinian resistance to the Israeli occupation (Shinar 1984) and eventual uprising (*intifada*) (Schiff and Ya'ari 1989, Nassar and Heacock 1991) (Plate 4.4). The differences are not limited only to motifs or style of presentation, but are found even in such variables as the demographic composition of the people depicted: on the nationalistic post cards young people, and especially young women, are much more frequently depicted than on the touristic photo post cards (cf Shinar 1984: 10–12). Plate 4.5 serves as a poignant example of the recontextualization involved in the transition from a touristic to a nationalistic representation of Palestinian women: the photo post card on Plate 4.5a represents two Palestinian women apparently returning from the market in the Old City of Jerusalem with their purchases; the post card on Plate 4.5b, a detail of the painting on the post card in Plate 4.4d captioned 'Fate', shows these same women, obviously copied by the artist from the earlier photo post card (Plate 4.5a), as Palestinian refugees in flight. The touristic image is transmogrified into a political one, by a mere change in the context of representation.

Plate 4.5 Recontextualization of the image of Palestinian women.
(4.5a) Left: Photo post card of Palestinian woman in the market of the Old City of Jerusalem. Produced by 'Palphot' (No. 9978). Photographer not indicated;
Caption: 'Jerusalem. Street scene in the Old City, a labyrinth of narrow streets and lanes, lined with innumerable small shops' (in Hebrew, England and French).
(4.5b) Right: Detail of painting on post card (4.4d) above by Isam Hillis; the two women in front of the painting are a mirror image of those in the photo on post card (4.5a).

Historical and contemporary touristic images

Touristic images vary over time, in response to a changing touristic clientele, and also to changing general attitudes towards native people. The greater tolerance for and appreciation of foreign cultures and growing opposition to chauvinism and racism, suggest that native people – or ethnics in general – will less often be represented as 'exotic' or 'comic', and more often as 'beautiful' or 'cute'. Indeed, it is difficult to imagine that anyone would nowadays produce such bitingly satiric or derogatory images of American blacks (or of any other ethnic group) as were common in the early twentieth century (cf Baldwin 1988, Pieterse 1990). The issue of historical trends in touristic images appears to have been examined systematically only by Albers and James (1983) in a diachronic study of the changing post card image of the Great Lakes Indians. Their very provocative findings will be tested on a comparative basis in the author's study.

Touristic images in different media of representation

This appears to be one of the most important, but also one of the least investigated, comparative aspects. Most studies of touristic images of any kind (not only of native people), deal with two kinds of mass media – post cards (Albers and James 1983, 1988, 1990; Peterson 1985, Baldwin 1988) and tourist brochures (Buck 1977, Cohen 1989, Dann (forthcoming)). Other media, and especially souvenirs and tourist arts and performances, even if studied for other purposes (e.g. Graburn 1976, Gordon 1986), were only rarely investigated as a source of touristic images (but see Blundell 1989 and forthcoming). Moreover, the most significant question on this issue was never really asked, let alone investigated: how does the image of a particular group differ across the various media of representation? This question can be looked into by different research methods but the most pertinent are the interpretative, and particularly the semiotic ones.

In the author's study, only the different materials on Thai hill tribes have as yet been systematically collected or otherwise examined. While young women predominate in representations of the hill tribes in the printed mass media, such as post cards, brochures and posters, they do so even more in most other media, and especially on souvenirs such as dolls and figurines and in touristic events. Men and even children appear rarely in those other media; when they do, they usually appear in conjunction with women, as, for example, on figurines of a hill tribe

Plate 4.6

Plates 4.6 and 4.7 Dolls, figurines, busts and a cup illustrating the diversity of representations of the women of a single hill tribe group – the Lisu – in several media.

couple or a woman carrying a baby on her back. However, there is considerable variety in the manner in which hill tribe women are represented in the different media. Though in all media metaphoric representations predominate, metanymic ones can occasionally be found in the printed mass media. They are very rare in the other types of media, even though some doll makers and touristic painters seek to represent the hill tribes 'as they really are', with only a negligible metaphoric 'hidden message'. Most representations are rich in metaphoric allusions. These vary widely in the different media between the categories of 'beautiful', 'cute', and 'comic' in the above classification (Figure 4.3), with only a few tending toward the 'exotic'.

This range of diversity of representation across the media is here illustrated by a series of images of women from just one hill tribe, the Lisu, in several media: dolls of different kinds, figurines, busts, and a souvenir – a cup (Plates 4.6–4.7). Examples could be multiplied either by adding other media featuring Lisu images or by presenting similar series of images of each of the other hill tribes.

Another point emerging from the comparison of representations across a wide range of media is the considerable variation in ethnographic precision. While hill tribes depicted in the printed mass media are almost always easily identifiable by their costumes, identifiability is generally less in most other types of representation, and tends to decline the smaller and cheaper the object on which they are represented becomes. The important point to note, however, is that this decline occurs in several distinct versions, which are to some extent related to the medium of representation:

1 A gradual reduction in the number of marks by which a representation is identifiable, until eventually only one such distinguishing mark, usually a headdress, remains, as on the figurines in Plate 4.8.
2 A growing vagueness of the marks themselves, so that the image becomes increasingly unidentifiable, until an indeterminate and unclassifiable image of a 'hill tribe', without further specification, emerges.
3 A tendency to combine elements of the costumes of different tribal groups, resulting in a hybrid image which is not classifiable into any tribal group, for example, the woman in the painting in Plate 4.9.
4 The invention of a fanciful 'tribal' costume which resembles those actually worn by some tribal groups in Thailand but differs

markedly from any of them. Such costumes are worn by girls in the border town of Mae Sai who pose for photographs for tourists; these girls also appear on some highly staged recent post cards. Similar pseudo-tribal costumes are often worn by non-tribal Thai school children in performances or parades during festivals in northern Thai cities.

Although such processes recall those described by Albers and James (1983: 134 ff.) for the American Indians, they differ in one principal respect: in the US the costume of one group, that of the Plains Indians, came to dominate the image of 'the Indian'. In Thailand, no tribe achieved such a position of dominance in the formation of the hill tribe image.

Tourist images of different native groups

Within a given country or society there may live more than one group of native people, differing from each other in language, culture, costume or habitat. Not all of these groups are touristically equally 'marked'. In Thailand there is a large number of native groups of diverse origins (Seidenfaden 1967: 105–26), among whom only six major, and some smaller hill tribes have become touristically 'marked' (McKinnon and Bhruksasri 1983, Lewis and Lewis 1984, McKinnon and Vienne 1989). Half a dozen larger Indian tribes, all of them to some degree touristically 'marked', are found along the West Coast of Canada (McMillan 1988: 170–211). In Israel, in addition to urban, rural and (in the past) nomadic Arabs (Bedouin), there is a range of smaller non-Jewish minorities, such as the Druze, but only the Arabs, and even more the Bedouins, are touristically significantly 'marked'. One problem of comparison, then, is to investigate the reasons for this differential 'markedness'. Another problem emerges from the fact that the majority population usually entertains differential attitudes and prejudices towards each of the various native groups. The question therefore arises: are the touristic images of these groups differentiated along the lines indicated by those attitudes and prejudices, or do they tend to become homogenized, as would follow from the studies of Albers and James (1983, 1988)? As pointed out above, at least in the hill tribe material, no such homogenization has been noted. The preliminary observations made by the author in Canada and the materials collected indicate that, in contrast to the tendency observed for the US Indians by Albers and James, no homogeneous image of a 'West Coast Indian' is emerging there; rather,

Plate 4.8 Three unclad wooden hanging dolls wearing the headdresses of Karen (left), Lisu (middle) and Yao (right) hill tribe women.

Plate 4.9 A painting of a woman carrying a baby of mixed tribal traits: headdress of Akha woman, skirt and apron of Meo woman.

the individuality of tribal groups has not been erased and is presently even re-emphasized. But a degree of homogenization or, better, fusion, has appeared in one area – totem poles erected for public or touristic consumption often combine symbols taken from different tribal groups. Finally, in Israel, a fairly homogeneous image of the 'Arabs' is presented in the touristic media, which is little related to the actual attitudes to them of the majority Jewish population. However, a distinction between the touristic image of 'Arabs' and 'Bedouins' has been maintained.

Tourist images of native people of different destinations

This aspect can be studied on two levels, a specific and a general one. There are native people, such as some South East Asian hill tribes and North American Indians or Inuit, who constitute minorities in more than one country. The comparative question, on the specific level, then, would be: is the same group similarly or differently represented to tourists in the media of those societies? Such specific comparisons would constitute interesting and precise test cases of the impact of contextual factors on the formation of touristic images. The comparative question formulated on the more general level would be: is there a tendency to represent the diverse native groups, differing widely in language, culture and costumes, and living among different majority populations, in a similar stereotypical manner to visiting tourists, or is there a significant variance in the manner of their representation? In a wider and less precise manner, this question, too, relates to the importance of contextual factors, as against the impact of some kind of general tourist culture, on the formation of touristic images of native people. These contextual factors are the subject of the following, and last, comparative issue.

Tourist images and social reality

This is perhaps the sociologically most significant comparative aspect, since it relates to one of the principal themes in the sociology of tourism: the tension between the way destinations are presented to tourists and the way they are 'in reality'. It thus touches upon the role of ideologies and interests – political, economic and cultural – in the creation of touristic images of native people.

From a methodological point of view it is important to stress that this kind of comparison necessitates not only a study of the touristic images but also a clear conception of the contrasting 'social reality', since both are constructs; there is no sheer reality 'out there' with which the touristic images could be simply compared. Indeed, in cases less extreme than those of the Andean highlands and the occupied West Bank, it may not always be a simple matter to perceive and gauge the extent and nature of the discrepancy between the image of a native group and the real conditions of its social existence.

The discrepancy between touristic images and social reality is pointed out succinctly in such statements as the one at the head of this chapter. However, it is not sufficient to state the existence of a discrepancy; it is necessary to establish precisely what the discrepancy consists of, how, and by whom it was produced, as well as the nature of the social mechanisms that produce and reproduce it in actual practice.

The discrepancy is often a consequence of the staging of the native people's authenticity by the touristic establishment (MacCannell 1973) or other interested institutions or individuals. Such staging is of crucial importance in the formation of tourists' impressions of a destination. However, while the fact of staging in itself creates the discrepancy, the manner of staging has to be looked into. Is it overt or covert (Cohen 1979b: 26–8)? Is it effected merely by a judicious selection and de-contextualization of situations and poses taken from the life of the subjects, by the interpretation (or misinterpretation) of the depicted situations or poses by means of captions, descriptions or other textual means, or is it achieved by outright fabrication of otherwise non-existent situations, customs or costumes (Cohen 1985b: 14–16), or even of whole native groups (cf Berreman 1991)?

However, the most important comparative problem relating to this issue concerns the wider social mechanisms which produce and reproduce the discrepancy. According to the present approach the discrepancy is a consequence of socio-historical conditions which helped to form the touristic image of the native people discussed on pages 51–5; and of the prevailing socio-political relationships between the native people and the majority population (elements (6) and (7) in Figure 4.1). For purposes of comparison between the touristic images and the social reality of native people, these conditions and relationships should be carefully determined on the basis of anthropological, socio-logical and political studies, as well as less formal but reliable informa-tion. One should beware of deriving them from popular counter-images, often purposely formulated to contest prevailing touristic images, which may be as much slanted as the latter.

The prevailing touristic image of native people may not be *directly* related to the prevailing relationships between native people and the majority population.

Thus, there is no direct connection between the tendency to present the Arabs of Israel and the occupied territories as if they were the contemporary prototypes of the people of the Bible, and the *intifada*, the Palestinian uprising against the Israeli occupation.

However, there may exist an indirect and more insidious connection: the presentation of the Arabs in biblical terms may be purposely intended to deflect the tourists' and pilgrims' attention away from the present predicament of the Arab population.

An extreme example of the oblique liaison between insidious political motives and economic interests and purposeful misrepresentation of a native people is the hoax perpetrated by Marcos' régime in the Philippines, of 'discovering' an innocent, lovable and peaceful 'stone-age' people, the 'Tasaday', which were then presented in a tightly controlled manner to selected foreign visitors (Berreman 1991). The ulterior motives of this elaborate hoax are difficult to establish unequivocally but one of the dominant ones appears to have been the desire of its perpetrators 'to make available to themselves and their cronies the natural resources' of the area in which the Tasaday were allegedly discovered, and which was declared a Special Forest Preserve upon that discovery (Berreman 1991: 21). The fabrication of the 'lovable' Tasaday was thus a trick intended to help to exploit the environment inhabited by other, 'real' tribal people. It appears, then, that the more a native people is exposed to political pressures or economic exploitation by outside agencies, the greater the ideological significance of their (spurious) touristic image, produced by interested outsiders, and the greater, also, the discrepancy between this image and reality.

A last point to note is that 'discrepancy' is not a simple variable, but may be broken down into several sub-variables. Thus, there is less of a discrepancy between the touristic image of Arabs or of the hill tribes and their *cultural* reality. For example, many Arabs and hill tribe people in their daily lives often wear the costumes in which they are represented and perform the activities or celebrations in which they are depicted. The discrepancy is much greater in the case of the West Coast Indians who are represented on post cards, dolls and in performances wearing pseudo-traditional costumes or performing reconstructed customs which have not been part of their usual practice for many years. However, the discrepancy between the touristic image and the *socio-political* reality is much greater in the case of Arabs or the hill-tribes than it is in the case of the West Coast Indians. The Arabs suffer from suppression of their national aspirations and from progressive economic dependency upon the Jewish majority, which destroys the socio-economic basis of their community life. The hill tribes are undergoing progressive deculturation and, in some instances, pauperization, as they are being forcibly settled and incorporated into the Thai state (see Kesmanee 1988, Eudey 1988, McKinnon 1987). The representation of these native groups as biblical people contentedly tending their sheep or ploughing their fields, or as colourful, exotic or cute primitives with quaint customs, completely falsifies the socio-political reality. The touristic image of the West Coast Indian tribes does not directly reflect their present political aspirations, especially not the reassertion of their national identities and rights, but it is not incongruent with these. Indeed, it may even assist them in their struggle, by drawing the awareness of the external touristic public to their separate existence and identity.

CONCLUSION

Touristic images of native people, according to Albers and James (1988: 154), underwent processes of homogenization, decontextualization and mystification. These authors argue that 'the diverse cultural motifs that tourism uses in its various productions' are woven together by a 'dehistoricized' thread, which is 'easily manipulated in the interests of a commodity-oriented leisure travel'. This is certainly a significant and, to a large extent, correct conclusion. There is little doubt that touristic images, at least from this perspective, can be seen as manifesting a growing similarity. The problem with this perspective, however, is not that it is incorrect but rather that it stops the investigation at a certain point and thus precludes the emergence of another perspective and of a new set of questions, which may perhaps mitigate the stereotype of the stereotype of native people as represented for touristic purposes and show that underlying the apparent homogeneity of touristic images there is nevertheless considerable diversity.

The underlying rationale of the argument presented here is that similarity and diversity, like continuity and change (Smith 1982, Cohen 1985c), are not fixed concepts but are essentially negotiable. A group of phenomena may from the perspective of one set of philosophical, ideological or theoretical interests appear very similar but from another perspective may appear highly diverse, depending upon the traits of the phenomena on which the observer's perspective fixes. Thus, the images which looked uniform and stereotypical from the perspective of researchers such as Albers and James, may from a fresh perspective look differentiated. Indeed, the mitigation of the stereotype of touristic images of native people was the principal aim of this chapter. In order to achieve it, it was necessary to develop a new theoretical, methodological and comparative perspective, leading to a research programme on touristic images which would generate novel theoretical problems and empirical questions.

In the preceding sections the principal elements on which such a programme could be built and the lines of comparative study along which it could proceed have been outlined. While the various elements and lines of comparison were discussed separately or in pairs, it should be stressed that viable research designs can be developed by combining them into larger constellations, responding to the theoretical interests of the researcher. Though emphases may vary, the principal issues of theoretical significance to be studied are, from the perspective developed here and in the author's own current work, those which relate to the specificities of the touristic images of various native people in different media, as they emerged under diverse socio-historical conditions and socio-political relationships.

NOTE

This paper is based on research conducted during several periods of field-work in the course of the years 1988–91 in Israel, Canada and Thailand. The work on Israel and Canada was supported by a grant from the Program of Canadian Studies, and the work on Thailand by a grant from the Harry S. Truman Institute, both at the Hebrew University of Jerusalem. This support is hereby gratefully acknowledged.

REFERENCES

Albers, P. C. and James, W. R. (1983) 'Tourism and the changing photographic image of the Great Lakes Indians', *Annals of Tourism Research* 10, 1: 123–48.
——(1988) 'Travel photography: a methodological approach', *Annals of Tourism Research* 15, 1: 134–58.
——(1990) 'Private and public images: a study of photographic contrasts in postcard pictures of Great Basin Indians, 1898–1919', *Visual Anthropology* 3: 343–66.
Baldwin, B. (1988) 'On the Verso: postcard messages as a key to popular prejudices', *Journal of Popular Culture* 22, 3: 15–28.
Behdad, A. (1990) 'Orientalist tourism', *Peuples Méditerranéens* 50: 59–73.
Bernatzik, H. A. (1947) *Akha und Meo*, Innsbruck: Wagner'sche Universitats–Buchdruckerei.

Berreman, G. D. (1991) 'The incredible "Tasaday", deconstructing the myth of a "Stone-Age" people', *Cultural Survival Quarterly* 15, 1: 2–44.

Blundell, V. (1989) 'The Tourist and the Native', in B. Cox, J. Chevalier and V. Blundell (eds) *A Different Drummer*, Ottawa: Carleton University Anthropology Caucus, 51–8.

——forthcoming: ' "Take Home Canada"; Representations of Aboriginal Peoples as Tourist Souvenirs', in S. Riggins (ed.) *The Sociosemantics of Things*.

Boorstin, D. J. (1964) *The Image: a Guide to Pseudo-events in America*, Harper & Row, New York.

Buck, R. C. (1977) 'The ubiquitous tourist brochure', *Annals of Tourism Research* 4, 4: 195–207.

Clifford, J. (1988) *The Predicament of Culture*, Cambridge, MA: Harvard University Press.

Cohen, E. (1972) 'Toward a sociology of international tourism', *Social Research* 39, 1, 164–82.

——(1979a) 'A phenomenology of tourist experiences', *Sociology* 13, 179–201.

——(1979b) 'Rethinking the sociology of tourism', *Annals of Tourism Research* 6, 1, 18–35.

——(1982) *The Pacific Islands from Utopia to Consumer Product: The Disenchantment of Paradise*, Cahiers du Tourisme, Ser. B, no. 27, Aix-en-Provence: Centre des Hautes Etudes Touristiques.

——(1985a) 'Tourism as play', *Religion* 15: 291–304.

——(1985b) 'The tourist guide: the origins, structure and dynamics of a role', *Annals of Tourist Research* 12, 1: 5–29.

——(1985c) 'Sociocultural change in Thailand: a reconceptualization', in E. Cohen, M. Lissak, U. Almagor (eds) *Comparative Social Dynamics*, Boulder: Westview Press: 82–94, reprinted in: E. Cohen, 1991: *Thailand in Comparative Perspective*, Bangkok: White Lotus (forthcoming).

——(1988) 'Authenticity and commoditization in tourism', *Annals of Tourism Research* 15, 3: 371–86.

——(1989) 'Primitive and remote: Hill tribe trekking in Thailand', *Annals of Tourism Research* 16, 1: 30–61.

——(1990) 'Hmong (Meo) commercialized refugee art: from ornament to picture', in D. Eban, E. Cohen, and B. Danet (eds), *Art as a Means of Communication in Pre-literate Societies*, Jerusalem: Israel Museum: 51–95.

——(forthcoming) *Arabs and Jews on Postcards in Israel*.

Crocombe, R. G. (1973) *The New South Pacific*, Wellington: Reed Education.

Dann, G. M. S. (forthcoming) *The People of Tourist Brochures*.

Dann, G. M. S., Nash, D. and Pearce, P. L. (1988) 'Methodological issues in tourism research', *Annals of Tourism Research* 15, 1: 1–172.

Eudey, A. (1988) 'Hmong relocated in Northern Thailand', *Cultural Survival Quarterly* 12, 1: 79–82.

Evans-Pritchard, D. (1989) 'How "They" see "Us", native American images of tourists', *Annals of Tourism Research* 16, 1: 89–105.

Fabian, J. (1983) *Time and the Other: How Anthropology Makes Its Object*, New York: Columbia University Press.

Girardet, E. (1991) 'Backstage jitters', *Contours* 5, 1: 18–19.

Gordon, B. (1986) 'The souvenir: messenger of the extraordinary', *Journal of Popular Culture* 20, 3: 135–46.

Graburn, N. H. H. (n.d.) 'Why Eskimos? Why Canada? The Fourth World in the First', unpublished ms.

——(ed.) (1976) *Ethnic and Tourist Arts*, Berkeley: University of California Press.

Jules-Rosette, B. (1984) *The Messages of Tourist Art: an African Semiotic System in Comparative Perspective*, London: Plenum.

Kesmanee, C. (1988) 'Hilltribe relocation policy in Thailand', *Cultural Survival Quarterly* 12, 4: 2–6.

Keyes, C. F. (1971) 'Buddhism and national integration in Thailand', *Journal of Asian Studies* 30: 551–68.

Keyes, C. F. and van den Berghe, P. L. (eds) (1984) 'Tourism and ethnicity', *Annals of Tourism Research* 11, 3: 343–501.

Lewis, P. and Lewis, E. (1984) *Peoples of the Golden Triangle; Six Tribes of Thailand*, London: Thames & Hudson.

MacCannell, D. (1973) 'Staged authenticity: arrangements of social space in tourist settings', *American Journal of Sociology* 79, 3: 589–603.

——(1976) *The Tourist: A New Theory of the Leisure Class*, New York: Schocken.

MacDowell, M. (coordinator) (1989) *Stories in Thread: Hmong Pictorial Embroidery*, Michigan Traditional Arts Program, Folk Arts Division, Michigan State University Museum.

McKinnon, J. (1987) 'Resettlement and the three ugly step-sisters, security, opium and land degradation: a question of survival for the Highlanders of Thailand', paper presented at the Conference on Thai Studies, ANU, Canberra, 3–6 July 1987.

McKinnon, J. and Bhruksasri, W. (eds) (1983) *Highlanders of Thailand*, Kuala Lumpur: Oxford University Press.

McKinnon, J. and Vienne, B. (eds) (1989) *Hill Tribes Today: Problems in Change*, Bangkok: White Lotus: ORSTROM.

McMillan, A. D. (1988) *Native Peoples and Cultures of Canada*, Vancouver: Douglas and McIntyre.

Mirante, E. T. (1990) 'Hostages to tourism', *Cultural Survival Quarterly* 14, 1: 35–8.

Moore, A. (1980) 'Walt Disney World: bounded ritual space and the playful pilgrimage center', *Anthropological Quarterly* 53: 207–17.

Nassar, J. R. and Heacock, R. (eds) (1991) *Intifada; Palestine on the Crossroads*, Birzeit: Birzeit University.

Nir, Y. (1985) *The Bible and the Image: The History of Photography in the Holy Land 1839–1899*, Philadelphia: University of Pennsylvania Press.

Peterson, N. (1985) 'The popular image', in I. and T. Donaldson (eds), *Seeing the First Australians*, Sydney: George Allen & Unwin: 164–80.

Pieterse, J. N. (1990) *Wit over zwart: beelden van Africa en zwarten in der westerse populaire cultuur.* [White over Black: Pictures of Africa and Blacks in the Western Popular Culture], Amsterdam: Koninkligk Instituut voor de Tropen.

Said, E. (1979) *Orientalism*, New York: Vintage Books.

Schiff, Z. and Ya'ari, E. (1989) *Intifada: The Palestinian Uprising – Israel's Third Front*, New York: Simon & Schuster.

Seidenfaden, E. (1967) *The Thai Peoples*, Bangkok: The Siam Society.

Shinar, D. (1984) 'Art and communications in the West Bank: visual dimensions of Palestinian nation building', *Studies in Visual Communication* 10, 2: 1–15.

Smith, M. E. (1982) 'The process of sociocultural continuity', *Current Anthropology* 23, 2: 127–42.

Smith, V. (1977) 'Introduction', in V. Smith (ed.) *Hosts and Guests*, Philadelphia: University of Pennsylvania Press: 1–14.

Starn, O. (1991) 'Missing the revolution: anthropologists and the war in Peru', *Cultural Anthropology* 6, 1: 63–91.

Turner, V. W. (1969) *The Ritual Process*, Harmondsworth: Penguin.

Young, G. (1962) *The Hill Tribes of Northern Thailand*, Bangkok: The Siam Society.

Chapter 5

Methodological and conceptual issues raised by the study of international tourism

A test for sociology

Marie-Françoise Lanfant

> We would do well to remind ourselves from time to time, that along
> the way we might fall in a well without being able to reach the bottom
> for a long time.
>
> (Heidegger 1971: 15)

INTRODUCTION: SOCIOLOGY AND TOURISM

The relationship between sociology and tourism is a never-ceasing source of amazement. It is a relationship that should be self-evident since it is a well-known fact that tourism, as a social practice and a representation, as well as a system of action and decision-making, is becoming an increasingly important dynamic of contemporary societies. However, the marriage between sociology and tourism is fraught with difficulties. It has become commonplace among those research scientists interested in this object of study – such as geographers, sociologists, anthropologists, as well as psychologists, semiologists, political scientists, historians and many others – to deplore the difficulties encountered in earning recognition for their research within their own respective disciplines (Crick 1989).

There are numerous cases of those who have suffered the mockery or the scepticism of their colleagues. Nash and Smith observed that:

> It has been suggested that it would be demeaning for an
> anthropologist to be identified with what many think is a frivolous
> activity or with people who look in a less authoritative way on other
> people's 'ways'.
>
> (Nash and Smith 1991: 14)

Francesco Frangialli, Deputy Secretary General of the World Tourism

Organization, echoes the difficulty in overcoming this impression of frivolity:

> If you try and indicate the fact that you are, in reality, studying the development of one of the world's primary economic activities, which demands a serious and attentive approach, you will usually only receive a slightly sardonic smile, clearly marked by the scepticism of your interlocutor.
>
> (Frangialli 1991: 1)

Sociology is like an elderly lady concerned about her respectability and with preserving her own identity while dealing with other related disciplines. Within the academic establishment, the bringing together of different disciplines necessitates delimiting the boundaries of each, which in turn entails referring back to its history and its conceptual underpinnings. Sociology cannot escape the rule to which the creation of any new field of research has to conform in order to be legitimized.

This academic position is destabilized when the study of tourism attaches itself to the phenomena of mobility. Sociology then escapes from predetermined points of reference and is opened up to the other, to the otherness of the other, to the unknown of the otherness of the other and of the Other. This is what give it its own identity. Sociology develops from this opening up.

The difficult relationship that sociology has with international tourism constitutes an epistemological obstacle which we must examine in order to be able to pursue our research. For we are now coming to that absurd situation where international tourism, a phenomenon that is increasingly being encountered by sociology, is disregarded by the discipline and really only studied by chance. Admittedly the social science special issue of the *Annals of Tourism Research* (18, 1, 1991) stresses that this field of research is gradually achieving some degree of maturity (Graburn and Jafari, 1991); that the study of tourism as a cultural phenomenon is increasingly imposing itself on anthropology (Nash and Smith 1991); and that the great diversity in approaches initiated by various sociological schools of thought is indeed a blessing (Dann and Cohen 1991). Nevertheless, it remains very difficult to assess, from the work that has been done in sociology and anthropology, the challenge which international tourism represents, as we still appear to be very attached to our established conceptual foundations.

Adding to this difficulty is the fact that surrounding this object of study there are mechanisms of projection, of identification and of denial which prevent us from standing back and which impair scientific objectivity. Within every sociologist is a tourist, something of which he is unaware, so the very fact of regarding the relationship which sociology has with tourism as an epistemological problem provokes resistance, even aggression. Here one comes into contact with that which Merleau-Ponty defined as the 'access to the other' (Merleau-Ponty 1960: 144), which is also perhaps the blind spot of sociology.

INTERNATIONAL TOURISM: A SOCIOLOGICAL OBJECT?

'Tourism is not a sociological object.' This declaration by the sociologist who had been appointed by the French National Centre for Scientific Research (CNRS), during the evaluation of a research project on tourism, was understood by the candidate as being the rejection of his work. The rejection of the object of the research during this 'rite of passage', which at the same time was a 'rite of legitimatization' and a 'rite of consecration' (Bourdieu 1982: 121), could 'discourage on a long term basis the temptation of the passage' (p. 128) and cast the object of research into the fringes of sociology. This declaration nevertheless raises one incisive question that merits scrutiny: what is a sociological object?

This question has occupied a central place in sociological epistemology since Durkheim. 'The first rule and the most fundamental' that he assigns to sociology is 'to consider social facts as things' (Durkheim 1968: 15). And this rule, despite the controversies that it aroused, to this day maintains its impact, inasmuch as it demands of the sociologist that he frees himself from 'sensitive images' from 'crudely formed concepts' (XV) and that he adopts a 'mental attitude of scientific objectivity' towards social facts (XIII). The sociology of international tourism cannot escape this rule despite the pitfalls awaiting it.

In the 1960s, when a sociology of leisure was being founded in France, Pierre Bourdieu was already sensitive to the predicament that the sociologist confronted in his concern for objectivity when he, as a subject, was implicated in the object of his investigation:

> It is not a coincidence if the domains of sociology such as the study of the means of communication or leisure are more receptive to the problematics and schemes of spontaneous sociology. In addition to already being obligatory themes of common conversation in modern society, these objects owe their ideological load to the fact that it is yet again with himself that the intellectual is dealing.
>
> (Bourdieu, Chamboredon and Passeron 1968: 60)

I fully agree with Bourdieu's point of view and if I understand him correctly, this means that the sociologist who dedicates himself to these objects of study should not only tear himself from surrounding ideologies, from common sense prejudices, but somehow tear himself from himself, renouncing the object of fantasy which gives consistence to discourse. Adopting a sociological attitude towards tourism means not taking up the literal meanings of common discourse but, on the contrary, disregarding these meanings and asking oneself how objects acquire meaning (Quine 1977: 13–37).

It is by the mediation of language that sociology encounters tourism as a social fact. The word tourism invades social discourse, it returns like a leitmotiv in the most banal conversations, as well as in the philosophical reflections of our contemporaries, it sinks into political discourse and plunges into the discourse of scientists. Tourism has become part of the network of linguistic exchanges and as such is connected to the structures which articulate these exchanges. It is from here that it draws its meaning as a social fact.

At the beginning of my studies in the field of tourism, almost twenty years ago, I insisted on rigorously setting up a system of hypotheses and demonstrating its predictive value by a verification procedure based on scientific rationality. But as my contact with this object of research continued to develop, I had to abandon my pretensions and listen ever more attentively to the urgent questions which emerged in my circle, as it soon became clear that it was there that a place for analysing this phenomenon presented itself. In this way I became aware of the potentialities which sweep along this field of research in the sociology of international tourism. The study of international tourism led me to a place which was unforeseen in the original project. Our field of research resembles more and more that 'elsewhere' of Michel Foucault, 'everything overloaded with complex figures, entangled paths, strange sites, secret passages and unforeseen communications' (Foucault 1966: 10–11).

THE LESSON OF EXPERIENCE

My adventure began during the 1960s when, as a sociologist attached to Joffre Dumazedier's Sociology of Leisure Team within the CNRS, I was invited to introduce the basics of this sociology by lecturing to university students at the Centre of Advanced Studies of Tourism (CEST) of the University of Paris I – Sorbonne. The CEST's mission was to train future tourist promotion executives. This institution trained

French and foreign students, the latter generally coming from developing regions which were opening their borders to international tourism. Some of the latter held scholarships from the government of their country of origin and were preparing themselves to assume top level professional responsibilities in their home countries. It was then that I sensed the stakes which tourism represented in the world economy and in international exchange. During my lectures over the years I have had students from almost all parts of the globe where tourism is important. This is how I became involved with the international reality of tourism.

That lecturing experience turned out to be decisive for the beginning of my research and immediately led me to conceive of tourism as being an essential mode of international exchange, with no distinction being made between its cultural and economic dimensions. Through this experience a fundamental contradiction became more pronounced: I was faced with two categories of students, the majority were French, imbued with the mounting values of leisure, particularly as their career choices were thus legitimized; the second group was from the Third World, for whom the words tourism and leisure did not even figure in the vocabulary of their own languages but who, nevertheless, had to acquire these terms when faced with the tourist development of their own countries. I was incapable of examining the whole range of social and cultural phenomena relating to the implantation of international tourism in the world, especially in developing countries. I had been asking myself if my lectures had other functions than those of indoctrinating my audience with an ideology of leisure aimed at masking the expansionist movements of the rich towards poor societies. I needed to stand back and judge the content of these lectures. This is how my book, *Theories of Leisure. Sociology of Leisure and Ideologies,* was born (Lanfant 1972).

With this is mind I attempted to deconstruct the code to which the different sociological theories of leisure and free time constantly refer. To this end I brought together a group of authors of both Marxist and liberal persuasions and, while taking the capitalist and socialist contexts in which their thought developed into consideration, I compared the epistemological and conceptual bases which sustained them. This analysis was based on the principles of structural analysis and led to the identification of the 'common conceptual framework' of all these different sociologies. This in turn gave rise to the question which still remains topical: while claiming the universality of leisure values which have originated in the context of Western industrialized societies, does not the sociology of leisure carry in itself the germs of a totalitarian ideology? This ideology is all the more dangerous as it is not perceived by authors who lay claim to this discourse and who often pose as anti-totalitarian and as apostles of modern individualism.

The concept of leisure elaborated by sociology is born in the context of Western societies and bears the stamp of ideals peculiar to Western culture. The phenomenon of tourism is viewed through a unilateral model of explanation which does not come to grips with the nature of the exchanges between the developed and the underdeveloped worlds engendered by the growth of international tourism.

The sociology of leisure deals with tourism as a special free time activity. It annexes tourism into its repertory of leisure activities; it defines it by relying on the properties which it attributes to leisure, such as the need for a break, to escape, to compensate and for personal accomplishment, and in this vein, it offers an explanation of the development of tourism based on the individual demand for leisure. But in fact the sociology of leisure did not really proceed to analyse the phenomenon of tourism as such in a systematic manner. It ignored the formidable organization of the apparatus of international tourist promotion which is aimed at increasing the mobility of industrial and urban populations and dispatching them to the tourist resorts of underdeveloped regions. It underestimated the new sense of free time spent in travelling undertaken in the context of mass tourism consumption.

Listening to the questions asked by these students and witnessing their intercultural confrontation led me to establish correlations between two series of facts, which at first seemed unrelated but which in reality do belong together. On the one hand, the increase of free time and the promotion of leisure in industrialized societies and, on the other, the desire for development in economically weak societies.

I let the students make their own decisions. According to their own personal experience they were free to choose the theme of the dissertation or paper to conclude their studies. By so doing, I gradually became aware of the profound implications that tourism has for the ethnic groups of host societies, disrupting their identities at the most existential level. At this stage of reflection, it became imperative to change the points of reference.

At that time in France research on the overall significance of tourism was virtually non-existent. The majority of sociological studies treated tourism as a leisure activity, or managed to reduce the phenomenon of tourism to that of holidaying. What is more, the models of explanation

and the concepts borrrowed from other domains were being transposed
to the study of tourism; the various disciplines interested in the study of
tourism borrowed from each other without having analysed their mutual
bonds, thereby repeating similar types of explanations. Research was
undertaken in a fragmented and unsatisfying fashion. This conclusion
concerning the state of affairs in tourism research was reached in the
1970s, and Dann and Cohen still found it valid in 1991.

From 1972 onwards I progressively initiated research in this domain.
My primary concern was to produce a framework of theoretical and
methodological analysis which would allow me to analyse tourism
using a global approach and respecting its pluridimensionality in order
to understand what logic lies behind its development on the international
scale. From 1972 to 1982 I launched five large international surveys
within the institutional framework of the CNRS. A research team, which
we later named URESTI, was founded at the same time.

The intention behind these surveys was less to produce and verify
facts than to construct, through an inductive approach, methodological
and conceptual tools based on empirical evidence. Our research was
carried out in stages, each new phase linked to the preceding one, and by
looking back it was possible to determine coherence in the results and
identify important points.

We adopted a strong hypothesis right from the start, defining tourism
as an 'international fact' and emphasizing its exchange value according
to concepts proposed by Durkheim and Mauss. For Durkheim (1969:
681–5) 'Certain phenomena are more related to exchanges between
peoples. They surpass a national territory . . . in a certain manner they
live a supranational life.' And for Mauss (1969: 243) 'One could divide
social phenomena into two big groups; some are incapable of travelling,
by nature the others are capable of doing so: they themselves transcend
the limits of any given society, limits which are themselves often
difficult to determine.'

To present tourism as an international fact is to break with all those
approaches based on marketing, which analyse tourism as being the
result of a demand for leisure to be found in industrial societies. It means
overcoming the separation established by the studies carried out either
in the countries who send out tourists or in those which are the tourists'
hosts, without linking the two. It is an attempt to develop an overall
concept of this phenomenon which is being formed at the point of
articulation of the modern and the traditional, the industrial and the
archaic, the rural and the urban worlds. By observing things at an
international scale, we are creating a global framework of analysis.

We initiated this analysis using the notion of 'total social phenomenon'. This notion, as it has been treated and put into practice by anthropology, proved to be a particularly appropriate way of operationalizing research in this field. To understand tourism as 'total social fact' means considering that the social element is always present in the object of analysis, even though this might be found in very tenuous areas of sociality or even outside the domain of sociology as such (e.g. demographic and economic questions). Finally, we employed a pluridimensional systemic approach. With systemic analysis, our reasoning is no longer based on a fixed point of reference, for example, of a national or local territory, but begins by defining the sociological object at the outset within a system of interrelations. In the field of international tourism the choice of systemic analysis as a working hypothesis proved to be determinant. It was to free us from an explanation of the tourist phenomenon as a purely Western ideal of leisure or as a symmetrical vision of terms of exchange.

DEVELOPMENT OF THE RESEARCH PROGRAMME

Our first investigation relied on statistics and highlighted issues regarding source materials to be used. Abundant statistical information about departures and arrivals, both national and international, does indeed exist. A synthesis based on the perspective I have adopted, that is, tourism as a means of international exchange, had not yet been undertaken. We sifted through all the data covering five continents, applying the methodological principles of graph theory, which enabled us to go beyond the linkages of sending and receiving societies and uncover a system of structural relationships. A graph of international tourist areas needed to be drawn to reveal the dominant links formed on a global level between sending and receiving regions, as well as the poles of domination and dependence. Based on this, we could elaborate hypotheses which then needed working through, on the nature of the international exchanges caused by tourism and their possible implications for internal economic and cultural systems and for social relationships.

This project ran up against the problems of data sources. Not only did statistics lack reliability due to compilation difficulties but the data carried the stamp of alarming normative assumptions. Elaborated to meet the objectives of foreign trade, they were based on definitions that met the criteria of profit making and the needs of tourist promotion. Our attention was then directed towards the official discourse of international tourism which we attempted to deconstruct (Lanfant and de Almeida Matos 1972). Structural analysis enabled us to identify significant articulations and the conceptual basis which underlay them. Tourism is officially regarded primarily as being an economic fact. Tourism is understood in terms of supply and demand, the tourist demand recorded in sending countries, the tourist product enhanced or promoted in the receiving countries. Questions are constantly raised about fluctuations of supply and demand on the market, but as these phenomena are seen in conjunctural terms, structural implications are lost. What is more, this notion contains the germs of an ideology. Official tourism thought is transcended by a notion of international exchange in which the relationships that tourism creates between the developed and the underdeveloped worlds are seen to be reciprocal. Host societies which offer their territory to tourists are understood to enrich themselves due to the foreign exchange brought in by those who come from wealthy countries. Tourism is portrayed as a means of redistributing disposable income from wealthy countries to those that are less well off. This ideological model is a substitute for a theory of exchange.

Dissociating itself deliberately from this supply and demand problematic, the research that followed emphasized the national and international centres of decision making which governed international tourist promotion, by considering them to be social actors. Content analysis of national and international tourist policies was undertaken using a framework which integrated sending and receiving societies into a network. In this way the decision-making system which coordinates tourist activity was reconstituted step by step. Tourist activity was analysed in terms of its diverse interactions, enabling us to reveal the complex organizational structure that underlies such activity on a global scale.

In terms of promotion, tourist activity is seen as the result of a combination of multiple and convergent forces: the tourist industry composed of networks of multinational firms, the centralizing tourist policies of international governmental organizations, the elaboration and diffusion of the economic doctrine which fosters tourism as a means of development for developing countries by linking such development to the growth of tourist consumption in the rich countries, the integrating and unifying effects of tourist promotion strategies which interfere with cultural, artistic and religious practices and with lifestyles which are not by nature tourist products. Thus one ends up by pointing out the 'international system of tourist action', that is, a network of agents belonging to various powers – financial, technical, scientific, cultural, educational, religious – which forms a complex whole (Lanfant and de Weerdt 1975).

From this perspective, the movement of millions of people across national borders to visit or stay in foreign countries becomes in effect a veritable displacement. This migrational movement cannot be seen as spontaneous. Prompted by promotional policies elaborated on an international scale, tourism is involved in a process of internationalization. Tourist activity cannot therefore be reduced to the question of travel. It becomes an instrument of integration in the process of globalization which results in a growing dependence of national policies on international instruments of planning. As more and more closely-knit interdependencies emerge between more and more regions of the world based on central decision making, national reference systems are rendered progressively invalid (Lanfant 1980).

From this a series of questions arises. What is the aim of international tourism? Which cultural model does it represent? What role does it play in disturbing national, regional or local identities? What is its universalist requirement? And the ever-urgent question: which sociology? Is a sociology of international tourism at all possible? Which theoretical, methodological and practical conditions does it have to fulfil to be able to analyse this phenomenon?

An attempt to answer these questions necessitated clarification of the role of sociology, in particular its relationship to decision making and its place in the international system of tourist action. Surveys centred around this system of action were set up in eleven countries, countries connected by scientific and technical cooperation agreements, developing countries opening up to international tourism and centrally planned economies. After visits to research institutes and documentation centres and discussions with research scientists in these countries, and after gathering information such as master plans and local surveys, our analysis enabled us to conclude that a research network is coming into being in close cooperation with decision-making powers. International organizations and teams of experts play the most important role here.

As a consequence of this, sociological research, its problematic and its methods are prisoner to an approach which is foreign to them. Informed by the economic problematic and mainly concerned with the conjunctural effects of tourism in the development process and development for the common good, this dominant approach only incidentally tackles the implications of tourist decision making for social systems. And it is only after problems emerge in host societies that sociologists are called upon to establish the negative effects in order to reduce them. Thus we have a simplistic reductive position from which sociology can only extract itself by showing that it is capable of asking the questions crucial to the evolution of societies being changed by tourism. This is the point we had reached at the end of the 1970s (Lanfant *et al.* 1978).

We attacked this task by elaborating a research project aimed at shifting the analysis towards the regions affected by international tourism. Starting out with three field studies, of which two were situated in rural France (Var and Perigord) and one in Indonesia (Bali), we attempted to explore the processes of dialecticalization which permeate economic, social and cultural systems, as they occur within the reality of local milieus which are as distinctive as possible in terms of their traditions and their cultures (Lanfant, Picard and de Weerdt 1982).

This research involved a real methodological change of direction. Not only did the classic sociological approach, which explains changes observed locally in terms of the results of an exogenous factor of change, become inapplicable, but we also had to explore a new method of conceiving things in order to grasp the way in which the process of internationalization worked through the social layers to reach the level of the subjects on the spot. The question of identity becomes critical because it concerns all levels and different dimensions of the processes engendered by tourism: reconversion and redefinition of territories; integration of national, regional and local communities in the larger context; protection, promotion and relocation of cultural heritage; requests for authenticity and fabrication of fakes; staging of tradition and modernity; creation of imaginary cities; tourism as a new religion; the return of the repressed image of 'the stranger'. . . . How is it possible to understand the question of identity given such diversity?

SOCIOLOGY IN THE PROCESS OF INTERNATIONALIZATION

Sociologists studying international tourism must take into account a large number of facts, both internal and exotic, and as far as possible do so simultaneously. Herein lies the first difficulty because with tourism we rub shoulders with diametrically opposed universes of discourse: urban/rural, post-industrial/primitive, traditional/modern. To understand something of these dialogical relationships one needs to take up a position at the intersections, at Mauss' (1980) 'crossroads of subjectivities'.

The worldwide diffusion of international tourism generates processes which cut across, divide and tear apart cultural systems and undermine the image that societies have of themselves. These processes of identification/*autrification* ('otherization'), of integration/separation, overlap each other, become entangled with each other, jostle each other, thwart each other and lead us to what Georges Balandier, as a true disciple of Georges Gurvitch (1957, 1962), would have called 'the anthropology of turbulences' (Maffesoli and Rivière 1985).

Faced with these realities of internationalization, we concluded that political and scientific thought remained locked into national points of reference as well as into the implicit judgements linked to each individual's experiences. Each individual ignores the existence in himself of a certain tourist, which is the same being one despises in others.

From 1984 onwards, we set out to enlarge our research network and to create institutions where scientific cooperation could become effective. The International Round Table held in Marly-le-Roi in June 1986 was part of this ambitious process. We wanted to create an interdisciplinary and international forum through the presence of scientists from all over the world (Problems of Tourism 1987). That meeting represented our first initiative and coincided with the project to develop an International Academy for the Study of Tourism under the leadership of Jafar Jafari and with the involvement of researchers from Eastern Europe, through the assistance of Krzysztof Przeclawski, who has never ceased to support us and with whom we have long been associated.

The logical outcome of this strategy of institutional creation, which was inaugurated by the International Round Table of Marly, was that we initiated and became party to the following:

(a) the International Network of the Analysis of Leisure and of Tourism (RIALTO), founded in France;
(b) the Thematic Group of the Sociology of International Tourism (TGSIT) which has since become the Working Group of International Tourism (WGIT), an affiliated structure of the International Sociological Association (ISA), which benefits from the status of an international association;
(c) TGSIT sessions within the framework of the Twelfth World Congress of Sociology of the ISA in Madrid in July 1990.

Besides these, we also support other initiatives such as the establishment of a Mediterranean Association of the Sociology of Tourism.

These institutions became places for collective research, but they also offer individual members the possibility of bringing together a wide range of results and research experiences which come from different geographical contexts and which are presented in different ways. These are vital methodological tools. The fields of research range from the local to the international, passing through the regional and the national levels, and the confrontation of these different levels of analysis in one forum offers extremely interesting possibilities for induction. One is forced to draw comparisons, to go beyond local characteristics and approach discourses from completely opposing corners of the earth. It then becomes possible to exchange opposite and conflicting points of view concerning the phenomenon in question. And this exchange of points of view, these variations of perspective, constitute, in my opinion, an essential methodological principle at the present stage of research and information (Lanfant forthcoming).

THE SOCIOLOGY OF NO

If the relationship that sociology cultivates with international tourism shows the effects of this characteristic of mobile/mobility, one can imagine the effects it has upon the discipline itself. Tourism appears to be a means of prying sociology from its binding points. Therefore the sociology of international tourism somehow threatens the discipline which is mainly concerned with staying orthodox.

Paraphrasing Gaston Bachelard and adapting his outlook to the concrete situation which is now manifesting itself in this field of research, we could say that what sociology needs in this period of agitation is a 'sociology of No' (Bachelard 1949, 1960, 1989). The 'sociology of No' is not a means of responding to a negation by a negation. It does not originate in a spirit of systematic contradiction faced with scientific codes acknowledged by the majority. The dialectic of Bachelard is a 'dialectic of No', which leaves us the possibility of 'a negation which does not annihilate, a detour which does not separate' (*Encyclopedia Universalis* 1968: 1007–8). It is characterized by 'a scientific opening which is supple and moving' (Bachelard 1949: 104) and it tries to think out its epistemological foundations accordingly.

Continuing the tradition of Gaston Bachelard, from the 1960s the philosopher Michel Serres anticipated the indicator of the new scientific spirit: its ability to adhere to the phenomena of mobility. 'The New Scientific Spirit is concentrated in a philosophy of No,' Serres (1972: 10) reminds us; 'the new scientific spirit develops into a philosophy of transport: intersection, interception, intervention . . . .' And later (p. 158) 'The place of the epistemologist, if he wishes to remain so and not a pure specialist of such and such a region of knowledge, is a mobile place, the very path of the circulation of concepts.'

In the light of what has just been stated, researchers should not fear setting themselves free from national points of reference. On the other hand, the inductive movement, which is at present asserting itself in this field of research, will only be able to achieve this broadening of knowledge if sociology can clearly indicate well-defined links between the different fields of observation which are developing haphazardly and simultaneously in various parts of the world.

The sociology of international tourism cannot be an *a priori* construction because the experience of a scientific subject is continually being dialecticalized by the experience of another and because the logic of global functioning is always elusive. One is planted in front of a sort of chaotic kaleidoscope, a mosaic of points of view which can divert the attention of the scientific spirit intent on having clear ideas. In international tourism we are not really dealing with a well-defined sociological object, but rather with what Gaston Bachelard would call a supra-object or an infra-object. We are not just in a realm of pure scientific rationality but also one of infra-rationality or even supra-rationality. We should not hesitate to take literally what is being said about international tourism. On the spot oral accounts of subjects, whatever their role in the system of actors, are of just as great an interest to us as the statistical data which enable us to note the major trends.

The sociology of international tourism should not fear embarking on a kind of supra-rationality at a certain stage, because it is important to have access to a vision of the whole of the phenomenon in its globality, its pluridimensionality and its contribution to civilization on the global level, which surpass the capacities of observation of a single person. In this case one should not fear relying on new paradigms or even on audacious metaphors (Brown 1989).

On academic grounds one could disapprove of the lack of orthodoxy but is this not the price one has to pay for a daring investigation into poorly mastered domains of the knowledge of social matters? But this sociology should not retreat into a sort of arrogant secrecy. For this reason we have created networks for research scientists which act as reception centres for the groping efforts of young explorers, places which not only provide understanding but which are also sensitive to the embarrassment and discomfort which they feel when faced with a phenomenon which is not reassuring. For what we need most at the moment is to discredit the conventional discourses, which, when it comes to tourism, are legion.

SOCIOLOGIST – TOURISTOLOGUE – ETHNOLOGIST

Recently we have noted research in the sociology of international tourism branching out in a new direction. This is the work of young researchers who carry out multi-faceted field studies of tourism. A new generation is born. The majority of these researchers come from the tourism generating countries but they have chosen to work in the host countries. Most have one foot in one country and one in another; consequently, like Descartes, they may experience a feeling of freedom. Straddling two cultures it is usual to think in terms of oppositions – the sociologist is able to take into account each of the two poles simultaneously and to try to analyse what holds them together under a tension between integration and separation. I come back to this because these oppositions are the nerve centres of international tourism: advanced societies/developing societies, post-industrial societies/ traditional societies caught up in tourist promotion.

Frequently the researcher chooses an insular area, an enclave or a peripheral region. These isolated areas are often traditional societies, a field of research greatly preferred by ethnographic surveys. The 'cultural niches', according to the beautiful expression of Claude Levi-Strauss (1973), the areas inhabited by ethnic groups, now attract tourists and researchers who mix on the spot. This phenomenon imposes itself upon the anthropologist–ethnologist and provokes upheavals within these disciplines. A tourist discourse is developing parallel to the scientific discourse which results in mixes which may embarrass the academics. For some, this in itself provides a subject of study.

Numerous difficulties are encountered by researchers exploring this new phenomenon, the product of modern times (Bruner forthcoming, Crick forthcoming). Viewed strangely by the natives who do not really understand which side they are on, now that they are so-called *touristologues*, our researchers have to find their way between two worlds. Strangers in the place because their centres of interest are in themselves perceived as being foreign, researchers who are interested in tourism are themselves taken for tourists by the locals. Thus identified with their subject of research, they could very well be considered intruders, exploiters or agents of contamination. *Touristologues* are ill at ease, particularly as they see themselves as ethnologists who respect the place and its customs. But here again a misunderstanding occurs because ethnology, just like sociology, does not look kindly on researchers attracted to the study of tourism on its own turf, who have come to disturb its perception of ethnology. Tourism is perceived by the ethnologist as being a nuisance, a plague, and the sociologist–anthropologist who is interested in a place while it is being changed by tourism is not regarded as a fully fledged researcher by the academic profession.

The *touristologue*, a newcomer in the scientific world, appears to be a bastard, a sort of hybrid incapable of choosing between two motivations, of which one appears to be legitimate and the other a subject of suspicion. In general these young researchers, who themselves are seeking to break away, who have often hit the road with only a vague idea of enjoying the landscape and trying to be different, found themselves in the midst of a scientific and academic career, or in the tourist industry as a cultural intermediary. Indeed, one could ask oneself if tourism is not just a pretext to stay in the chosen place. Is it really out of interest in tourism or is it out of interest in the place that the researchers are making it their object of study? To which problems asked in their countries of origin are they going to look for the answers in those faraway places? Which are the questions which are taking them to countries yet unknown? These are important questions to investigate even as we try to create this field of research. These were the first subjects of the RIALTO's research, role of the choice and involvement of the researcher as elements shaping research. For it is at a personal level that these researchers, who often take the pains to learn the local language, carry out their research between two or more cultures. What motivations do they have?

These well meaning researchers who seek to become part of traditional societies become the target of criticism from the better established (Dumont 1983). Are *touristologues* like Sartre's hero who wanders from town to town where nobody is waiting for him, a stranger to others and to himself (Sartre 1990)? Would they not be more likely to experience something of the cosmopolitism which has become part of our modernity?

Why should we not give the same credit to these researchers as we would willingly give to someone who follows a safer career? In the field, *touristologues*, even if involved with tourists who wish to break with routine, never lose sight of the ethnologist's rule of keeping one's distance. And if they are not adverse to undertaking common experiences, scientific work will encourage them to make these experiences the focus of research. In my opinion these experiences, complex as they are, constitute the true ferment of this field of research. In conclusion, I will quote Gaston Bachelard yet again: 'When one searches for the psychological conditions of the progress of science, one soon comes to the conviction that it is in terms of obstacles that one has to formulate the problem of scientific knowledge' (Bachelard 1960: 13). Translated from the French text.

REFERENCES

Bachelard, G. (1949) *La Philosophie du Non. Essai d'une Analyse du Nouvel Esprit Scientifique*, Paris: PUF.
——(1960) *La Formation de l'Esprit Scientifique. Contribution à une Psychanalyse de la Connaissance Objective*, Paris: PUF.
——(1989) *La Poétique de l'Espace*, Paris: PUF.
Bordieu, P. (1982) *Leçon sur la Leçon*, Paris: Minuit.
Bordieu, P., Chamboredon, J. C. and Passeron, J. C. (1968) *Le Métier de Sociologue*, Paris: Mouton.
Brown, R. (1989) *Clefs pour une Poétique de la Sociologie*, Arles: Actes Sud.
Bruner, E. M. (forthcoming) 'The Ethnographer/Tourist in Indonesia', in J. B. Allcock, E. M. Bruner and M. F. Lanfant (eds) *International Tourism: Identity and Change. Anthropological and Sociological Studies*, London: Sage Studies in International Sociology.
Crick, M. (1989) 'Representations of international tourism in the social sciences: sun, sex, sights, savings and servility', *Annual Review of Anthropology* 18: 307–44.
——(forthcoming) 'The anthropologist as tourist: an identity in question', in J. B. Allcock, E. M. Bruner and M. F. Lanfant (eds) *International Tourism: Identity and Change. Anthropological and Sociological Studies*, London: Sage Studies in International Sociology.
Dann, G. and Cohen, E. (1991) 'Sociology and Tourism', *Annals of Tourism Research* 18, 1: 155–69.
Dumont, L. (1983) 'La communauté anthropologique et l'idéologie', in *Essais sur l'Individualisme. Une Perspective Anthropologique sur l'Idéologie Moderne*, Paris: Seuil: 107–221.
Durkheim, E. (1968) *Les Règles de la Méthode Sociologique*, Paris: PUF.
——(1969) 'Note sur la notion de civilisation', *Journal Sociologique* : 681–5.
Encyclopedia Universalis (1968) 'Gaston Bachelard (1884–1962)', Paris: *Encyclopedia Universalis*: 1007–8.
Foucault, M. (1966) *Les Mots et les Choses. Une Archéologie des Sciences Humaines*, Paris: Gallimard.
Frangialli, F. (1991) *La France dans le Tourisme Mondial*. Paris: Economica.
Graburn, N. H. H. and Jafari, J. (1991) 'Introduction: Tourism Social Science', *Annals of Tourism Research* 18, 1: 1–11.
Gurvitch, G. (1957) *La Vocation Actuelle de la Sociologie*, Paris: PUF.
——(1962) *Dialectique et sociologie*, Paris: PUF.
Heidegger, M. (1962) *Die Frage nach dem Ding*, Tübingen: Niemeyer.
——(1971) *Qu'est-ce qu'une Chose?*, Paris: Gallimard.

Lanfant, M. F. (1972) *Les Théories du Loisir. Sociologie du Loisir et Idéologies*, Paris: PUF.

——(1980) 'Tourism in the process of internationalization', *International Social Science Journal* 32: 14–42.

——(forthcoming) 'International tourism: A test for identity in the process of internationalization', in J. B. Allcock, E. M. Bruner and M. F. Lanfant (eds) *International Tourism: Identity and Change. Anthropological and Sociological Studies*, London: Sage Studies in International Sociology.

Lanfant, M. F. and de Almeida Matos, H. (1972) *Les Jeunes dans les Echanges Touristiques Internationaux. Dossier d'Informations Statistiques Comparées*, Paris: CNRS.

Lanfant, M. F., de Weerdt, J. *et al.* (1975) *Signification du Tourisme International: Fait et Acte Social*, Paris: CNRS.

Lanfant, M. F., Mottin, M. H., Picard, M., Rozenberg, D. and de Weerdt, J. (1978) *Sociologie du Tourisme: Positions et Perspectives dans la Recherche Internationale*, Paris: CNRS.

Lanfant, M. F., Picard, M., de Weerdt, J. *et al.* (1982) *Implications Locales du Tourisme International*, Paris: CNRS.

Levi-Strauss, C. (1973) 'Humanisme et humanité', in *Anthropologie Structurale Deux*, Paris: Plon: 319–422.

Maffesoli, M. and Rivière, C. (1985) *Une Anthropologie des Turbulences. Hommages à Georges Balandier*, Paris: Berg International.

Mauss, M. (1969) 'Les civilisations. Eléments et formes', in *Essais de Sociologie*, Paris: Minuit.

——(1980) 'Essai sur le don. Formes et raisons de l'échange dans les sociétés archaïques', in *Sociologie et Anthropologie*, Paris: PUF: 145–379.

Merleau-Ponty, M. (1960) *Signes*, Paris: Gallimard.

Nash, D. and Smith, V. L. (1991) 'Anthropology and Tourism', *Annals of Tourism Research* 18, 1: 12–25.

Problems of Tourism (1987) '*L'impact social et culturel du tourisme international' en question: réponses interdisciplinaires*, Actes de la Table Ronde Internationale de Marly-le-Roi, 9–11 Juin 1986, *Problems of Tourism*, 10, 2 and 3.

Quine, W. V. O. (1977) 'Parler d'objets', in *Relativité de l'Ontologie et Autres Essais*, Paris: Aubier: 13–37.

Sartre, J. P. (1990) *Les Mouches*, Paris: Gallimard.

Serres, M. (1972) *Hermés II. L'Interférence*, Paris: Minuit.

Chapter 6

Limitations in the use of 'nationality' and 'country of residence' variables

Graham M. S. Dann

INTRODUCTION

Over the years, travellers have become accustomed to, if not perhaps a trifle annoyed at, having to complete international entry and departure (E/D) cards. Although these forms represent a far cry from the optimal level of desired standardization sufficient to facilitate comparisons (Caribbean Tourism Organization 1989a), in practice they usually feature a core of questions requesting information on nationality, country of birth, country of residence and ports of embarkation/ disembarkation. These items, which at first sight may appear to be overlapping, or even synonymous, in reality are quite distinct and used for different purposes. It should be noted that, since the E/D card is a legal document required by participating signatory countries to the International Civil Aviation Organization, it often necessitates an act of the destination's legislature to change its format.

'Nationality' is similarly a legal concept determined by the state. It is variously defined as being based on such diverse criteria as parental/ paternal status (*ius sanguinis*), place of birth (*ius soli*) or naturalization/ citizenship requirements (Brubaker 1990). Typically, this information is monitored at point of entry by government officials for immigration purposes, and there is often the additional necessity for the incoming foreign traveller either to provide evidence of an onward/return ticket, or else a work permit or some other acceptable grounds for residence in the receiving society. A passport is usually indicative of nationality, though matters naturally become complicated where individuals hold two or more passports or where two or more persons share the same form of identification. Additional problems arise where the passport requirement is waived and a substitute document (e.g. driver's licence) is deemed acceptable.

'Country of birth', which often coincides with nationality, and therefore also comes under the scrutiny of immigration personnel, can sometimes be quite different, particularly in those instances where an individual's parents had been temporarily or permanently residing outside their own territorial boundaries. Occasionally, too, 'country of birth' is misinterpreted as 'country of origin'.

More normally, however, and certainly as far as tourism statistics are concerned, 'country of origin' denotes 'country of residence', that is, place of customary domicile (usually stipulated in terms of current abode for a minimum annual period of six months and a day). Residence thus defined indicates the point of touristic generation and departure. Tourism researchers frequently employ such a measure in analysing fluctuating market shares over different time periods. In such a manner it is also possible to compare the similarities and differences between domestic (now known as 'home') tourists and international tourists with respect to bednights, patterns of expenditure, employment generation, government revenue, and both the geographical spread and impact on regions within the receiving country (see Pearce 1990b). However, difficulties can arise in those instances where the period of residential sojourn is exceeded (e.g. overseas university students, expatriate retirees returning from their former homeland, illegal immigrants) and where such individuals are counted as tourist arrivals.

'Home address', which is also frequently requested on the E/D card, acts as confirmation or as a surrogate for country of residence. At the same time, especially when accompanied by an area or zip code, it provides useful information for market segmentation analysts who can make inferences about socio-economic status from such details.

'Port of embarkation' and 'port of disembarkation' can be useful as well, to the extent that they supply itinerary points and permit comparative analyses of travel according to whether it is of the 'destination' (one stop) or 'circuit' (two or more stops) variety. Douglas Pearce's (1990a) examination of patterns of travel in the South Pacific typifies this sort of approach. Information can additionally be extrapolated from these data which can be helpful in understanding variation in air transport demand, hub densities and flight bottlenecks. Unfortunately, many travellers, particularly those who are required to change planes in order to reach their destinations, do not record point of embarkation accurately, if at all, thus rendering this variable somewhat hazardous for the compilers of derivable statistics.

These working distinctions now clarified, it is maintained that in some tourism research a great deal of conceptual fuzziness still reigns, thereby limiting the methodological applications of the foregoing predictor variables. Examples will be supplied which serve to highlight such imprecision of thought and its associated problems. Additionally, a theoretical case will be made for the increasing limitations of employing nationality and country of residence as lone discriminating factors in tourism research, and the corresponding need to look for alternative approaches.

EXAMPLES AND LIMITATIONS OF NATIONALITY AND COUNTRY OF RESIDENCE IN TOURISM RESEARCH

While nationality has up to this point been considered largely the prerogative of the immigration department, it is occasionally also used by tourism authorities in their compilation of arrival statistics. In Grenada, for instance, arrivals are broken down according to this variable. In Jamaica, on the other hand, returning nationals are filtered *out* of the analysis, thereby effectively reducing the annual number of visitor arrivals by some ten per cent. Similarly, visitors from the United States to Puerto Rico and the US Virgin Islands, and French visitors to Martinique and Guadeloupe, do not even complete E/D cards, since their travel is considered to be domestic or home based.

Such practice, needless to say, counteracts prevailing norms, to the degree that nationals residing overseas are generally incorporated into arrivals by country of residence. Thus, Barbadians living in New York, for example, who return for the annual Crop Over festivities on the island, are customarily treated as United States entries by the compilers of tourism statistics. At the same time, marketers of Barbados as a destination usually downplay such 'Bajan Yankees' in their promotional efforts.

The actual practice of recording nationality for each incoming visitor has further been found to vary according to the prevailing ideology and political history of the authorities in the host society. In this regard, Richter (1989: 107) notes, for instance, that Pakistan and Nepal often omit Indian arrivals, while Indian statistics frequently exclude visitors from Pakistan and Bangladesh. Just why this should be so has to be seen in the geo-political context of the pre-1947 situation. At the same time, however, it does raise questions about the validity of the data and the whimsical interpretation given to the concept of nationality.

Nationality is also arguably implied in these accounts which inappropriately employ single territory epithets to describe visitors. Thus, Americans are meant to gravitate immediately towards such photogenic sites as Trafalgar Square, St Mark's and the Arc de Triomphe (Jafari 1974: 242), while the British, grotesquely personified in the infamous El Sid (Coren 1986: 7–13), would presumably head for the nearest pub, regardless of the surrounding attractions. Not unsurprisingly, such caricaturing frequently becomes the object of academic humour (Cohen 1972), and this largely anecdotal material has been justifiably criticized for lacking a sufficient theoretical base, particularly whenever it is gratuitously asserted that different nationalities have their own distinct ways of travelling, and hence, by implication, specific impacts on a given destination area (Mathieson and Wall 1982).

Nationality as a predictor variable is additionally utilized in studies of stereotyping. Reigrotski and Anderson (1954), for instance, examined in some detail national attributes of Europeans in which they asked various national samples to rate themselves and others according to selected characteristics. Unfortunately, the stimuli used for the basis of comparison were derived from the culture of the researchers, and consequently often connoted different meanings for the subjects. Thus, 'hardworking', for example, was considered to be a positive attribute by German participants, while it tended to be viewed as a negative quality by French respondents. In such a manner, the researchers inaccurately attributed to nationality the unexplained indigenous cultural variation of their subjects.

Others have concentrated their attention on the changes in visitor attitudes brought about as a result of the travel experience (see Pool et al. 1956; Smith 1955, 1957). More recent examples of this work can be found in Philip Pearce (1982). He refers, for instance, to a study of his own (Pearce 1977) which sought to compare pre- and post-trip attitudes of British holidaymakers to Greece and Morocco, as well as to the investigation of Triandis and Vassiliou (1967) who performed a similar analysis among Greek and American travellers. Here it seems that the focus once more centred on nationality. The Triandis and Vassiliou (1967) study, for example, concentrated on Greek students and American military personnel, where both groups were likely to have been homogeneous with respect to nationality. Confirmation of this assumption is made when the analysis was said to turn on the use of heterostereotype (images of another's nationality) and autostereotype (images of one's own nationality). In Philip Pearce's (1977) study of British tourists, two of the four central research questions hinged on change in overall evaluation of the visited nationality and change in belief about the visited nationality, while the remainder concentrated on change in attitude towards their fellow countrymen (the British people). The use of a multidimensional scaling technique to determine stereotypical descriptions of Moroccans and Greeks further reconfirms that nationality was the principal focus of the study. However, not wishing to be pinned down to this variable alone, Pearce interestingly explored the further possibility that his tourists might be able to differentiate sub-groupings of the Greeks and Moroccans based on such considerations as social class and ethnicity. The fact that his subjects did not significantly perceive these strata in the visited communities does not alter the contrary reality of the situation, nor the realization that nationality on its own often fails to capture the richness and complexity of a host society.

In some other studies it is unclear whether it is country of residence or nationality that is being investigated. The research conducted by Yuan and McDonald (1990), for instance, which utilized data from a larger project carried out by the United States Travel and Tourism Administration and Tourism Canada on approximately 1,500 inter- views, is a typical example. Here respondents were described as overseas travellers aged 18 years or older who had either taken a long haul vacation of four days or more in the past three years or else planned to do so in the next two years. The four targeted countries were Japan, the United Kingdom, (then) West Germany and France, and the travellers were subsequently referred to as Japanese, British, German and French. That nationality was the focus of attention may be gleaned from the manner in which the samples were drawn. In Japan, the method employed was described as a 'national' probability cluster sample, in which geographical areas, and later households and their members, were randomly selected. In the remaining countries, samples of telephone subscribers were chosen. Yet closer inspection of the foregoing methodology suggests that country of residence, rather than nationality, was the subject of investigation, since both zones and households, if as representative as claimed, would certainly (with differing degrees of probability in the four territories) have included non-nationals among their number, a point seemingly overlooked by the researchers. The subsequent finding that motivational 'push' and 'pull' factors were variously predicted on this single poorly operationalized variable, and that the results had implications for marketing in Japan, the United Kingdom, West Germany and France, could be very misleading and costly for the relevant destination areas towards which these travellers were heading.

A similar sort of problem can be experienced when the focus

switches to impact research, and how the inhabitants of a given destination area differentially regard the tourists in their midst. In Pi-Sunyer's (1989) frequently cited work, for instance, we are told of the transformation of Cap Lloc by mass tourism from a former small fishing village to a modern resort, and the system of categorization employed by locals to discriminate between 'natives, strangers and different sorts of foreigner'.

Here the destination people are said to produce 'personality profiles distinctive to a variety of nationalities and ethnic groups' (Pi-Sunyer 1989: 193), and that responses tend to be more uniform the closer the country is to Spain. Such images, which combine negative and positive evaluations of behavioural patterns and personal qualities, are in some instances anachronistic, and become quite complex when predicted on such non-tourism forces as the media, international politics and the presence of expatriates. Whereas it would be tempting to classify Pi-Sunyer's account as just another example of stereotyping research based on nationality, further perusal suggests that his study of interpersonal contact, since it is both processual and dynamic, cannot simply refer to the rigid and static categories of stereotype. Rather, the emphasis has shifted to the richer and more elusive concept of culture, which is not necessarily coterminous with either nationality or country of residence.

Another anthropological account, that of Brewer (1978), complements the position adopted by Pi-Sunyer. This time, however, the analysis concentrates on 'ethnicity'. More specifically, it focuses on the methods employed by local entrepreneurs in San Felipe, Baja, California, as they attempt to categorize their customers. In practice, their strategy amounts to the interfacing of two classification devices – one based on race, the other on residential status. The most important distinction, however, is said to be that of 'Mexicano' versus 'Americano', which, in addition to differences of appearance and language, hinges on variation in purchasing behaviour, and the differential strategies utilized by the storekeepers in dealing with the often misunderstood associated peculiarities. What is particularly fascinating is the presence of a Mexican-American (Chicano/Pocho) group, which becomes even more problematic for the businessmen on account of its marginality. In relation to the present argument, the existence of this third group further highlights the difficulties inherent in classifying tourists by nationality or country of residence, and even the ethnic stereotyping of the remaining two suggests that the race/ethnicity dimension needs to be added to the scenario for a fuller appreciation of the various forces at work.

There have also been several surveys which have sought to measure the impact of tourism on one or more host communities. Generally, these studies are quite sophisticated and employ a number of working hypotheses. One thinks, for instance, of the work of Sheldon and Var (1984) in North Wales, and that of Bélisle and Hoy (1980) in relation to host attitudes displayed towards visitors in Santa Marta, Colombia. Here it becomes quite clear that the local society can no longer be considered homogeneous in terms of country of residence or nationality, and that such additional factors as proximity to the hotel sector, employment of the inhabitants and the use of native language, have to be further explored in order to make adequate sense of the interaction between tourists and locals.

The most ambitious of these projects to date is probably the seven country multiphase Vienna Centre study (Bystrzanowski, 1989), where both residents and tourists were questioned. Interestingly, and in spite of a number of methodological and theoretical deficiencies (referred to by D. Pearce in Chapter 3 and in Dann 1991: 39–44), many of the local investigators concluded that the inhabitants of the various sampled territories saw very few differences in the attitudes and behaviour of their visitors (i.e. tourist nationality/country of residence was no longer a key variable at their level of perception and judgement). Whether it was in Lanzarote (Lazo and Quintana 1989: 78) or in Yugoslavia (Dragicevic *et al.* 1989: 146), for instance, the tourist's place of origin was far less important than the fact of being a tourist, and hence of displaying different attitudes from locals towards leisure, time and morality. Also more significant than considerations of nationality or country of residence were frequency of travel, duration of sojourn, repeater status and the population size of place of domicile. Naturally, it is this awareness that explanations are more often than not multifactorial that raises doubts over studies which rely solely on the variables of nationality and country of residence.

Another example of a survey approach to country of residence reinforces the danger of identifying one condition as both necessary and sufficient for another. During the first half of 1991, the Tourism Development Corporation of Barbados commissioned a local research organization (Systems Caribbean 1991) to conduct monthly visitor exit satisfaction surveys. The principal twin mandate was to obtain demographic information on tourists which was not recorded on the E/D cards and, coterminously, to gauge their attitudes towards various features of the so-called 'tourism product'. In the event, only repeater status, number of previous visits, location of accommodation and types of accompanying persons, were added to the list of E/D independent variables, and no motivational questions were asked beyond the customary inadequate distinction between business and leisure travel. At the analysis stage, disappointingly, only country of residence was employed as a predictor variable, the lone exception being the issue of beach harassment (where repeater status, location of hotel, age and sex, were brought into the equation). Unfortunately, a marginal breakdown of the distribution of country of residence revealed a disproportionate emphasis on visitors from the United States and Canada and a corresponding undue percentage shortfall in the Caribbean market (Caribbean Tourism Organization 1989b), thereby posing unresolved questions of the reliability and representativeness of this sole variable. Once bi-variate cross-tabulations were provided and explanation was attributed to country of residence, regrettably no statistical tests of significance were taken. Thus 'findings' were highlighted as being important when it was not possible to ascertain whether or not these were simply chance fluctuations in the data. That no type of sampling, random or otherwise, was reported in the methodology section, reinforces this view.

However, and more germane to the current argument, perhaps the worst feature of the study was the unacknowledged possibility that spurious relationships were being presented. In the absence of controls for simultaneous effect by associated variables, one was therefore not in a position to assess the causal validity which had been uniquely attributed to country of residence. A typical instance was a table showing the evaluations of airport immigration personnel by visitors from different countries of origin, where those from the United Kingdom were seen to be more critical than their North American counterparts. What was not stated, yet may have been the real reason behind the situation, was that negative attitude could simply have been a function of distance of travel. That is, the tolerance level of those spending eight or nine hours in a plane would be lower than for those travelling half that time. As a matter of interest, once country of residence is treated as a spatial or temporal variable, rather than as a social factor denoting assumed homogeneity, its importance would surely be far easier to justify.

Happily, there are some studies which do not unilaterally focus their attention on either country of residence or nationality. A good example of this sort of work is Douglas Pearce's (1990b) previously mentioned statistical analysis of tourists to New Zealand from 1980 to 1990. Basing his presentation on international arrivals, he was able to observe fluctuations in the market share during the period under review and to note that, whereas those from Australia in 1980 constituted almost one half of all arrivals, by the end of the decade their figure had dropped to 35 per cent. In contrast, the Japanese statistics had risen from 3.9 to 10.8 per cent over the same time interval, while the British contribution had remained relatively constant. Comparisons in daily patterns of expenditure were also broken down by country of residence, as indeed were person-nights, spatial concentration and predominant types of motivation. Thus far the study was just like many others of its kind.

However, there were a number of provisos made by the author which introduced several useful notes of caution into the interpretation of these and similar tourism statistics. The first caveat has to do with the percentage share of the overall long haul market according to country of origin. We are told, for instance, that New Zealand manages to attract only 1 per cent of United States and Japanese travellers. That being the case, one appreciates that, while it may be a perfectly legitimate exercise to compare the characteristics of those Americans and Japanese who do visit New Zealand, unless one has recourse to additional recent and reliable data for these respective populations one cannot extrapolate to the population of these countries. Second, the previous question becomes all the more salient with the further realization that only about 7 per cent of all Americans travel abroad, since it suggests that it is not so much their nationality or even the fact of residing in the United States which is so important, but that in all likelihood some other variable or mix of factors has contributed to the situation. Realizing the difficulty and its potential solutions, Pearce (1990b: 35) refers to a study by McDermott and Jackson (1985) where income is shown to be a 'major determinant of long haul arrivals in New Zealand, with other factors, such as fares and exchange rates, varying in strength from market to market'. In other words, he highlights the limitations in dealing with country of residence as a lone independent variable, preferring instead to treat it as dependent on other factors. Third, after comparing differences in purpose of visit, and in seeking to explain the slackening of demand in the Australian market, Pearce points to changes in preference from long haul wanderlust to short haul sunlust, and adds that outbound travel was also depressed by the parallel strengthening of domestic demand due to the Bicentennial celebrations and Expo. In these cases, then, it becomes essential to examine other factors, which in reality now have the effect of transforming country of residence into an intervening or dependent variable.

NATIONALITY AND COUNTRY OF RESIDENCE: THEORETICAL CONSIDERATIONS

So far we have seen the limited methodological usefulness of relying solely on nationality or country of residence as the explanatory factor in tourism research. Here we will briefly explore the corresponding theoretical deficiencies. They are discussed under the following headings:

1 the globalization of tourism
2 the cosmopolitan nature of tourist generating societies
3 the pluralistic nature of tourist receiving societies
4 limited host–guest interaction along the lines of nationality and country of residence.

The globalization of tourism

With the annual number of international tourists swiftly approaching the estimated 460–480 million mark, and international tourism displaying consistent and robust patterns of growth (Lanfant 1989: 178–9), we are currently witnessing a world phenomenon of unprecedented dimensions and accessibility, where much power resides in transnational corporations whose all embracing decisions often pay scant regard to national interest (Lanfant 1990). In such a manner, both developed and developing countries have become locked into a new international economic order, where supply and demand yield to the symbiotic practices of mass advertising, information technologies, marketing segmentation, consumerism and data bank networking, whose multinational operators seek no more or less than the world itself (Lanfant 1980). Thus, Mowlana and Smith (1991: 215) are able to maintain that 'modern international relations have become characterized by a number of new participants, institutions and issues beyond that of the conventional nation-state system. Outstanding among these is international tourism.'

What takes place at the political level, certainly in so far as international tourism is concerned, is more often than not predicated on global commercial interests. As Olsen observes:

While the buyer grows in strength and the providers combine resources more formally, firms will become global, combining resources and investing where opportunities exist. The caution is this,

that such global organizations often are not bound by the laws and
regulations of any individual nation.

(Olsen 1991: 124)

Furthermore, with the world already forming into new major political
and economic trading blocs, such requirements as passports, visas,
currency controls, customs, preferential treatments, and so on, will
rapidly become relics of the past (Lee and Malek 1991). The
'democratization' of Eastern Europe may well be accompanied by loss
of territorial identity as former Soviet satellites madly scramble to join
the European Community. With factionalism in the former USSR,
Yugoslavia, Iraq, Canada, Sri Lanka, South Africa and elsewhere, it
may no longer make much sense to speak of national identification with
such societies, and both current and former colonies and *départements*
may suddenly find themselves cut loose and looking for partners.

While the foregoing scenario may be alarming for the inhabitants of
such areas, many of which incidentally are tourism destinations, it
apparently presents little difficulty for the operators of international
tourism. By now they have grown accustomed to transnational banking
and telecommunication high technology, and actually seem to thrive on
the change they have largely engineered. Nowhere is this more evident
than in the sphere of central reservation systems, where national carriers
and hotel chains cheerfully surrender their erstwhile identities on the
altar of progress. Thus, we find, for example, that such transportation
giants as United Airlines, British Airways, Swiss Air, US Air, KLM,
Alitalia and Air Canada, are all linked under the Apollo CRS, while
Thisco, Amadeus and Galileo account for the key players in multinational accommodation establishments (Lee and Malek 1991). Those
who wish to abstain from such global corporatization are, of course, free
to do so, but, in selecting such an option, they will inevitably find
themselves out on a proverbial economic limb. Hence, whatever resistance is offered, token or otherwise, it would seem that the globalization
of tourism is now very much a politico-economic reality. Those who
choose to ignore this fact do so at their peril.

The implications for the dwindling importance of nationality and
country of residence are spelt out by Øyen (1990: 2). She believes that,
since the world is divided into administrative units called 'countries', it
becomes 'seductively convincing to use such units in comparative
studies'. In spite of this, she nevertheless points out that:

National boundaries are different from ethnic, cultural and social
boundaries . . . (since within all countries, even the very old and

homogeneous ones, we may find several sub-societies which on some variables may show greater variation than comparisons across national boundaries can demonstrate: that is, within-variation may sometimes be greater than between-variation.

(Øyen 1990: 7)

Scheuch (1990: 30), instancing the biannual EEC cross-national studies, agrees with Øyen. Such Euro-barometer surveys, he notes, rarely show variation in excess of 10 per cent. Yet, by contrast, within-country differences may be much higher. Indeed, in reference to 'Galton's Problem' (originally surfacing at a meeting of the Royal Anthropological Institute in 1889!), Scheuch has even queried whether it makes sense any more to talk about a given national culture as 'causing something', when a far more likely explanation is one of cultural diffusion.

Scheuch's thesis is quite straightforward in its corollary and implications for this discussion. Whereas before it might have been quite reasonable, in terms of national politics, national big business interests and national research funding, to have isolated nationality, country of residence or national culture as an independent variable in tourism research, the inescapable contemporary fact of the matter is now the globalization, rather than the nationalization, of problems. As Øyen relatedly and pertinently observes:

The air we breathe is polluted from faraway sources. An understanding of poverty in the Third World cannot be isolated from a consideration of the wealth accumulated in rich countries. The suppression of minorities becomes public property throughout the world when caught by television. Within such a perspective, the use of countries as units in comparative research may not appear to be the most fruitful approach.

(Øyen 1990: 2)

The cosmopolitan nature of tourist generating societies

Since international tourism is a function of discretionary income and relative affluence, it clearly follows that the greatest bulk of this trade flows between the Northern and Western Hemispheres – in practice to and from North America and Europe. Indeed, in 1989, Europe was calculated by the WTO to account for some 63.4 per cent of world arrivals and one half of all tourism receipts, while the Americas respectively constituted some 19.7 and 27 per cent of each (Frechtling

1990: 7; Oyowe 1990: 53). Thus, even though the latter region includes Latin America and the Caribbean, there is nevertheless a predominant majority situation in which those from metropolitan societies visit each other.

Yet, when one seeks to analyse any given country forming part of this vast configuration, problems are encountered whenever one begins to speak of nationality, national identity, national consciousness, or even country of residence. The United States, for instance, which has for decades built up its population largely from immigrant sources, can no longer realistically be viewed as a single national entity. Instead, there are generations of Irish, Italians and Poles from the old world, and rapid inflows of Cubans, Vietnamese and Filipinos from the new. When one further adds the racial factor, as indeed one must in order to obtain an accurate picture of this pluriform society, one comes across Afro-Americans, West Indians of African and Indian extraction, Chinese and others who collectively represent an antithesis to the supposedly ubiquitous White Anglo Saxon Protestant.

In Canada a similar situation exists in most of the major urban centres, while the overall scenario becomes more complex and divisive due to the presence of Indians and Inuit, and the perennial movement towards the possible reality of a Québec Libre and the confusing establishment of a society within a society.

In the so-called 'United' Kingdom, where nationality is often regarded in terms of being English, Welsh, Irish or Scots, there is an analogous history of immigration, particularly from the former Empire and Commonwealth countries. With racial tensions running high in many inner city areas, and erupting periodically as ethnic reactions against official discrimination towards immigrant minorities, one can only with difficulty speak of the British population in a nationalistic framework.

Over the Channel in Germany, with its national appendages of Southern European and Turkish *gästarbeiter*, matters are further complicated by events since the crumbling of the Berlin Wall and the assimilation of those from the Eastern bloc. France, too, sees its distinctiveness eroded by playing host to generations from former and present colonies, as indeed do the Netherlands and Belgium.

In fact, wherever one turns in North America or Europe, the question of nationality becomes highly problematic. Apparently not even the holding of a passport any longer resolves the issue, since, in the case of the EEC at least, there is but one document for all. Labour, trade and, of course, tourism, roam where they wish, and soon there will be a common currency to blur former distinctions still further.

The pluralistic nature of tourist receiving societies

What applies to generating countries for the most part also pertains to destination areas, given that in the majority situation these are usually one and the same. However, when the remaining Third World receiving societies are considered (which in 1989 collectively managed to obtain some 22.1 per cent of worldwide arrivals and 23.2 per cent of global receipts – Oyowe 1990: 54), the question of nationality can sometimes be even more problematic. In India and Africa, for instance, where to speak of homogeneous countries is more than a simple stretch of the imagination, polarization additionally occurs with respect to tribal origin, caste, religion and language. Moreover, Third World poverty and political conflict in these parts of the world can also lead to massive out-migration and brain drains, just as they can frequently represent a refugee problem of horrendous proportions. In this regard one thinks, for example, of the difficulty in establishing national identity for Kurds and Shiites in Iraq, foreign workers in Kuwait or the Jamaat-al-Muslimeen in Trinidad.

At one time it was sociologically fashionable to analyse developing countries along the lines suggested by the plural society thesis (Smith 1965). Here, groups of indigenes divided by race were treated like many cultural layers, agreeing to separate for the major institutional domains of life, and only congregating for essential economic exchanges. If it were hard enough to fit an analysis of nationality into that framework, now that the model has been largely discredited and replaced by a conflict paradigm (Craig 1982), it is even more difficult to speak of the minimum consensus required for national identity. When one adds to this the now all too familiar scenario of emigration and claims for refugee status, the overall picture becomes even more perplexing.

Limited host-guest interaction along the lines of nationality and country of residence

Just as consideration of nationality or country of residence becomes a problematic exercise when examining guests and hosts separately, *a fortiori* it presents further difficulties when the two parties interact or fail to interact at the point of contact in the destination area. Of these two alternatives, arguably the latter is the more salient to the task at hand, and will therefore be dealt with first in this necessarily brief discussion. The worst case scenario, that of North–South travel (English 1986) is highlighted in the hope that encounters of lesser culture shock can be better understood.

Lack of interaction between host and guest

Many first time tourists to regions of the developing world have very rudimentary images of the destination area and its people, and often depend for such knowledge on the content of video presentations and brochures produced in the Metropole. The latter, however, devote considerably more space and attention to displays of resorts, hotels and beaches than ever they do to the representation of locals. Furthermore, host people are, more often than not, depicted either as mobile scenery to authenticate various sites, or else displayed in a number of servile roles, rather than shown as interacting with visitors on an equal footing (Dann 1988a). Tourists are thus conditioned by the discourse and pictorial content of promotional material *not* to fraternize with the natives or, if they must, to do so through a series of temporary asymmetrical encounters. They are additionally encouraged through a language of social control either to remain within the hotel compound (where locals are defined as maids and waiters), or else to venture forth as a group in the isolating company of such marginalized culture brokers as couriers, guides and taxi drivers, in order to enjoy certain prescribed attractions (Dann 1988b).

With such a pre-conditioning, it is not surprising that many visitors become virtual prisoners of their enclaves and 'environmental bubbles', perhaps failing to recognize that many of these artificial home from home establishments have been specially prepared to minimize the trauma associated with unfamiliarity and strangerhood (Cohen 1972: 166). In a sense, too, 'The places of the glossy brochure of the travel industry do not exist; the destinations are not real places and the people are not real either' (Crick 1988: 59). These locations have not been selected out of friendliness for the natives, but rather because they are cheap (Thurot and Thurot 1983: 187; Crick 1988: 58). Indeed:

> Most Third World tourism destinations are highly substitutable for one another. It only requires political difficulties for the travel organizers in the tourist generating countries simply to reroute their clients to other destinations, leaving many people out of work and drastically under-occupied tourist accommodation.
>
> (Crick 1988: 45)

Seen in this light, any mixing of hosts and guests in order to promote international understanding is both highly contrived and unrealistic.

Knowledge of the participants' nationality or country of residence now only becomes useful to the extent that it facilitates their categorization into touristically independent and dependent groups.

Limited interaction between host and guest

Given the above inequalities, where 'With every encouragement from the travel industry, the tourist is prone to behave as a master in his own home rather than a guest in someone else's' (English 1986: 53) and where there is an increase in status merely by being a tourist and being served (English 1986: 56), it is hardly likely that host–guest interaction will be any different in terms of quality, at least as far as North–South tourism is concerned. As a consequence, argues Van den Berghe (1980), attitudes and behaviour between visitors and the visited will tend to be characterized by suspicion, distrust and resentment. He further maintains (although admittedly without the necessary empirical evidence) that, if tourists come from areas which are known for their racism, they will often extend such stereotyping and prejudice from the home society to the people of the destination country by treating them as similarly despised minorities merely on grounds of resemblance (Van den Berghe 1980: 379).

The exploitative and transitory nature of encounters between tourists and locals is thus best understood, not in terms of the nationality or country of residence of the participants, but what these terms stereotypically represent and how they are defined. The unit of analysis therefore more appropriately passes from 'American' to 'gringo' and from 'Chinese' to 'wog', with all that these labels richly imply in the self-fulfilling contexts of their utterance.

ALTERNATIVE APPROACHES TO NATIONALITY AND COUNTRY OF RESIDENCE

From the foregoing it seems clear that tourism research which rests its case solely on analyses of nationality or country of residence faces a number of theoretical and practical problems. For this reason a number of alternative approaches have been suggested. While they relate almost exclusively to generating countries, they could with some imagination be applied to receiving societies as well. They are very briefly discussed here under the headings of personality, role, culture, social class and lifestyle. A combination of approaches is also examined.

Personality

Since this is the most individual-directed approach, its psychological orientation stands in sharpest contrast to any treatment by nationality or country of residence. Pool (1958), for example, devotes the second half of his article on 'What American Travellers Learn' to an examination of personality characteristics as they emerge from a number of case studies. Here it is argued that attitudes of xenophobia or xenophilia are very much bound up with the handling of individual emotional problems, so much so that what travellers find in Europe depends on what they personally need to discover. A similar, although more elaborate, line of thinking can also be found in Mayo and Jarvis (1981).

However, closer inspection of these works quickly reveals that personality is structured according to the expectations of various reference groups (e.g. familial, occupational, religious). Thus the scenario of an American tourist wearing shorts in a European cathedral or shouting at a Portuguese waiter takes its meaning from similar behaviour in his/her home town. So too is the recounting of travellers' tales predicated on type of audience, whether it be the Chamber of Commerce or the League of Women Workers. In both instances, however, the references are local rather than national, and the need to supplement explanations at the macro-level with interpersonal definitions of situations becomes fairly evident.

Role

As the smallest element of culture, role also addresses attitudes and behaviour which are predicated on the expectations of others. Thus Cohen's (1972, 1974) early work which focuses on conceptualizing the tourist does so by means of a typology of tourist roles which are arranged on a continuum extending from familiarity to novelty. Since there is no reference to either nationality or country of residence, the implication is that tourist roles transcend spatial and temporal boundaries to the same degree that Simmelian forms which they portray, and on which they are based, are also universal and perennial (Simmel 1950). In such a manner, one can just as easily, and perhaps more validly, compare the role behaviour of tourists as women, bankers, middle class or Catholics, as one could by referring to their nationality or country of residence.

Culture

In spite of occasionally being placed in apposition (Mathieson and Wall 1982: 135), nationality and culture are not synonymous. The mountain dwellers of the Andes, for instance, enjoy a different culture from the inhabitants of Lima, and, whereas both groups may still unhelpfully be referred to as Peruvian, it is important to recognize that each comes under separate systems of belief, norms, values and sanctions, which ultimately guide their role behaviour. So too can variation be found between other sub-cultures.

However, what arguably makes the analysis of tourism so fascinating is that some participants often choose to suspend home based culture as ludic and liminoid actors 'out of culture' (Crick 1988: 61), while for others 'Tourism is very much about our culture, not about their culture or the desire to learn about it' (Crick 1988: 58). A fuller anthropological treatment of this intriguing, though complex, variable, and the different ways that tourists try to overcome the tension between liminality/ exploration versus nostalgia/the familiar through such non-ordinary, society transcending, shared human behaviour as play, ritual and pilgrimage, can be found in Graburn (1983).

Social class

Whereas the operationalization of social class is a vexatious issue (Dann 1984) beyond the scope of this discussion, there can be no denying that, by treating it as an independent variable, much can be learned about tourist attitudes and behaviour. Gottlieb's (1982) inversionist analysis of Americans' vacations, for example, throws a great deal of light on the proletarian quest to be a king or queen for a day, just as it does on the upper echelon pursuit of becoming a temporary peasant. The discourse of promotional material has also been shown to be class-related (Thurot and Thurot 1983), mirroring social structure through time. More contentious is the question of whether class is relative to a given culture (nationality?) or whether it can somehow transcend physical boundaries. In this regard, and although MacCannell (1976) has been criticized by Schudson (1979) for paying insufficient attention to social stratification in his new theory of the leisure class, what his analysis of symbols and attractions surely does suggest is that this semiotic world relates to modern secular man in general rather than to the citizens or residents of any given country.

Lifestyle

As Allcock (1988: 36) in a partial analysis of MacCannell (1976) points out, consideration of social class leads to an examination of the relations of production (occupation) and the relations of consumption (lifestyle). Interestingly, the latter, rather than the former, have become the focus of tourism research and marketing practice (Middleton 1988: 74–5). Thus, Mayo and Jarvis (1981: 234–343), while stressing the importance of social class as a key variable in predicting travel decisions, nevertheless make it quite clear that they are emphasizing consumer behaviour. This premise leads them naturally to a discussion of life cycle and types of family relationships (Nolan and Nolan 1978), and how these variously affect touristic choice. McIntosh and Goeldner (1984: 261–2), however, prefer to highlight the changing patterns of life brought about by the sexual revolution and the women's movement. These modifications in lifestyle, they argue, are no longer simply predicated on considerations of social class or demographics, since millions, in becoming more and more financially and physically mobile, have overstepped these narrow confines. At the same time, and in spite of the fact that they mainly address the American scene, the corollary to their observations is surely that to varying degrees lifestyle itself similarly transcends the limited boundaries of nationality or country of residence.

CHANGING MARKETS AND NEW MARKETING STRATEGIES

One way of combining the foregoing approaches, thereby enhancing the data set provided by the traditional E/D card, is to undertake complementary surveys including such lifestyle variables as newspaper readership, use of credit cards and leisure pursuits. Poon (1990), for instance, has argued convincingly that the best marketing practice is one which has replaced mass production with flexible specialization. Mass standardized and rigidly packaged (MSRP) tourism is giving way to flexible segmentation and diagonal integration (FSDI) tourism (Poon 1988). The accent is now on permanent innovation in the industry and ceaseless change in the marketplace, and how high technology can cope with fundamental alterations in leisure time, work patterns, income distribution, economic uncertainty and increasing globalization.

Drawing a lesson from the successful Benetton formula, she maintains that all-inclusive hotels which have rapidly built up a clientele based on individual interest are financially well ahead of their traditional rivals catering to package tours. Of course, much of this has been made possible by central reservation systems which, when combined with 'the globalization of major companies and international expansion . . . will lead to increasing numbers of companies and related outlets being accessible through CRS networks' (Leslie 1991: 84). One thus finds Scandinavian hotels tapping into the London market and the Japanese utilizing the Intercontinental network at the mere touch of a button.

Coterminously, and perhaps even more significantly, the market becomes segmented to cater to individual and group needs by use of multivariate analysis and other statistical techniques (Leslie 1991). Conceivably it would not take long for linked computers to rush through the various permutations and design a potential vacation to suit the recreational requirements of a 30-year-old eligible male bachelor, the single son of a widowed mother, who is also a hypochondriac left-wing journalist interested in mountaineering and watersports. While the unique solution might be a unisex vegetarian commune on the shores of Lake Bled in Slovenia, there would still be other appropriate options from which to exercise free will. Yet rarely would nationality or country of residence be entered into the equation; they would simply no longer be relevant.

As a corollary to the foregoing, it would also follow that NTOs equipped with similar software would scarcely need to promote their destinations on a country by country basis. Instead, they might more suitably direct their activities to targeting interest clusters within and without territorial boundaries. For that matter, they could even jointly market with two or more other boards of tourism, as is already being contemplated in the Caribbean for instance, and, eventually, cease to exist in their own right.

ALTERING THE PROMOTIONAL DISCOURSE

Just as nationality and country of residence are becoming less and less important to tourism marketing, so too does such a realization have implications for promotion. Whereas formerly tour operators could be considered as 'belonging' to a given territory, international mergers and takeovers increasingly point to a smaller number of multinational companies directing linkage operations from central hubs. Thus, provided the communication networks are satisfactory, it matters little where such centres are established, or even whether they are set up on land, in the sea or in the air.

Such manoeuvring naturally will have some effect on the way that promotional messages are conveyed and the discourse of such advertising. It may have been simple enough once, for example, to have promoted Gibraltar in Britain by merely emphasizing cups of tea, Union Jacks, bobbies, EIIR pillar boxes and telephone kiosks, with the odd Barbary ape thrown in to distinguish the Rock from Blackpool or Brighton. Now and in the future, however, such a strategy will become decreasingly feasible as EEC membership and Spanish neighbourliness begin to blur erstwhile national markers and as the physical and psychological distance from Tangiers and Algeciras becomes correspondingly reduced.

In a similar fashion (and in spite of fond memories of former stark differences in immigration procedures), it may soon be forgotten that Alaska belongs to the United States or the Yukon to Canada, as marketing similarities begin to obliterate national differences.

A like effect may also be experienced in travelogues, or in whatever form of electronic communication replaces them. Whereas messages based on the metaphor of homespun familiarity were once targeted by same country authors at fellow nationals, in the years ahead it is quite probable that the discourse will increasingly be anonymously generated and directed towards specific interest groups regardless of where they happen to be domiciled. In other words, nationality and country of residence will no longer be such important spatial or cultural considerations in promoting tourism under the new economic order.

CONCLUSION

Cohen (1979) has recommended that tourism research be processual, contextual, comparative and emic. In other words, such investigations should optimally be longitudinal in nature, take into account the prevailing economic, political and socio-cultural circumstances of the situation, be related to other studies, and be conducted from the perspective of the participants (P. Pearce 1982: 19). While adherence to these properties raises a number of philosophical issues, which have been treated elsewhere under the questions of values and subjectivity (Dann 1991: 32–4), what can and should be noted here is that the last three qualities no longer solely refer to nationality or country of residence.

This chapter has attempted to elaborate this point theoretically and in relation to tourism research. It has tried to demonstrate that, as part of the new economic order, tourism is now well and truly a global phenomenon in the hands of multinational corporations which pay scant attention to the national boundaries circumscribing either host or guest. In any case, such generating and destination societies are no longer culturally uniform, if indeed they ever were, and, for this reason, it becomes more appropriate to employ alternative approaches to the analysis of tourism. Furthermore, these proposals are not so radical or novel as they might at first appear, when one appreciates that they are quite consonant with best marketing practice and new forms of promotion.

To a certain extent, this chapter has an autobiographical motivational component, in that the author is an expatriate residing in a well established Third World tourism destination. He is also on occasion a tourist visiting a variety of places other than his own country of birth. The preceding account should therefore be contextualized within the framework of such reflection. At the same time, however, it should be noted that there are many other tourism researchers who share a similar lifestyle and perspective.

This autobiographical bias aside, other contributors to this volume reinforce the general position adopted here. Lanfant (Chapter 5), Hawkins (Chapter 10) and Ritchie (Chapter 11), in particular, underline trends towards the increasing internationalization of tourism and the emergence of global operations and issues. However, by way of final summary, it is perhaps more than fitting that the concluding remark should be left to Cohen, who so aptly and prophetically commented in an earlier paper (1972: 173) that 'A development complementary to ecological differentiation of the tourist sphere is the gradual emergence of an international tourist system, reaching across political and cultural boundaries.' One has no quarrel with that sentiment, except possibly in his use of the word 'gradual', but then that epithet was attached almost twenty years ago.

ACKNOWLEDGEMENTS

The author acknowledges with thanks the comments received on the original version of this chapter when presented as a paper at the Calgary meeting of the International Academy for the Study of Tourism and subsequently the useful critiques and suggestions provided by Richard Butler, Nelson Graburn, Douglas Pearce, Arley Sobers and Paul Wilkinson.

REFERENCES

Allcock, J. (1988) 'Tourism as a sacred journey', *Loisir et Société* 11,1: 33–48.

Bélisle, F. and Hoy D. (1980) 'The perceived impact of tourism by residents: a case study in Santa Marta Colombia', *Annals of Tourism Research* 7, 1: 83–101.

Brewer, J. (1978) 'Tourism, business and ethnic categories in a Mexican town', in V. Smith (ed.) *Tourism and Behavior, Studies in Third World Societies*, Williamsburg: William and Mary Press, 83–100.

Brubaker, W. (1990) 'Immigration, citizenship and the nation state in France and Germany: a comparative historical analysis', *International Sociology* 5, 4: 379–407.

Bystrzanowski, J. (ed.) (1989) *Tourism as a Factor of Change: National Case Studies*. Vienna: European Coordination Centre for Research and Documentation in Social Sciences.

Caribbean Tourism Organization (1989a) *Statistical Report*. Barbados: Caribbean Tourism Organization.

——(1989b) *A Conceptual and Methodological Guide for the Collection and Analysis of Tourism Statistics. Report on the Deliberations of the Task Force on Tourism Economic Statistics*. Barbados: Caribbean Tourism Organization.

Cohen, E. (1972) 'Towards a sociology of international tourism', *Social Research* 39, 1: 164–82.

——(1974) 'Who is a tourist? a conceptual clarification', *Sociological Review* 22, 4: 527–53.

——(1979) 'Rethinking the sociology of tourism', *Annals of Tourism Research* 6, 1: 18–35.

Coren, A. (1986) *Tissues for Men*, London: Sphere Books.

Craig, S. (1982) *Contemporary Caribbean: A Sociological Reader*, Maracas: College Press.

Crick, M. (1988) 'Sun, sex, sights, savings and servility: representations of international tourism in the social sciences', *Criticism, Heresy and Interpretation* 1, 1: 37–76.

Dann, G. (1984) *The Quality of Life in Barbados*, London: Macmillan.

——(1988a) 'The people of tourist brochures', paper presented at the First Global Conference on Tourism as a Vital Force for Peace, Vancouver, October.

——(1988b) 'Images of Cyprus projected by tour operators', *Problems of Tourism* 11, 3: 43–70.

——(1991) 'Issues in international tourism research', in M. Bäckström and M. Hanefors (eds) *Turism och Resande i Teori och Pratik*, Borlänge: Institutet für Turism & Reseforskning: 29–50.

Dragicevic, M. *et al.* (1989) 'Yugoslavia', in J. Bystrzanowski (ed.) *Tourism as a Factor of Change: National Case Studies* : 131–58.

English, E. (1986) *The Great Escape: An Examination of North–South Tourism*, Ottawa: North–South Institute.

Frechtling, D. (1990) 'Indicators: World Review, Regional Trends', in D. Hawkins (ed.) *Background Papers – Tourism Policy Forum*, Washington DC: International Institute of Tourism Studies: 4–15.

Gottlieb, A. (1982) 'Americans' vacations', *Annals of Tourism Research* 9, 2: 165–87.

Graburn, N. (1983) 'The anthropology of tourism', *Annals of Tourism Research* 10, 1: 9–33.

Jafari, J. (1974) 'The socio-economic costs of tourism to developing countries', *Annals of Tourism Research* 1: 227–59.

Lanfant, M.-F. (1980) 'Introduction: tourism in the process of internationalisation', *International Social Science Journal* 32: 14–33.

——(1989) 'International tourism resists the crisis', in A. Olszewska and K. Roberts (eds), *A Comparative Analysis of Free Time*, London: Sage: 178–91.

——(1990) 'Tourisme international: phénomène social total', paper presented to the Thematic Group on International Tourism, World Congress of the International Sociological Association, Madrid, July.

Lazo, C. and Quintana, V. (1989) 'Social impacts of tourism on the island of Lanzarote' in J. Bystrzanowski (ed.) *Tourism as a Factor of Change: National Case Studies*: 65–87.

Lee, J. and Malek, A. (1991) 'Multinational trade negotiations and the tourist industry', in *World Travel and Tourism Review* 1: 139–40.

Leslie, D. (1991) 'Trends in centralized reservation systems', *World Travel and Tourism Review* 1: 139–40.

MacCannell, D. (1976) *The Tourist: A New Theory of the Leisure Class*, New York: Schocken.

McDermott, P. and Jackson, L. (1985) *The Determinants of Tourist Arrivals in Australia and New Zealand*, Wellington: New Zealand Tourist Industry Federation.

McIntosh, R. and Goeldner, C. (1984) *Tourism: Principles, Practices, Philosophies*, 4th edn, Columbus: Grid.

Mathieson, A. and Wall, G. (1982) *Tourism: Economic, Physical and Social Impacts*, London: Longman.

Mayo, E. and Jarvis, L. (1981) *The Psychology of Leisure Travel*, Boston: CBI.

Middleton, V. (1988) *Marketing in Travel and Tourism*, Oxford: Heinemann.

Mowlana, H. and Smith, G. (1991) 'Tourism as international relations: linkages between telecommunications, technology and transnational banking', *World Travel and Tourism Review* 1: 215–18.

Nolan, S. and Nolan, M. (1978) 'Variations in travel behavior and the cultural impact of tourism', in V. Smith (ed.) *Tourism and Behavior, Studies in Third World Societies*, Williamsburg: William and Mary Press: 1–17.

Olsen, M. (1991) 'Environmental scan: global hospitality industry trends', *World Travel and Tourism Review* 1: 120–4.

Øyen, E. (1990) 'The imperfection of comparisons', in E. Øyen (ed.) *Comparative Methodology, Theory and Practice in International Research*, London: Sage: 1–18.

Oyowe, A. (1990) 'Dossier tourism', *The Courier*, no. 122 (July-August): 50–5.

Pearce, D. (1990a) 'Tourist travel patterns in the South Pacific: analysis and implications', in C. Kissling (ed.) *Destination South Pacific – Perspectives on Island Tourism*, Cahiers du Tourisme, série B, no. 59, Aix-en-Provence: Centre des Hautes Etudes Touristiques: 31–49.

——(1990b) 'Tourism, the regions and restructuring in New Zealand', *Journal of Tourism Studies* 1, 2: 33–42.

Pearce, P. (1977) 'The social and environmental perceptions of overseas tourists', unpublished D Phil. dissertation, University of Oxford.

—(1982) *The Social Psychology of Tourist Behaviour*, Oxford: Pergamon.

Pi-Sunyer, O. (1989) 'Changing perceptions of tourism and tourists in a Catalan resort town', in V. Smith (ed.) *Hosts and Guests, The Anthropology of Tourism*, 2nd edn, Philadelphia: University of Pennsylvania Press: 187–99.

Pool, I. (1958) 'What American travellers learn', *Antioch Review* 18, 4: 431–46.

Pool, I., Keller, S. and Bauer, R. (1956) 'The influence of foreign travel on political attitudes of American businessmen', *Public Opinion Quarterly* 20, 1: 161–75.

Poon, A. (1988) 'Information technology and tourism' *Annals of Tourism Research* 15, 4: 531–49.

—(1990) 'Flexible specialization and small size: the case of Caribbean tourism', *World Development* 18, 1: 109–23.

Reigrotski, E. and Anderson, N. (1954) 'National stereotypes and foreign contacts', *Public Opinion Quarterly* 24, 4: 515–28.

Richter, L. (1989) *The Politics of Tourism in Asia*, Honolulu: University of Hawaii Press.

Scheuch, E. (1990) 'The development of comparative research: towards causal explanations', in E. Øyen (ed.) *Comparative Methodology, Theory and Practice in International Research*: 18–37.

Schudson, M. (1979) 'Review essay on tourism and modern culture', *American Journal of Sociology* 84, 5: 1249–58.

Sheldon, P. and Var, T. (1984) 'Resident attitudes to tourism in North Wales', *International Journal of Tourism Management* 5, 1: 40–7.

Simmel, G. (1950) *The Sociology of Georg Simmel*, K. Wolff (ed.) Glencoe: Free Press.

Smith, H. (1955) 'Do intercultural experiences affect attitudes?', *Journal of Abnormal and Social Psychology* 51, 3: 469–77.

—(1957) 'The effects of intercultural experience. A follow up investigation', *Journal of Abnormal and Social Psychology* 52, 2: 266–9.

Smith, M. (1965) *The Plural Society in the British West Indies*, Berkeley: University of California Press.

Systems Caribbean (1991) *Research Report. Visitor Satisfaction Survey, Sixth Round*. Bridgetown: Tourism Development Corporation.

Thurot, J. and Thurot, G. (1983) 'The ideology of class and tourism: confronting the discourse of advertising', *Annals of Tourism Research* 10, 1: 173–89.

Triandis, H. and Vassiliou, V. (1967) 'Frequency of contact and stereotyping', *Journal of Personality and Social Psychology* 7: 316–28.

Van den Berghe, P. (1980) 'Tourism as ethnic relations: a case study of Cuzco, Peru', *Ethnic and Racial Studies* 3, 4: 377–91.

Yuan, S. and McDonald, C. (1990) 'Motivational determinants of international pleasure time', *Journal of Travel Research* 29, 1: 42–4.

Chapter 7

Fundamentals of tourist motivation

Philip L. Pearce

The purpose of this chapter is to outline a blueprint for tourist motivation; in effect it will be a consideration of critical factors and issues that an adequate account of this area must consider. The issues raised do not provide a theory of tourist motivation but they do give the architectural specifications, a knowledge of the key materials and the desired feel of the built form. The seven specifications discussed will then be used to evaluate three existing approaches to tourist motivation, specifically the work of Plog (1974, 1987), Iso-Ahola (1980) and Pearce (1988, 1991a).

THE CONCEPTUAL NICHE OF TOURIST MOTIVATION

An initial consideration of the conceptual place of tourist motivation within the specialism of tourism studies must be made. The term tourism demand should not be equated with tourism motivation. Tourism demand is the outcome of tourists' motivation, as well as marketing, destination features and contingency factors such as money, health and time relating to the traveller's choice behaviour (Morrison 1989). Tourism demand can be expressed as the sum of realistic behavioural intentions to visit a specific location. This generic statement is usually expressed in or reduced to existing travel statistics and forecasts of future traveller numbers. Tourist motivation is then a part rather than the equivalent of tourist demand.

Tourist motivation is also a hybrid concept; it is a term borrowed from the individual orientation of psychology (and to some extent from the group and social structure emphases of sociology) and applied to a specific domain of human action. Accordingly, its conceptual place in tourism studies might not be exactly equivalent to the position occupied in psychology, where in the past it has been seen as the prime organizer of human personality and a basic determinant of goal directed behaviour (de Charms and Muir 1978). The great classical theories of psychology, developed from the works of Freud and Jung (psychodynamic approaches), Hull and Skinner (learning theory) and Tolman and Lewis (cognitive theories), while treating motivation very differently, recognized it as a core topic in theories of human behaviour. The learning theories explicitly avoided using the term, preferring to focus on the external control of behaviour, but cognitive and psychodynamic perspectives are rich in ideas about individual motives and dominant forces controlling personality (Mehrabian 1968 and Boring 1950). The influence of these significant figures in the history of psychology lives on in the biosocial, holistic and cognitive research on motivation to be discussed later in this chapter.

The conceptual place of motivation within tourism surfaced as an issue of debate a decade ago in the interchange between Graham Dann and Seppo Iso-Ahola (Dann 1981, Iso-Ahola 1982, Dann 1983). In essence Dann argued for the position that tourist motivation was a hybrid concept, a new application of existing understandings of human action in a particular sphere which justified an eclectic and multi-disciplinary approach. The Iso-Ahola argument pushed the perspective that psychological research was fundamental to this area, that such research had been but should not be ignored and to some extent was sufficient to explain the phenomenon.

The intellectual contributions of psychology and the traditions of inquiry it represents are to be respected, but tourist behaviour and tourism as an area of human action have particular features which create new theoretical challenges. Some of the novel features pertaining to tourist motivation are that tourists select a time and place for their behaviour often well in advance of the event, that the behaviour is episodic across the life-span, influenced by one's close relationships, that satisfaction may result in the behaviour being repeated or a new form of holiday attempted, and that there is a constantly evolving interplay between how well tourist motivation is understood and what is provided to satisfy this motivation. In summary, tourist motivation is discretionary, episodic, future oriented, dynamic, socially influenced and evolving. These novel features of tourist motivation require a new focus and some attempts at synthesizing existing knowledge rather than simply applying existing psychological research. An appropriate analogy here is the area of leisure studies where some novel adaptations of psychological perspectives have been achieved (Neulinger 1974, Csikszentmihali 1977). While the achievements of the leisure researchers are admirable (Mannell and Iso-Ahola 1987), tourist motivation has sufficient novel features, as outlined above, which are only partly shared by leisure, to be worthy of independent attempts at theory building. In brief, the conceptual place of tourist motivation is a distinctive one, being both a component of tourist demand and a specialized facet of the general study of motivation.

A BLUEPRINT FOR TOURIST MOTIVATION

Seven key specifications which together might be said to constitute a blueprint for tourist motivation are identified and examined in this section.

The role of tourist motivation analysis

A discussion of the conceptual place of tourist motivation leads directly into a second and related issue governing a blueprint for a sound tourist motivation theory. One has to address the issue of the tasks of tourist motivation – what does this concept have to do, what must it explain? Within general motivation writing there is a view that motivation, rather like attitudes, 'has been expected to and been used to explain too much' (Cofer and Appley 1967). This comment is equally applicable to tourist motivation with the range of phenomena to be explained including why humans like to visit sunny places, how people choose holidays, why some people prefer peripatetic holidays to single location vacations, why vandalism occurs in national parks, how satisfaction can be explained and how to engineer one's marketing strategy for a target region so that it appeals to the needs of potential visitors. These tasks share one fundamental objective; they all recognize the importance of psychological factors and processes in tourism and they attempt to use motivation theory to understand better the choices, preferences and requirements of visitors. Additionally, the use of motivation theory for these purposes is also accompanied by the parallel use of terms such as attitudes, behavioural intentions, values, preferences, beliefs, needs and goals. In short we have an academic spaghetti of overlapping and interlocking concepts. So not only do we have a concept which is being asked to do too much, but we also have a concept which is competing with related concepts to establish its usefulness.

One possible resolution of these difficulties is to view tourist motivation as the basic tapestry, the prototype, the DNA structure or the geological bedrock which informs and integrates the related concepts.

According to this perspective, tourist motivation is the global integrating network of biological and cultural forces which gives value and direction to travel choices, behaviour and experience. Tourist motivation, in emphasizing biological and cultural components, is a more generic and fundamental term than its sibling term, values, which tends to downplay biological imperatives and gives less force to the energizing of behaviour and the patterning of behaviour generating forces. Indeed, the link between values and motives can be made even more explicit by recognizing that many of the models of values (such as Rokeach 1968 and 1973, Allport 1935) can be mapped on to the broader intellectual terrain carefully described in social motivation theory (see McClelland 1958, Maslow 1959, White 1959, Weiner 1972, Atkinson and Raynor 1975).

Pizam and Calantone (1987) and Calantone and Mazanec (1991) discuss and have begun to explore, profitably, the use of values in tourism market segmentation studies. This promising line of work could be further enhanced by a recognition and development of the links between research in value and motivation research. These developments reinforce the perspective that values might be an accessible component of psychological inquiry but this accessibility does not negate the view that values are related to and embedded in a broader landscape of motivational analysis (Feather 1975, Ajzen and Fishbein 1977, Pearce 1988, and Pearce and Stringer 1991). Similarly, the work on tourist expectations and satisfaction is understood by seeing motivation theory as the mould which forms and shapes the directions of the work undertaken in such studies.

The task of tourist motivation theories and perspectives is, then, to provide a rich and full tapestry of tourist needs, a reservoir of ideas for researchers to use in specific studies of satisfaction, decision making and marketing. Further, the task of tourist motivation analysis is to provide both short term and limited-in-scope perspectives (I want a drink right now) through to long term and broader motives (I want to see all of Canada's theme parks). Additionally, the task of tourist motivation is to provide some form of integration and synthesis amongst tourist motives (and the more specific term values) such that the patterns of behaviour and experience can be understood in a cumulative rather than a piecemeal fashion.

The ownership of tourist motivation explanations

In itemizing these fundamentals of tourist motivation it has just been suggested that the task of tourist motivation should be to provide a tapestry of short and long term needs differing in scope and preferably able to be understood within some hierarchical or integrative framework. The latter phrase raises the next issue to be addressed – able to be understood by whom? The issue to be addressed here is the 'ownership' of explanations in relation to tourist motivation. Motivational accounts of tourist behaviour, in common with other theoretical perspectives (e.g. perception, attitudes), have no ultimate recourse to the 'correct' explanation of the phenomenon. Accordingly, explanations and our investment in these explanations must be tempered by the anticipated biases of observers versus actors, of tourist researchers versus tourists, and of armchair speculators versus quantitatively minded data-gatherers. Some sophisticated components of attribution theory provide a metatheoretical framework with which to evaluate the motivational accounts of the above groups. For example, one should be alerted to the view that tourists themselves will be more likely to give favourable explanations of their own behaviour, in terms of socially acceptable motives, than will tourist observers (Jones and Nisbett 1971).

In order to illustrate the problems raised by this issue of the ownership of tourist motivation explanation, one can consider Cohen's (1983) criticism directed at this author's own early work on tourist motivation (Pearce 1982). One chapter of the 1982 book was titled *Inside the Tourist's Perspective* and provided some forty direct quotes from over 400 travellers' accounts of their best travel experiences with an interpretive gloss commenting on the patterns contained in these stories. It was, if one likes this terminology, an early form of discourse analysis (Potter and Wetherell 1987). Cohen observed: 'There is a deep significance to an emic view, it is more than "mere reporting by tourists of their personal impressions and reactions".' He elaborated: 'The emic perspective [is] one emerging from the understanding from within of the totality of a cultural world view,' and recommended: 'in depth studies of the meaning of tourism within the culture in the manner conducted by anthropologists'.

Cohen's observations and insights suggest at least three issues pertaining to the ownership of tourist motivation theories – in order, the principle of parsimony, the principle of reflexivity and the principle of ethnocentrism. These principles are related to the issues of ownership as follows. Scientific and research perspectives will value parsimony, that is, an elegant, efficient and usable tourist motivation theory. A distinction can also be drawn here between specialist and non-specialist scientific users. Psychologists and sociologists will demand precision and specificity from a motivational theory because using such approaches is central to much of their work. Other researchers in tourism may be satisfied with an approach which seems comprehensive and broadly describes an area of tourism in which they are not centrally interested. Consumers and more general readers of the tourist motivation literature will be attracted by theories in which they can see themselves, that is, the theories which are reflexive or insight generating for a wider audience. Where the tourist motivation theory is being applied across national groups, ownership of the theory will be heightened for the target groups if they do not detect cultural bias or ethnocentrism in the theoretical formulation. For example, an overemphasis on the importance of achievement motivation to explain tourist motivation in the South Pacific would be seen as inappropriate by societies dominated by group cohesiveness, affiliation motivation and complex personal reciprocal obligations (Sofield 1991).

Ease of communication

These ownership issues blend into another fundamental concern for tourist motivation theories, specifically the ease with which the theory can be communicated to any of the potential owners. There are many fascinating and overdue studies to be undertaken in the area of how and exactly why some theoretical formulations in social science (e.g. alienation, I.Q., stereotype) become active research areas and others are neglected (e.g. overmanning, de-individuation, social episodes (Knorr-Citena 1981)). Some of the forces to be included in such an analysis would be the power of research funding agencies, the prestige of the originator of the concept and the timeliness of its derivation and public launch as well as the more usually stated issues of power, testability, generality, congruence with existing research findings and the role of competitive and overlapping terms Becher (1989). The motivational approach of Plog, to be reviewed later in this chapter, has been accorded attention partly for reasons of timeliness and an absence of competitors.

In summary, it can be argued that a good tourist motivation theory must communicate efficiently and be readily understood by its potential owners. This principle would weigh against abstruse new terms, complex multivariate formulations and approaches which involve sharp revisions of existing understandings. The latter are quite extensive in existing tourism and travel writing. Thus travel motivation has been described as a travel bug, an itch, lust (as in wanderlust and sunlust), a herd instinct, the flocking of the masses, a spiritual re-birth, escape, enhancement, desire and, finally, consummation (Twain 1869, Steinbeck 1962, Dichter 1967, Owen 1968, Alderson 1971, Neville 1971, McIntosh 1972, Young 1973, Lundberg 1974, Eco 1989). While these social representations are somewhat fanciful, such views must at least be respected or incorporated as a part of the communication of a sound travel motivation theory.

The measurement issue

The next problem area, namely that of measuring tourist motives, is a familiar psychological issue in another context. The essential problem is whether the data gathered are meant to have predictive value or whether they are directed towards obtaining a *post-hoc* descriptive account of travel motivation. If prediction of some future behaviour is the aim, then questions concerning the precision of the prediction and its reliability emerge. If *post-hoc* accounts of behaviour are at issue, there is an alarming tendency to be able to bend any theoretical perspective to fit the observed outcome (Gergen 1983). Since it can be justifiably claimed that these issues are not settled within the field of psychology itself, it is rather demanding to expect that they are satisfied in the context of tourist motivation. Clearly, though, there is a need to differentiate between predictive and *post-hoc* accounts of tourist motivation and to consider seriously the breadth and reliability issues if one is concerned with prediction. The most useful guiding principle to follow in this respect might be the attitudinal research of Petty and Cacioppo (1986) who have chosen to move in the direction of greater specificity of both action and situational context in their attempt to predict behaviour. On the other hand, a broad-ranging *post-hoc* account of travel motivation might benefit from summarizing across the specific situations and actions with the kind of generalized value orientation promoted by Rokeach (1968) and Feather (1975).

Multi-motive versus single trait approaches

Another fundamental issue is that of viewing tourist motivation as multi-motive versus single trait or unidimensional. The strait-jacket of positivist methodology which requires (or used to require) the interpretation of data with neat trait-based approaches to the assessment of individual differences has been a limiting force (Harré 1979, 1983). Increasingly there is a recognition that much human behaviour (including travel behaviour) is multi-motive or over-determined (Harré, Clark and de Carlo 1985). Expressed differently, people will frequently have more than one motive operating in any social setting and the challenge for a good theory of tourist motivation is to have this tapestry, this interlocking pattern of shifting and fluctuating motives represented and treated within the theoretical formulation. Additionally, some efforts or capacity to explain these shifting patterns of motivational dominance would add explanatory power to a good motivation theory.

The issue of the multi-motive factor in tourist behaviour is one of the most intractable for quantitatively minded researchers. Nevertheless, if researchers recast their thinking of tourist motivation as multi-motive, then greater rapprochement between research and public ownership of tourist motivation theory will be achieved. For example, it is highly consistent with Cohen's emic perspective (Cohen 1983) that travellers explain their behaviour in place, social context and time with a multiplicity of causes and accounts. For example, a visitor to Hawaii questioned on her reasons for visiting a small theme park might observe: 'I went to Hawaii's Sea Life Park to entertain my 2-year-old, relax in a pleasant safe setting, and to develop my professional understanding of exhibit technologies'. It can be noted that to choose one motive from this list is to view a one-dimensional person and to underestimate the complexity of tourist needs and behaviour. Such limiting one-dimensional motivational views may partly explain why many current psychographic groupings are less effective predictors and explainers of travel behaviour than they might be.

A dynamic approach

A further issue for tourist motivation theory is that it must be dynamic. The perspective or theoretical formulation must be flexible enough to incorporate individual changes across the life-span and to consider the effects of broad cultural forces on tourist motivation. For example, if travellers from a particular source region are becoming consistently more environmentally conscious in their travel choices, then our tapestry of tourist motivation theory must be able to accommodate and hopefully interpret such changes. Similarly, if individuals change their travel preferences as they move through a family career and life cycle then tourist motivation theory should be able to chart such progress or change. As with the multi-motive perspective, the demand for tourist motivation theory to be dynamic and sensitive to individual and social group change weighs against simple fixed trait approaches and argues for an integrative, cumulative and organizing tapestry or theoretical mould.

Intrinsic and extrinsic motivation

The area of leisure, holiday taking and tourism is also a fertile field for the development of ideas pertaining to intrinsic motivation. The final issue to be discussed for an adequate tourist motivation theory is to weave the interplay between intrinsic and extrinsic motivation into one tapestry of understanding. Intrinsic motivation may be briefly defined as behaviour conducted for its own sake whereas extrinsic motivation is behaviour under the control of outside rewards. De Charms and Muir (1978) and Csikzentmihali (1977) argue that intrinsic motivation makes us pay attention to the issues of personal control and choice in travel motivation, thus providing a non-reductionistic view. By way of contrast, Harré, Clarke and de Carlo (1985) develop the view that an understanding of human action must attend to people's competencies, their understandings of the moral order in their society and the autonomy and power of actors to present their behaviours for social recognition from others. For Harré, Clark and de Carlo most social action is extrinsically motivated in that people account for and explain their choices and actions with reference to judgement by others. Additionally, Valentine (1982) develops the view that teleological or future oriented concerns must not be neglected in understanding people's current actions. Her position fosters the interpretation that some travel behaviour may be motivated by the satisfaction derived from the experience at a later point in time, by way of recollection, reflection, mental souvenirs and social status issues, rather than by the immediate enjoyment of the event. Valentine thus offers a kind of delayed intrinsic motivation in her emphasis on teleological explanations of conduct. These psychological ideas are reflected in much existing leisure research, notably the early work of Clawson and Knetsch (1966) and followers in that tradition who emphasized the recollection phase of leisure recreation.

It is clear from this brief account that both extrinsic and intrinsic motivation are relevant to tourist behaviour and experience. It may be necessary and valuable for future leisure and tourist motivation studies to rethink the conceptual distinction between these terms for the tourism sphere, as they were developed in part to distinguish between leisure and work settings rather than to understand leisure settings alone. One should not, for example, glibly assume that all leisure and tourist behaviour is intrinsically motivated simply because it is chosen and is outside of a work context (Vroom 1964).

Pearce (1991b), for example, has revealed that travellers can be very selective about to whom they tell their travel stories, a finding which suggests that for some travellers extrinsic motivation factors figure prominently in their motivational profile. An example of the subtle effects of extrinsic and intrinsic motivation in a tourist setting illustrates the potential importance of considering this distinction. Every year 200,000 people climb to the top of Ayers Rock, one of Australia's most remote tourist destinations in Central Australia. This arduous and usually very hot tourist activity was studied by Fielding, Hughes and Pearce (in press). On the basis of tourists' answers to a panel of questions, over 300 climbers were categorized as intrinsically or extrinsically motivated. Those who were extrinsically motivated were highly satisfied if they reached the summit and very disappointed if they failed to make it all the way. Intrinsically motivated climbers were equally satisfied with the climb whether they made it to the top or only completed a small segment of the total climb.

THEORETICAL APPROACHES TO TOURIST MOTIVATION

The preceding section has outlined a blueprint for a good theory of tourist motivation. While there have been many papers in the leisure research and tourism research literature dealing with motivation, there are few widely quoted theoretical approaches. This chapter will conclude by contrasting three theoretical approaches – the psychographic model (Plog 1974, 1987), the developing travel career model of Pearce (1988, 1991a) and the intrinsic motivation–optimal arousal approach of Iso-Ahola (1980). Each approach will be presented briefly and their attributes will be compared in a table based on the blueprint outlined.

The psychographic profile

Plog (1974, 1987) developed his tourist motivation work in a commercial consulting setting by initially working with airline business clients. He was concerned to detect and describe differences between flyers and non-flyers and used extensive telephone based interviews to develop the notion of psychocentric (self-inhibited, nervous and non-adventuresome people) and allocentric (variety seeking, adventurous, confident people) types. This work was generated at a time when unitary trait based approaches to motivation and personality were, though declining, still dominant in psychological thinking (Eysenck 1967, Mischel 1969). Plog (1974) reported that the psychocentric and allocentric types also varied in their media use (psychocentrics being heavy television watchers with allocentrics more print-oriented). From a 4,000 person national survey, Plog asserted that the population from allocentrism to psychocentrism is normally distributed. Further, he observed that income was not related to the trait except at the extreme ends of the scale where high scoring allocentrics have higher incomes and the lowest income levels have a greater proportion of psychocentrics. Plog transferred this basic market segmentation scheme to a range of tourism settings and observed that the two groups differed in travel characteristics as follows: psychocentrics prefer the familiar in travel destinations, they have low activity levels, they like to drive, enjoy familiar atmospheres and appreciate tour packaging. Allocentrics prefer less tourist-developed areas, they like novel destinations and cultures, they prefer independent tour arrangements and are more likely to fly to destinations. The core components of approach are presented in Figures 7.1 and 7.2.

Plog (1974) relates the psychocentric-allocentric distinction and its gradations to destinations, with allocentrics being the first wave and the psychocentrics being the last wave in the tourist succession process. For the purposes of the present analysis it is important to observe that the paper was presented at a meeting of The Travel Research Association (California chapter) in 1972 and published in the prestigious *Cornell Hotel and Restaurant Administration Quarterly* in 1974. Core tourism text books have referenced the work since that time (see McIntosh and Goeldner 1990). Plog (1987) does not develop the system but summarizes the advantages and advances in psychographic work since the 1974 studies. Some methodological details are reported in 1987 – it

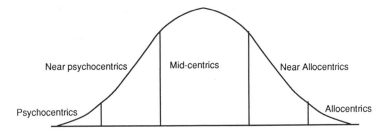

Figure 7.1 US population distribution by psychographic type

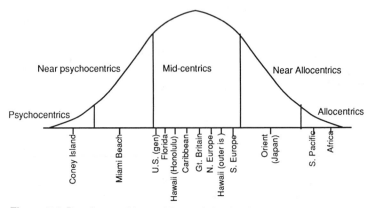

Figure 7.2 Psychographic positions of destinations

is stated that eight questions are needed to establish an individual's position on the psychocentric–allocentric scale – but presumably the commercial sensitivity and value of the work precludes explicit information. A dynamic element is added to the 1974 article with the assertions that allocentrics pick up new products first and then 'introduce the products to the near-allocentrics, and then the near-allocentrics will "pass" the products on to the mid-centrics, each group becoming a mover and shaker for the personality type that is a little more conservative in its consumer behaviour than the group which passed the product on' (1987: 212).

The travel career tapestry

Pearce (1988 and 1991a), Pearce and Caltabiano (1983), and Moscardo and Pearce (1986) have developed a tourist motivation framework in an academic setting with some commercial applications, notably in the theme park and tourist attractions sector. Basing their ideas initially on Maslow (1959), Pearce and Caltabiano demonstrated the applicability of a five-fold hierarchical system for ranking tourists' *post-hoc* motivational descriptions pertaining to their holidays. Maslow's system was employed in the initial studies because of its ability to combine biological motives (which are frequently ignored) and social ones within a single framework and because it involves a dynamic element whereby people can change their motivation over time or across situations. Additionally, it does not preclude people from having more

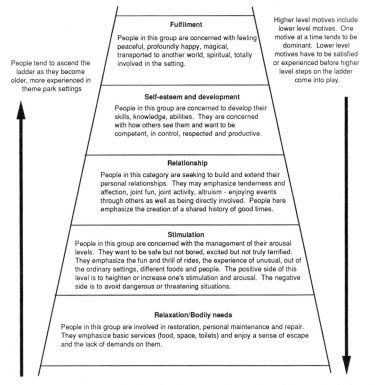

People tend to ascend the ladder as they become older, more experienced in theme park settings

Fulfilment
People in this group are concerned with feeling peaceful, profoundly happy, magical, transported to another world, spiritual, totally involved in the setting.

Higher level motives include lower level motives. One motive at a time tends to be dominant. Lower level motives have to be satisfied or experienced before higher level steps on the ladder come into play.

Self-esteem and development
People in this group are concerned to develop their skills, knowledge, abilities. They are concerned with how others see them and want to be competent, in control, respected and productive.

Relationship
People in this category are seeking to build and extend their personal relationships. They may emphasize tenderness and affection, joint fun, joint activity, altruism - enjoying events through others as well as being directly involved. People here emphasize the creation of a shared history of good times.

Stimulation
People in this group are concerned with the management of their arousal levels. They want to be safe but not bored, excited but not truly terrified. They emphasize the fun and thrill of rides, the experience of unusual, out of the ordinary settings, different foods and people. The positive side of this level is to heighten or increase one's stimulation and arousal. The negative side is to avoid dangerous or threatening situations.

Relaxation/Bodily needs
People in this group are involved in restoration, personal maintenance and repair. They emphasize basic services (food, space, toilets) and enjoy a sense of escape and the lack of demands on them.

Figure 7.3 The leisure ladder for theme park settings (domestic visitors)

than one motive at a time. The five motivational levels described in the scheme are: a concern with biological needs, safety and security needs, relationship development and extension needs, special interest and self-development needs and finally fulfilment or self-actualization needs. Pearce (1988, 1991a) argued that people have a career in their tourist behaviour. Like a career at work, people may start at different levels, they are likely to change levels during their life-cycle and they can be prevented from moving by money, health and other people. They may also retire from their travel career or not take holidays at all and therefore not be a part of the system. Moscardo and Pearce (1986) demonstrated that visitors at a historic theme park had different satisfaction levels depending on their career level. Recently Pearce (1991a), in connection with Brian Dermott and Associates (1991), developed a specific form of the travel career tapestry or system, the

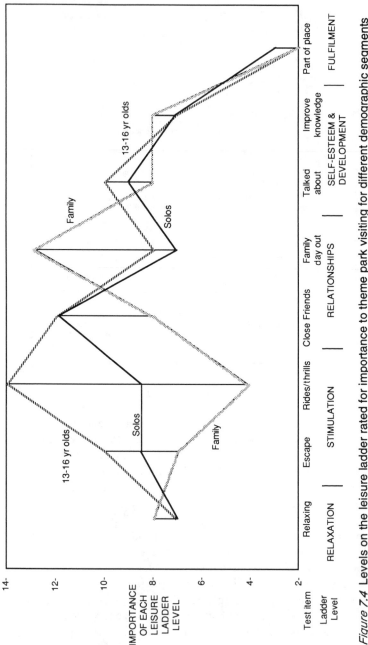

Figure 7.4 Levels on the leisure ladder rated for importance to theme park visiting for different demographic segments

Table 7.1 Questions and codes pertaining to the travel career system (leisure ladder adaptation for theme parks)

Code		Question content	Career level
relaxing	=	relaxing in a nice safe setting	relaxation
escape	=	escaping from the everyday world	stimulation
rides/thrills	=	enjoying the adventure and excitement of the rides	
close friends	=	seeing and doing things with friends	relationships
family day out	=	enjoying a day out with the family	
talked about	=	visiting a well known and talked about attraction	self-esteem and development
improve knowledge	=	improving my knowledge and understanding of people, places, events	
part of place	=	really feeling a part of the place	fulfilment

leisure ladder, for theme park research. By specifying more precise situationally relevant questions for the theme park context, but still retaining the core ideas of the travel career concept, the authors were able to predict and explain theme park attendance at three competitive theme parks as well as evaluate new development proposals for one of the parks. Figure 7.3, which depicts the leisure ladder for theme park settings, represents a specific generic derivation from the travel career tapestry.

Figure 7.4 illustrates how Pearce and Dermott matched demographic groups (young children, single adults and families) to motivations for theme park visitors. This graph illustrates how the demographic segments are different in their dominant motivation but that all groups are multi-motive to some extent. The specific items measuring each level of the leisure ladder are on the x axis and the importance of the attribute is on the y axis. The data come from a 4,000 person national survey of tourist behaviour and theme park visiting. As expected, the dynamic element of the travel career system is evident in the data with the shift in dominant motivation level moving from left to right across the page. The key questions which are referred to in Figure 7.4 and which represent levels on the leisure ladder are presented in Table 7.1.

The intrinsic motivation-optimal arousal perspective

A third theoretical approach to studying tourist motivation can be extrapolated from the analysis of leisure motivation by Iso-Ahola (1980). This approach, which may be labelled the intrinsic motivation–optimal arousal perspective, offers not so much a theory but a generalized style for examining leisure motivation. Iso-Ahola notes that leisure needs (and by implication tourist needs) can be explained at different levels of causality. He argues that future studies should be done within the framework of intrinsic leisure motivation and further emphasises that leisure behaviour takes place within a framework of optimal arousal and incongruity. That is, while individuals seek different levels of stimulation they share the need to avoid boredom while eschewing overstimulation and mentally exhausting settings. He argues that leisure needs should not be viewed as static and stable but as changing qualities. In particular, leisure needs change during the life span and across places, situations and social company. Important categories of leisure needs which should be considered include improvised or spontaneous needs as opposed to stable trait-like needs, as well as *a priori* as distinct from *a posteriori* needs.

Following Nisbett and Wilson (1977), Iso-Ahola warns against culturally supplied explanations of motives, that is, mindless or stereotypic responses to motivation questions which mask the personal individual motives for behaviour. He advises researchers to keep the motivation questions for leisure close to the actual participation in time, to limit the masking role of culturally supplied explanations.

The fundamental perspective of Iso-Ahola's approach to motivation for tourism and leisure is illustrated in Figure 7.5, which emphasizes the importance of understanding intrinsic motivation within the framework

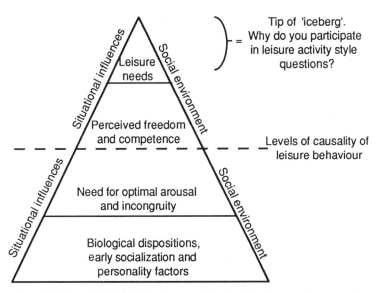

Figure 7.5 Iso-Ahola's intrinsic motivation/optimal arousal approach to motivation

of the need for optimal arousal. It is the task of managers and academics, Iso-Ahola argues, to facilitate participants' feelings of self determination and competence in leisure settings since attention to these factors ensures satisfaction. Iso-Ahola's work is clearly developing a leisure based perspective on tourist motivation.

An overall assessment on fundamentals

The three tourist motivation theories which have been described above – the psychocentric–allocentric model, the travel career model and the intrinsic motivation–optimal arousal approach – are compared in Table 7.2 within the blueprint for tourist motivation outlined earlier.

CONCLUSION

In summary, the blueprint for tourist motivation outlined in this article has directed attention to a number of fundamental issues. An adequate and insightful tourist motivation theory must pay attention to the issues of the conceptual place of tourist motivation, its task in the specialism of tourism, its ownership and users, its ease of communication,

Table 7.2 A comparison of three motivation theories using the blueprint for tourist motivation – fundamentals.

	(Plog 1974, 1987) Psychocentric– Allocentric model	(Pearce 1988, 1991) Travel career model	(Iso-Ahola 1980) Intrinsic motivation– Optimal arousal perspective
Role of the theory	Market research oriented	Both academic and commercial targets	Predominantly academic goals
Ownership of the theory – to whom will it appeal	1 Marketers 2 Non-specialist researchers 3 Popular use	1 Specialist researchers 2 Specific commercial settings 3 Marketers	1 Academic leisure and tourism researchers 2 Some recreation managers
Ease of communication	Now well known and integrated into tourism texts. North American bias in all examples is the strongest feature of the model	More complex to explain. Suits more sophisticated audiences and a multivariate approach to tourist behaviour. Universal in application	Somewhat complex to explain
The measurement issue	Measures not widely available. Use of measures to produce dimensional view highly questionable	Clear and situationally varied. A family of measurements to suit contexts is emerging	Eclectic; warns against stereotypic responses to obvious questions. Optimal arousal difficult to specify

Multi-motive versus single-trait approach	Dominated by single-trait approach. No continuing evidence that the distribution of the trait is normal	Explicitly mult-motive. Forces a consideration of the pattern of visitor motivation not the dominant motive	Motives seen as unitary but different levels of explanation recognized
Dynamic versus snap-shot approach	A single snap-shot view. May be historically dated. No capacity for individuals to change. Over time a tourism product is 'passed' from allocentric to psychocentric groups	Individuals can change and are expected to change. The role of societal changes can be assessed with relevant content at each travel level	An emphasis on changing needs with situation and over life-span
Extrinsic and intrinsic motivation	Not considered. The model fails to make an important distinction which is emerging in much leisure and tourism research	Explicitly considered. Each travel level has an external and internal component. Can be articulated as sub-components within each level of the travel career model	Dominant emphasis on intrinsic motivation. In danger of ignoring extrinsic motivation
Overall summary	Historically has generated an interest in psychographics	Likely to be used more widely	Future use limited unless more precise measures of optimal arousal can be articulated

pragmatic measurement concerns, the development of multi-motive perspectives, adopting a dynamic approach and resolving and clarifying intrinsic and extrinsic motivation approaches. The power of this blueprint in distinguishing between three approaches to tourist motivation was demonstrated, with the travel career model having more strengths than the allocentric–psychocentric approach. The intrinsic motivation–optimal arousal perspective was positively assessed on a number of fundamentals but some measurement issues and a recreation researcher ownership may limit its usefulness in tourism studies. In the future, different approaches to tourist motivation might be assessed against the blueprint outlined here.

REFERENCES

Ajzen, I. and Fishbein, M. (1977) 'Attitude–behaviour relations: a theoretical analysis and review of empirical research', *Psychological Bulletin* 84: 888–914.
Alderson, F. (1971) *The New Grand Tour – Travelling Today Throughout Europe, Asia Minor, India and Nepal*, Newton Abbot: David & Charles.
Allport, G. (1935) 'Attitudes', in C. Murchison (ed.) *Handbook of Social Psychology*, vol. 2, Worchester, MA: Clark University Press.
Atkinson, J.W. and Raynor, J. O. (1975) *Motivation and Achievement*, Washington, DC: Winston.
Becher, T. (1989) *Academic Tribes and Territories*, Milton Keynes: The Society for Research into Higher Education and the Open Learning Press.
Boring, E. (1950) *A History of Experimental Psychology*, New York: Appleton Century Crofts.
Calantone, R. and Mazanec, J. (1991) 'Marketing management and tourism', *Annals of Tourism Research* 18, 1: 101–19.
Clawson, M. and Knetsch, J. (1966) *Economics of Outdoor Recreation*, Baltimore: Johns Hopkins.
Cofer, C. N. and Appley, M. H. (1967) *Motivation: Theory and Research*, New York: Wiley.
Cohen, E. (1983) 'The social psychology of tourist behaviour', Publications in review, *Annals of Tourism Research* 10, 4: 580–2.
Csikszentmihali, M. (1977) *Beyond Boredom and Anxiety*, San Francisco: Jossey Bass.
Dann, G. (1981) 'Tourism motivation and appraisal', *Annals of Tourism Research* 9, 2: 187–219.
——(1983) 'Comment on Iso–Ahola's "Toward a social psychological theory of tourism motivation: A rejoinder" ', *Annals of Tourism Research* 10, 2: 273–6.
De Charms, R. and Muir, M. S. (1978) 'Motivation: social approaches', *Annual Review of Psychology* 29: 91–113.
Dermott, Brian and Associates (1991) *The Development of Dreamworld; A Strategy*, Melbourne: B. D. A. Associates.

Dichter, E. (1977) 'What motivates people to travel?', address to the Department of Tourism of the Government of India, Kashmir, India, October 1967.

Eco, U. (1989) *Travels in Hyper–reality*. London: Paladin

Eysenck, H. J. (1967) *Biological Basis of Personality*, Springfield, Illinois: C. Thomas.

Feather, N. (1975) *Values in Education and Society*, New York: Free Press.

Fielding, K., Hughes, K. and Pearce, P. L. (in press) *Satisfaction with Climbing Ayers Rock*.

Gergen, K. (1983) *Toward Transformation in Social Psychology*, New York: Springer–Verlag.

Harré, R. (1979) *Social Being*, Oxford: Blackwell.

——(1983) *Personal Being*, Oxford: Blackwell.

Harré, R., Clarke, D. and de Carlo, N. (1985) *Motives and Mechanisms*, London: Methuen.

Iso-Ahola, S. (1980) *The Social Psychology of Leisure and Recreation*, Iowa: William Brown.

——(1982) 'Toward a social psychological theory of tourism motivation: a rejoinder', *Annals of Tourism Research* 9, 2: 256–62.

Jones, E. E. and Nisbett, R. E. (1971) *The Actor and the Observer: Divergent Perceptions of the Causes of Behavior*, Morristown, NJ: General Learning Press.

Knorr–Citena, K. D. (1981) *The Manufacture of Knowledge*, Oxford: Pergamon.

Lundberg, D. (1974) *The Tourist Business*, 2nd edn, Boston: Cahners.

McClelland, D. C. (1958) *The Achieving Society*, New York: Van Nostrand.

McIntosh, R. (1972) *Tourism: Principles, Practices, Philosophies*. Ohio: Grid.

McIntosh, R. and Goeldner, C. (1990) *Tourism: Principles, Practices, Philosophies*, 6th edn, New York: John Wiley & Sons.

Mannell, R. C. and Iso–Ahola, S. E. (1987) 'Psychological nature of tourism and leisure experience', *Annals of Tourism Research* 14, 3: 314–331.

Maslow, A. H. (1959) *Motivation and Personality*, New York: Harper and Row.

Mehrabian, A. (1968) *An Analysis of Personality Theories*, New Jersey: Prentice Hall.

Mischel, W. (1969) 'Continuity and change in human personality', *American Psychologist* 24: 1012–18.

Morrison, A. (1989) *Hospitality and Travel Industry Marketing*, New York: Delmar Publishers.

Moscardo, G. M. and Pearce, P. L. (1986) 'Historical theme parks: an Australian experience in authenticity', *Annals of Tourism Research* 13, 3: 467–79.

Neulinger, J. (1974) *The Psychology of Leisure*, Springfield, Illinois: Charles C. Thomas.

Neville, R. (1977) *Playgoer*, London: Paladin.

Nisbett, R. E. and Wilson, T. D. (1977) 'Telling more than we know: Verbal reports on mental processes', *Psychological Review* 84: 231–59.

Owen, C. (1968) *Britons Abroad*, London: Routledge & Kegan Paul.

Pearce, P. L. (1982) *The Social Psychology of Tourist Behaviour*, Oxford: Pergamon Press.

——(1988) *The Ulysses Factor*, New York: Springer–Verlag.

——(1991a) *Dreamworld. A Report on Public Reactions to Dreamworld and Proposed Developments at Dreamworld*, Townsville: Department of Tourism: James Cook University.

——(1991b), 'Travel stories: an analysis of self–disclosure in terms of story structure, valence, and audience characteristics', *Australian Psychologist* 26, 3: 172–5.

Pearce, P. L. and Caltabiano, M. L. (1983) 'Inferring travel motivation from travellers' experiences', *Journal of Travel Research* 22: 16–20.

—— and Stringer, P. (1991) 'Psychology and tourism', *Annals of Tourism Research* 18, 136–54.

Petty, R. E. and Cacioppo, J. T. (1986) 'The elaboration likelihood model of persuasion', *Advances in Experimental Social Psychology* 19: 123–205.

Pizam, A. and Calantone, R. (1987) 'Beyond psychographics – values as determinants of tourist behaviour', *International Journal of Hospitality Management* 6, 3: 177–81.

Plog, S. (1974) 'Why destination areas rise and fall in popularity', *Cornell Hotel Restaurant and Administration Quarterly*: 55–8.

——(1987) 'Understanding psychographics in tourism research', in J. R. B. Ritchie and C. Goeldner (eds) *Travel Tourism and Hospitality Research*, New York: Wiley: 203–14.

Potter, J. and Wetherell, M. (1987) *Discourse and Social Psychology: Beyond Attitudes and Behaviour*, London: Sage.

Rokeach, M. (1968) *Beliefs, Attitudes and Values*, San Francisco: Jossey–Bass.

——(1973) *The Nature of Human Values*, New York: Free Press.

Sofield, T. (1991) 'Sustainable ethnic tourism in the South Pacific: some principles, *Journal of Tourism Studies* 2, 1: 56–72.

Steinbeck, J. (1962) *Travels with Charley, in search of America*, London: Pan.

Twain, M. (1869) *Innocents Abroad*, New York: Airmont, reprinted 1969, Harmondsworth.

Valentine, E. R. (1982) *Conceptual Issues in Psychology*, London: George Allen & Unwin.

Vroom, V.H. (1964) *Work and Motivation*, New York: Wiley.

Weiner, B. (1972) *Theories of Motivation*, Chicago: Markham.

White, R. W. (1959) 'Motivation reconsidered: the concept of competence', *Psychological Review* 66: 297–333.

Young, G. (1973) *Tourism: Blessing or Blight?*, Harmondsworth: Penguin.

Chapter 8

Pre- and post-impact assessment of tourism development

Richard W. Butler

Historically, most tourism developments were undertaken without assessment or consideration of potential impacts except for anticipated economic benefits. In recent years, in many countries, tourism developments have become subject to impact assessments before permission is given for construction. Few developments, however, have been subjected to post-impact assessments or monitoring to determine if the impacts generated were what were forecast and planned for. Impact studies have tended to be systematic and concentrate on 'tourism' as a phenomenon rather than on specific projects. It can be argued that, given the state of development of research into tourism and its effects, it may prove more beneficial and effective to conduct specific *post hoc* impact assessments of specific developments rather than general impact studies at a regional or community scale. In that way, consistent methodologies and comparable studies could be developed which could produce more rigorous and reliable results. In particular, the little-explored aspect of cumulative impact could be examined and insights gained on the perennial problem of the capacity of tourist destinations to absorb tourists.

This chapter will concentrate upon problems which have emerged in assessing impacts from tourism and tourism-related developments. It will not describe or discuss specific cases except where they serve to illustrate particular points. Some general comments are appropriate by way of introduction. Impact assessments of tourism and related developments, for the most part, have been few and far between. *Post hoc* assessments are so few as to be almost non-existent, except for studies done by academics. The academic studies, for the most part, have been case studies using a variety of methodologies, operating at different scales and conducted within the parameters, models and concepts of different disciplines. Nevertheless, some common conclusions do emerge and these will be commented on. A second general comment is that there are some fundamental differences about tourism compared to many other forms of activity and development which do not appear to be widely known or accepted by decision makers. Third, many of the comments and criticisms of the assessment procedures do not apply specifically to tourism alone but to the whole assessment process (Smith *et al.* 1988), particularly the general ignoring of cumulative impacts until relatively recently. Thus, while there now exists a sizeable body of research upon the impacts of tourism (see Mathieson and Wall 1982), little of it has been incorporated into what passes for tourism planning. In part this is because much of what is called planning in the tourism context is, in fact, marketing and promotion, a point also made by Pigram (Chapter 9). This has resulted in much inappropriate development and in many cases overdevelopment of tourist areas. Ignorance, politics and economics seem to work contrary to the attainment of the goal of sustainable development as far as tourism is concerned. This is perhaps even more regrettable in the case of tourism than for some other activities, because tourism, as Gunn (1979) and others (see Sadler 1989) have pointed out, is one activity which would benefit greatly from operating on a sustainable development basis.

This chapter attempts to explain why impact assessment has not resulted in improved planning for tourism and raises specific concerns about the assessment process, suggesting some aspects which need to be changed if things are to be improved. If there are lessons to be learned from past studies and current trends it is surely that procedures for assessing the impacts of tourism are inadequate and do not provide sufficient information for appropriate decision making (Mings 1978).

IMPACT ASSESSMENT

Impact assessment is intended 'to reduce the frequency of unexpected change, to reduce unexpected and undesirable consequences of planned or inevitable change, and to permit mitigation planning (or compensation) for unavoidable negative changes' (Meredith 1991: 239). The concept of impact assessment is hardly new, most agencies, corporations and individuals consider the implications of proposed actions before they take those actions. In an unconstrained situation, however, proponents of developments normally only take into active consideration those effects which have direct implications for themselves. In many cases they may only consider direct economic effects, the conventional benefit–cost exercise. Such thinking was common in decision-making in the pre-1960 period, especially in the private, corporate sector. Compounding this narrow viewpoint were a short-term perspective and the remnants of the 'frontier' mentality which dictated that when a problem arose, one moved on to pastures new, leaving the problem behind.

In the context of tourism some additional problems existed. Relative ignorance about even the economic effects of tourism resulted in some wildly inaccurate predictions, even in the established benefit–cost format, for example, the Zinder report on tourism development in the Caribbean (Zinder 1969). While such forecasts were quickly discredited, problems with economic predictions still continue (Archer 1973, Environics 1985). Second, the nature and scale of tourism, its international components, and the fact that major decision makers were often located very considerable distances from destination (development) regions, meant that many proponents of development were unaware of, or unconcerned about, negative or unanticipated impacts which resulted from development. Third, as discussed later, tourism may have been viewed as a 'clean' industry without impacts, except beneficial economic ones, by the residents of areas of such development.

The formal origins of impact assessment date back to the 1960s, and reflect a growing public concern, especially in the developed world, over environmental degradation. The National Environmental Policy Act (NEPA 1969) is the first example of legislation concerning impact assessment. As is the case with many legislative responses, this act was designed to meet public concerns over environmental quality. As such, it had the unfortunate effect of creating the impression that the environment and humans were separate entities and unrelated except for the effect of the actions of one on the other (Christie *et al.* 1986). The inclusion of human (social) impacts in assessment processes did not take place in most jurisdictions for a number of years after environmental impact assessment had become accepted (Lang and Armour 1981). It is more common now to see references to impact assessment, which implicitly includes both environmental impact assessment (EIA) and social impact assessment (SIA).

The complete range of impacts of development may only become apparent after a considerable time has passed and different effects may appear at different stages of development and operation. Impact assessments, therefore, may distinguish between impacts which will occur during planning and construction (e.g. speculation, environmental change), during operation (e.g. pollution, employment), and during or following closure or scale down (e.g. declining land values, hazardous waste).

A second aspect to consider is screening or scoping (Meredith 1991), that is, the decision on what to study. Two major parameters are normally considered, the likelihood of occurrence of an impact, and the significance of the impact, which may include the dimensions, severity and permanence of the impact. The significance element can become more complicated by the fact that it may be difficult to determine. Small impacts may produce cumulative major effects, and in some cases may combine to produce small or large critical changes depending upon circumstances. In all cases it is of crucial importance to understand the processes at work, how elements interact, and to be able to predict results. In the case of tourism and the impacts resulting from related development, it is clear that this is not the case (Mathieson and Wall 1982, Pearce 1989).

It should be noted that there tends to be a noticeable difference between impact assessment studies of tourism undertaken by academics and those undertaken by and for public sector agencies (including those imposed on potential developers by relevant agencies). The studies by academics, for the most part, have been post-development assessments, and have often focused upon the negative or undesired effects of tourism and related developments (see Boissevain 1979, Milman and Pizam 1988, Dogen 1989). They have also tended to focus on the social and cultural impacts generated by tourism. Private sector studies, most often done by consultants, have traditionally been predictive studies, generally concentrating on economic impacts, particularly in the early years of modern tourism development, and also focusing on the benefits of tourism to the proponents and communities. The traditional impact assessment studies done as a precondition of development, often in accordance with environmental protection guidelines or legislation, have almost all been predictive in nature and have generally contained many more environmental aspects than either of the other types discussed above. This relationship is illustrated in Table 8.1.

It should be emphasized that the categorization implied is highly generalized. There are examples of academic studies which are predictive, or which cover environmental and economic aspects, private sector studies which cover social issues (see Abt Associates 1975) and post-development public sector studies which also examine social or economic impacts. However, the point needs to be made that none of the sectors regularly examines all aspects of proposed developments nor conducts post-development appraisals or monitoring.

Table 8.1 Major characteristics of types of impact assessment studies

Characteristics	Agent		
	Public sector	*Private*	*Academic*
Principal focus	Environmental	Economic	Social
Timing	Pre-development	Pre-development	Post-development
Tone	Neutral	Mostly positive	Mostly critical/negative
Breadth	Exhaustive in detail, focussed in topic	Focused in topic, detailed	Broad in issues, less detailed
Context	Specific case study	Specific case study	Specific case study and general studies on themes or regions
Decision making role	Major	Major	Minor, if any
Dissemination	Rarely published, may be available to interested parties	Rarely published or disseminated except when required	Usually published and disseminated

Another aspect to consider is the formal and informal nature of these studies. Reflecting the impact assessment setting, almost all formal impact assessment studies, that is, those required by a public sector body or by legislation, are predictive studies undertaken before development. In many cases they are proprietary, being undertaken by or for the private sector and often are not released, at least in their entirety, for public examination. Many studies done by and for public agencies are also treated as confidential and are not easy to obtain. Most academic studies, on the other hand, tend to be informal, have no standing in a legal or regulatory sense, and are after-the-fact studies. Many of them are published in the academic press but may have little impact upon policy or regulation in a direct way.

PROBLEMS WITH IMPACT ASSESSMENTS

It was noted earlier that there are problems with the procedures for and the effectiveness of impact assessments in the context of tourism. The reasons are relatively simple to itemize but much more difficult to explain.

The relative absence of examples

Good comprehensive impact assessments, either pre- or post- development, of tourism developments are generally absent from the literature. This may be for a number of reasons, one being that many tourism developments are small scale, especially in rural areas, which may result in them being below a minimum threshold necessary to require impact assessment under legislation. Another may be that in many areas in which tourism development is occurring, impact assessment is not mandatory, especially in developing countries. A third reason may well be that tourism is regarded in some quarters as environmentally friendly and not requiring impact assessment. Another factor is the proprietary or confidential nature of many studies noted above. Finally, some developments that impinge on or are related to tourism are not 'tourism' developments and some may not be subject to impact assessment. For example, in the United Kingdom, two major land uses, agriculture and forestry, are not covered by planning legislation, but clearly have major links with tourism and the environment in which it occurs.

The inadequacy of many studies

Wall and Wright (1977) articulated clearly the problems of assessing the impact of recreation from an environmental perspective. The lack of benchmark studies for comparison, the lack of longitudinal data, the absence of control studies, an inability to ensure that impacts are caused solely by tourism, the problem of units and methods of measurement as noted by Douglas Pearce (Chapter 3), and the lack of long term commitment to studies, were some of the major points of concern as far as environmental impacts were concerned. Several of these points are of critical importance. If there are no benchmark studies to demonstrate what a location was like before development, or even the prospect of development, took place, there is great difficulty in demonstrating convincingly what has changed, and what elements of change are due to tourism. The lack of longitudinal studies deprives researchers of the opportunity to measure change over time. As noted earlier, impacts occur at different stages in a project's development and some may not be identified for a number of years after development has taken place. With regard to the attitudes of local residents towards tourism, it has been argued that these change over time (Doxey 1975), although there is not universal acceptance of a simple linear relationship (Butler 1975). Pearce (1989: 228) comments on the potential value of longitudinal studies, but notes that there are limits as to how far back retrospective studies can be made. Macfarlane (1979), in a longitudinal attitude study of a regular event, successfully recorded change in attitudes over a twenty-year period by retrospective questioning, but in such studies there is no method of controlling or identifying respondent error. Other longitudinal studies include those of Préau (1983, cited in Pearce 1989) and Getz (1986), but in both cases the focus is on change in the human system and not the overall environment. When one combines environmental effects with the highly subjective human/social aspects of tourism the situation becomes much more complicated and difficult to deal with adequately when assessing impacts, especially as tourism is often treated as a homogeneous entity.

The non-comparability of studies

The fact that many studies have been one-off case studies conducted in a variety of disciplines at varying scales in widely differing physical and social environments means that direct comparability is not easy, as Pearce (Chapter 3) notes. While certain general predictions may be made with reasonable certainty, for example, residents' concerns about the potential impacts of tourism will almost certainly include crowding, litter and traffic, and while there will probably be agreement that tourism provides employment and income, the dimensions and nature of the effects may be as uncertain as the general understanding of what tourism development really implies. There has been very little written, for example, on the criteria which could be utilized as a basis for evaluating the impact or performance of tourism developments (Haywood 1975).

The problem of fragmentation

One of the major problems which makes the assessment of impacts and the planning and managing of tourism difficult, is the fragmentation of the industry. The tourism industry consists of a wide variety of separate components, including travel, accommodation, food and retail services, information services, publicity and attractions. While some of these elements may have strong lateral links between them, airlines owning hotels for instance, many are separate entities with no links to any other beyond sharing a similar location. The very large number of enterprises and their very different characteristics make impacts difficult to predict and a common set of mitigating guidelines and policies very difficult to envisage or to operate. Thus, a variety of frameworks for assessment may need to be established (OECD 1981). There are widely differing goals involved, from pure commercial profit to pure preservation, from individual self interest to national priorities, different time scales, different regional goals, and different political and philosophical beliefs. Overriding goals and objectives at a national, regional or local level may be possible (see Tourism Canada 1989, for example), but are unlikely to be much more than that and lack real teeth or regulation. In most cases, as noted, both in the public and private sectors, the stated goals and objectives are to encourage the growth and development of tourism.

Conflicting nature of impacts

Almost all studies find both positive and negative impacts of tourism developments. Rarely do they successfully produce a bottom line or balance sheet acceptable to all parties. Balance of payment benefits will occur at a national/international level, while garbage pick-up costs are incurred at the local level; employment will occur at the local level (but not always of locals) but airport development costs take place at the national level and so forth. Not only do the benefits and costs accrue to different groups at different levels (local, regional, national, etc.) but the benefits and costs, as in most assessments, are often widely different in nature (e.g. dollars versus aesthetics, or pollution versus better transport). Each interested party can point to what it wishes to make its case. Rarely can it be convincingly concluded that tourism development is 'good' or 'bad' in specific cases, but more likely only that certain effects may result, depending on such factors as the type and scale of tourism, which does not give the decision makers the categoric definitive answer they may want.

A fundamental problem with any impact assessment is what to assess. In some situations the anticipated effects may be simple and direct, but inevitably, as studies are made, the innate complexity of ecological, economic and social systems becomes apparent. In the context of tourism this is particularly true, as tourism, by its very nature, involves the three conventional systems noted above, ecological or environmental, economic, and socio-cultural. While a considerable body of research exists on the impacts of tourism (OECD 1981, Mathieson and Wall 1982, Pearce 1989), there are still major problems in identifying reliable indicators of change and the level of significance of such changes. In many cases, both with respect to tourism developments and in the wider context, an impact may be characterized as both a benefit and a cost by different parties. Some impacts may be viewed as insignificant to proponents, while local residents may feel they are catastrophic. A great deal will depend on who is conducting the assessment as to what is examined and what significance will be given to specific impacts. There is a tendency to concentrate on measuring what is easy to measure and ignoring what is viewed as intangible and not easily quantifiable.

PROBLEMS WITH IMPLEMENTATION

Even when impact assessments have been conducted and results may be relatively unambiguous, decisions on development may be made which are at odds with assessment results for a variety of reasons.

Development may be predetermined or unavoidable

International pressure from creditors and financial institutions, or from domestic sources such as the unemployed or business sectors, may result in a government or agency approving or continuing with a development despite assessments predicting very significant negative effects. Foreign currency requirements may make tourism expansion unavoidable if few alternative sources of revenue exist. Pressure from airlines and hotel companies to have an airport expanded may have to be accepted in order to preserve international air services or to keep hotels (often linked to the airlines) open, as occurred in Turks and Caicos Islands (Butler 1992). Local pressures for jobs and income may override acknowledged needed limitations on tourist numbers or type of development, as Kenchington (1989) has noted in an examination of development and change in the Galapagos Islands.

Tourism is not integrated in the overall system

All too frequently tourism is treated, if it is considered at all, as a self-contained activity. In fact, it is one of the most highly linked economic activities with many strong interdependencies with other elements of the economic, social and environmental spheres. Agriculture, forestry, fishing, transportation, education, information flows, taxation, environmental quality and crime and many other elements of society are interwoven with tourism. Treating tourism as an independent item or, worse, ignoring it, when it may be directly affected by or have a significant impact upon other elements, only aggravates problems. Impact assessments which are limited in scope and do not recognize this are severely deficient and rarely accurate.

The lack of clear responsibility and control over tourism

In many countries, tourism is hardly controlled or managed. The predominant feature of government involvement is often the stimulation and development of tourism, not the controlling or managing of it. The assumption, common to most governments, seems to be that more tourism is always beneficial, and that controls, if needed, can come at the local level, although Morris and Dickinson (1987) have shown that such local controls may well not be put into place or, if they exist, may be circumvented. An alternative assumption is that the industry will be self-governing. The industry would like to agree with this, but there is no method of self-regulation for an industry like tourism, made up of the complete range of size of operations from one person enterprises to multinational corporations, most of whom are in competition with each other. Virtually all government tourism departments at every level have mandates to market their area and increase tourism. A very few may have established development plans or strategies but in many cases these are ignored if potential developers' wishes are contrary to the stated objectives of the plans, or even in some cases ignored when they do match objectives. This may stem from a series of fallacies, among them, that tourism just happens; that governments should only be reactive not proactive; and that there are really no problems created by tourism, a philosophy embodied in advertisements claiming that 'tourists take nothing but photographs and leave nothing but footprints' produced for the Ontario government in the 1970s. With such attitudes being prevalent, it is not likely that much responsibility will be assigned to restrict tourism. Thus impact assessments which produce negative recommendations or recommend severe restrictions on development are likely to be ignored or not fully implemented.

Inconsistency in response

Perhaps resulting partly from the last point, many governments act in an inconsistent manner with respect to tourism. While governments may promote conservation, for example, they often seem unaware that tourism may have negative impacts upon some protected areas or communities. Tourism ministries in Canada and elsewhere, for example, regularly promote national parks as tourist attractions, regardless of the fact that certain parks may experience extremely high and excessive visitation. Current increased emphasis on economic efficiency and overall cost reductions may make such inconsistencies more common and more serious in the future. Impacts from tourism seem to be viewed as more acceptable in areas such as parks than would impacts from industrial development, for example. No industrial development, forestry or mining are now allowed in national parks in Canada, but visitor facilities are frequently expanded to meet increased visitation, and this trend seems likely to continue (CPS 1991). Again, this may be due to a failure to appreciate that there are often severe negative impacts of tourism, or it may be due to the fact that national parks and similar areas have traditionally been associated with tourism for so long that such impacts are accepted as inevitable and politically necessary.

Lack of commitment to the long term view

A major difficulty in the broad field of impact assessment is the lack of institutions and agencies with responsibility for dealing with long term change. This is illustrated by present day concern over global warning and the 'greenhouse effect', and the lack of formal responses in this area (Wall 1992). The relative frequency with which ministers and departments change responsibilities in many jurisdictions works against long term commitments and policies, as does the relatively short time scale (four–five years in many cases) within which a government has to operate before it has to face the electorate. A similar situation, but for different reasons, faces many academic researchers who may contemplate long term studies and impact monitoring. Research requires funding, and most funding agencies only fund research for limited periods (one–three years in many places). Few results will be available, and even fewer published, before a request for renewed funding must be made, and agencies are not keen to fund longitudinal studies from which results may not appear for a decade or more. The private sector's time scale tends to be extremely short with respect to research before development and opportunities for investment may have very limited windows of opportunity, although the private sector generally monitors its operations efficiently and regularly to ensure at least economic efficiency of operation. These factors make the monitoring of developments difficult to undertake, even where there is knowledge of what should be monitored. This, however, is at best a partial explanation of the lack of monitoring and certainly not an excuse. Where considered necessary and appropriate, public sector agencies can and do monitor processes regularly or even continuously, often in considerable detail, for example, drinking water quality, air quality, water levels in flood prone areas, bacterial levels in sewage treatment plants, food quality in abattoirs and food preparation establishments, and radiation levels at nuclear establishments. The difference in most of these cases is that public safety is viewed as important to the electorate at least, and public sector agencies are prepared to pay for the costs of monitoring by allocating resources from the public purse, even where the facilities involved may be privately owned and operated. In other cases, for example, production of alcohol in distilleries, or importation of goods at border crossings, the monitoring and enforcement is undertaken because in its absence the public sector may lose considerable revenue. Unfortunately, tourism generated impacts are rarely critical to the public's health nor do they usually cost the public sector large amounts of money. As a result, monitoring of the impacts of tourism developments are rarely undertaken.

MITIGATION

Reference has already been made to the difficulty of controlling and managing tourism growth and development. There are considerable difficulties also relating to mitigating the undesirable effects of such development. First there are the problems noted above related to incomplete and in some cases inaccurate knowledge about the impacts. Second, there is a lack of knowledge about how to reduce or remove those negative impacts that can be identified and anticipated (OECD 1981). Despite programmes such as the Visitor Activity Management Program (V.A.M.P.) of the Canadian Parks Service (Graham 1989), which attempts to control visitor impact and behaviour in a logical and appropriate manner, there are few successful examples of how to manage tourism and tourists in a way which meets both their desires and the needs of the host population and environment. Much is left to restrictions on access, regulation, and design, without any subsequent evaluation of success or failure of such measures. Yet much has been done in outdoor recreation areas (Jim 1989). The work over the last two decades of researchers in the US Forest Service, for example, supplies considerable evidence of effective research on managing visitors to satisfy the two basic needs, a quality recreation experience and maintaining environmental integrity (Hendee, Stankey and Lucas 1978). In Britain the work of the Countryside Commission demonstrates how large numbers of visitors can be accommodated at sites by innovative management approaches (Edwards 1987). A key difference here, however, is that these recreation uses take place in designated areas under the control of specific agencies or the private sector. There is, in such cases, clear responsibility for management and regulation. In many tourist destinations there is no single agency, public or private, with such responsibility, and thus little action is taken.

Perhaps the major stumbling block to effective mitigation is the fact that in many cases it usually involves two elements that most tourist agencies find unappealing, namely restrictions on visitors and/or reduction in visitor numbers. Restrictions are unattractive to proponents of tourism because of the potential message which they send to visitors, namely that they are not entirely welcome to come to a place and be free to do as they wish, which, it is feared, may deter them from coming. Most people desire freedom from regulation on vacation, rather than continued control. More importantly, many of the problems resulting from tourism do stem very directly from excessive numbers of tourists. However, to reduce numbers of tourists almost always results in reducing the amount of expenditures, unless the smaller numbers of tourists spend more per capita. To achieve this latter situation would normally involve either an increase in the opportunity for tourists to spend more, and their desire to do so, which has limitations, or a shift in the market being attracted to the destination, to one of a higher income group or at least one with a higher propensity to spend, as suggested for Bermuda (Hayward, Gomez and Sterrer 1981). While this can be accomplished, it is not done easily, and it is impractical to expect it to be achieved by all tourist destinations. They cannot all cater to the élite – some tourists are always going to be in the low spending categories, because of their income if not their desires, and not all destinations will be successful in attracting an up-market clientele. Few public or private agencies are prepared to run the risk of rejecting or making feel unwelcome a potentially large proportion of their market in order to attempt to shift to a higher income market of a smaller size. Not all facilities are capable of improving quality and attracting a more up-market clientele and, therefore, many operators will be reluctant to agree to a reduction in the size of the market. Mitigation of impacts of tourism on the basis of a reduction in numbers of tourists is, therefore, not very likely in many areas. It may, of course, be desirable and practical for a new destination to begin by deliberately aiming at a small and high spending market and deciding to maintain exclusivity and quality at a high price, but it is much more difficult for an established area to change its image and market (Hinch and Butler 1988).

CUMULATIVE AND DERIVED IMPACTS

One of the problems of most impact assessment procedures is that assessments are normally of specific projects only. Rarely, if ever, are projects evaluated not only for their specific impacts, but also for the cumulative impacts which will occur (CEAC 1988). In the case of tourism this is particularly critical and yet there appear to be no specific references in the tourism literature to cumulative impacts. Many destinations can absorb limited tourism development and some tourists. Few, if any, can absorb unlimited numbers of tourists. While the concept of a fixed capacity of an area for tourists is no longer generally accepted as valid (Stankey 1982), few people will argue that destinations cannot be overdeveloped. At some point a development is one too many. Current impact assessment procedures rarely tackle that problem but concentrate instead on the specific attributes of a proposed development and whether these pose specific problems. It is necessary to examine the effects of each proposed development on an area, not simply whether this new development is adequate in terms of such items as sewage treatment, sufficient water, and parking. 'Zero sum gain in pollution' type limits may not be practical in the context of tourism in many areas but the issue of cumulative impact is crucial.

Related to the problem of cumulative impact is the one of secondary or derived impacts. An assessment of the impact of a new hotel, for example, is normally confined to the site of the proposed hotel and its associated facilities. Yet hotels are not built in isolation. To be successful, a hotel must be utilized by guests. The guests will require transport to the area (by air, road or sea), within the area (by road or water), access to attractions in the area and a range of associated services. Thus while a new hotel may by itself have few direct impacts which might negatively affect a request for approval, the results of the hotel attracting visitors may have severe impacts upon the areas visited by those visitors en route and on holiday. Those areas may be in different jurisdictions to the one giving approval for the project to take place. A new hotel in Calgary, for example, would almost certainly result in increased visitation to Banff National Park, a location already receiving more than the desired numbers of tourists, and yet a traditional impact assessment of such a hotel, pre- or post-development, would rarely consider the destinations of tourists and their impacts upon those destinations, even if those destinations were known.

POST-DEVELOPMENT ASSESSMENTS AND MONITORING

It would seem logical that developments which were viewed as significant enough to require an assessment of anticipated impacts would also be significant enough to warrant ongoing monitoring of operations and/or post-development audits or assessments to determine if unexpected impacts are occurring, and/or if mitigation measures have been effective, yet such actions in the context of tourism developments do not appear to exist.

It is appropriate therefore to consider why even mandatory impact assessments are rarely accompanied by mandatory post-development assessments. There are a number of possible reasons. One is the assumption that the initial assessment will be complete and correct, and thus follow-up assessments are unnecessary. Those undertaking assessments will argue in favour of this assumption, at least on credibility grounds, although they may be depriving themselves of potential additional work. Proponents of development, who often have to pay for impact assessments, can also be expected to support this assumption and thus avoid further costs and constraints. All parties involved probably want to believe this assumption, and in most cases few have firm grounds on which to challenge either the assumption or the impact predictions.

A second reason may relate to the problems of who would have responsibility for undertaking post-development audits or assessments, and at what point they should be undertaken. A third reason may be lack of agreement over what the purpose of such assessments should be, and what could be done if the initial assessment proved to be incomplete or inaccurate. The cost, scale, complexity, detail and difficulty of comprehension of many early impact assessments (Elkington 1981) may also have acted as a deterrent to the requirement of subsequent follow-up studies, as well as giving a sometimes misleading impression of completeness of material and accuracy.

In some cases the possibility of error or omission has been implicitly accepted by the requirement of monitoring operations to ensure that negative unanticipated impacts do not occur or can be addressed if they do. Post-development monitoring is most common for environmental impacts such as pollution, for example from oil spills at terminals and refineries (SOTEAG 1987), although monitoring of social change is not unknown (Butler and Nelson 1992). A major problem with monitoring in general is that it is an ongoing process, which needs to continue throughout the operational life of a development, and in the case of projects such as nuclear power stations, for a very long period after operations have ended. The costs of such monitoring exercises can be extremely large, and require a long term viewpoint, aspects which do not appeal to most political decision makers.

Additional problems exist again in the context of tourism impact assessment because, as already noted, there may be ignorance of what should be monitored as well as what impacts should be identified and how they should be characterized. Furthermore, it may be extremely difficult to ascribe correctly the recorded changes solely or even partly to the specific development.

IMPLICATIONS AND CONCLUSIONS

Unless impact assessments are mandatory under legislation they are unlikely to be conducted, and unless it is required that the results of assessments be incorporated into regulations and approval, they are likely to be ignored. Political and economic realities, combined with the short term viewpoint of many decision makers and stakeholders (or would-be stakeholders) mean long term pain or loss for short term gain may well occur. It is essential, however, that impact assessment be integrated into the decision making process. However good the assessment, if it is not utilized to assist in making decisions on development, such as whether approval is given or not, what changes in design, location or operation may be necessary, or what compensation may have to be made, then it becomes at best a harbinger of change, but offers little relief to those to be affected.

In the United States, where impact assessment has a legislative basis, it is enforceable through the legal process. In Canada, however, at the federal level the Federal Environmental Assessment and Review Process (EARP) and Review Office (FEARO) apply only to areas under federal jurisdiction, and are based on voluntary compliance (FEARO 1987). If an impact assessment is required, FEARO establishes a panel of experts to produce study guidelines, monitor the study and produce recommendations, and it is the ministers responsible who make the final decisions on development. Other areas have different arrangements. For example, in Western Australia, while assessment has legal backing and there is a legal obligation on local authorities and others to refer proposals to the Environmental Protection Agency, this obligation occurs 'if it appears likely that the development would have a significant effect on the environment' (WATC 1989: 4). However, the determination of level of significance is not specified and it is acknowledged that this will vary across the state and with the subject matter being investigated. Inevitably such arrangements can result in inconsistency in application, and in many areas be very subject to political intervention, especially with respect to the determination of what is significant.

The above problems with impact assessment procedures are common to many areas. It is clear, however, that even if many of these problems were resolved, and better predictive impact assessments could be conducted, that there would still be a clear need for post-impact assessments of many developments to determine how accurate the predictions had been and how successful mitigation measures, if any were taken, had been. A major problem still remains. While tourism has finally begun to be accepted as a major phenomenon with economic, social and environmental ramifications, the great diversity of tourism has rarely been recognized. Thus, at the policy level, discussion is of tourism as if it were a single entity with consistent impacts. In reality, people who study tourism know that it is anything but uniform and that it has a wide variety of effects which vary greatly.

The assumption that tourism is a homogeneous activity creates major problems and explains in part why the impacts of tourism are often misunderstood. While mass or conventional tourism may have many common elements, even then there are significant variations in impacts between mass beach oriented tourists, mass urban sightseers and mass winter sports enthusiasts. When one considers that over ninety sub-categories of tourism have been described in the literature in the last two decades (Boyd 1991) the complexity and variety of tourism becomes apparent. Inevitably, impacts from different types of tourism will vary. The fact that a development being assessed may be a hotel does not mean that the impacts from a hotel catering to one type of tourist will be the same as those from a hotel catering to other types. In many cases it is the impacts of the guests which need to be assessed rather than the impacts of the construction and operation of the specific developments. Such an assessment would require a much more detailed and spatially wide ranging assessment, including aspects such as sources of food and travel patterns, as discussed earlier.

Predictions of tourism-related impacts, such as employment or income generation at any scale, cannot be made without determination of what type of tourism is anticipated and at what level. Is it mass tourism, ecotourism, visits to friends and relatives, long haul visits or day visits, for example? To be able to produce definitive answers to questions about the anticipated effects of tourism development in an area, it is necessary to conduct far more studies of a detailed nature on a variety of developments as Innskeep (1987) has argued. This has to be done with consistent methodologies to ensure results are comparable (Pearce, Chapter 3), and we need to conduct specific studies in a variety of locations at a variety of scales to control for social, environmental and quantitative influences (Przeclawski, Chapter 2). In addition, it is of crucial importance to undertake replication studies on a longitudinal basis, as noted above, to see if initial predictions were accurate and to assess the effects of inevitable small and unexamined changes and development which have taken place since initial development. Only then can there be any confidence in the anticipated impacts of tourism in a predictive sense, allowing agencies to address the joint problems of cumulative and derived impacts discussed above.

The need both to improve the process of impact assessment of tourism developments and to incorporate the results of such assessment and monitoring into decision making processes will become even more crucial in the future as tourism continues to grow, and especially as it places increasing pressure upon previously undeveloped areas, many of which may be highly vulnerable to development related impacts. Tourism planning will need to become more proactive rather than at best reactive, as Pigram notes in Chapter 9. In addition, the single discipline, single case study approach which has characterized much tourism research will have to be supplemented, if not replaced, by a broader multidisciplinary approach which would allow examination of a wider variety of topics and explore the linkages and dependencies between systems, in the way suggested by Przeclawski (Chapter 2).

This discussion has ranged far from the specific topic of pre- and post-impact assessments in a tourism context. However, it is felt that one of the problems of impact assessment in the context of tourism is the far too narrow framework in which such assessments have been carried out, when they have been carried out at all. In the case of assessments of tourism related projects, or projects which will attract, even coincidentally and not primarily, significant numbers of tourists, they need to be much wider in scope than the traditional impact assessment which concentrates upon a single site at a specific time. There needs to be an acknowledgement of the much broader nature of tourism and its impacts on all elements of a destination area and its population, and the fact that tourism is an industry with all sorts of impacts, some very beneficial and some very harmful, which occur at a variety of scales, often in opposing directions to different populations and environments.

Such acknowledgement will need to be accompanied by a recognition of the importance of impact assessment and monitoring and the inclusion of these items in policies relating to tourism. Hawkins (Chapter 11) notes the gradual incorporation into decision making of the environmental and social concerns of community residents about tourism. He argues that these have now become critical and are clearly on the policy agenda, as the results of some two decades of impact studies are finally being acknowledged. To be really successful, however, impact assessments and monitoring need to be viewed as appropriate and necessary elements in tourism development, not as problems or hindrances which have to be overcome or avoided. It is very much in the long term interests of developers, local residents and tourists that tourism developments be appropriate in scale, location and effect, in order to ensure the long term survival of a sustainable tourism industry. If anything, *post hoc* assessments of tourism developments, few as they are, have demonstrated that tourism is not an easy option or a panacea for the development of areas which do not have other resources. It is a major activity with a full range of economic, social and environmental implications and deserves to be treated as such.

REFERENCES

Abt Associates (1975) *Prince Edward Island Tourism Study*, Boston: Abt Associates.

Archer, B. (1973) *The Uses and Abuses of Multipliers*, Tourist Research Paper TURI, Bangor: University College of North Wales.

Boissevain, J. (1979) 'The impact of tourism on a dependent island', *Annals of Tourism Research* 6, 1: 76–90.

Boyd, S. (1991) 'Towards a typology of tourism and experience', paper presented at Annual Meeting of East Lakes Division, Association of American Geographers.

Butler, R. W. (1975) 'Tourism as an agent of social change', in *Tourism as a Factor in National and Regional Development*, Occasional Paper 4, Peterborough: Trent University: 85–90.

——(1992) 'Tourism development in small islands: past influences and future directions', in D. G. G. Lockhart and D. Drakakis-Smith (eds) *Small Island Development*, Keele: Keele University (in press).

Butler, R. W. and Nelson, J. G. (1992) 'Evaluating environmental planning and management: the case of the Shetland Islands', *Geoforum* (in press).

Canadian Environmental Advisory Council (1988) *Evaluating Environmental Impact Assessment: An Action Prospectus*, Ottawa: Ministry of Supply and Services.

Canadian Parks Service (1991) *National Parks Policies*, Ottawa: Ministry of Supply and Services.

Christie, W. J. (1986) 'Managing the Great Lakes Basin as a home', *Journal of Great Lakes Research* 12: 2–17.

Dogen, H. Z. (1989) 'Forms of adjustment: socio cultural impacts of tourism', *Annals of Tourism Research* 16, 2: 216–36.

Doxey, G. (1975) 'A causation theory of visitor-resident irritants: methodology and research inferences', in *Impact of Tourism, Sixth Annual Conference Proceedings*, San Diego: Travel Research Association.

Edwards, J. R. (1987) 'The U.K. Heritage Coasts – an assessment of the ecological impacts of tourism', *Annals of Tourism Research* 14, 1: 71–87.

Elkington, J. B. (1981) 'Converting industry to environmental impact assessment', *Environmental Conservation* 8, 1: 23–30.

Environics Ltd (1985) *Recreation – The Sleeping Giant*, Toronto: Ontario Ministry of Tourism and Recreation.

Federal Environmental Assessment Review Office (1987) *Reforming Federal Environmental Assessment: A Discussion Paper*, Ottawa: Ministry of Supply and Services.

Getz, D. (1986) 'Tourism and population change: long term impacts of tourism in the Badenoch and Strathspey district of the Scottish Highlands', *Scottish Geographical Magazine* 102, 2: 113–26.

Graham, R. (1989) 'Visitor management and Canada's national parks', in R. Graham and R. Lawrence (eds) *Towards Serving Visitors and Managing our Resources*, Waterloo: Tourism Research and Education Centre, University of Waterloo: 271–96.

Gunn, C. A. (1979) *Tourism Planning*, New York: Crane Rusak.

Haywood, M. (1975) 'Criteria for evaluating the social performance of tourism development projects', in *Tourism as a Factor in National and Regional Development*, Occasional Paper 4, Peterborough: Trent University: 94–7.

Hayward, S. J., Gomez, V. H. and Sterrer, W. (1981) *Bermuda's Delicate Balance*, Nassau: Bermuda National Trust.

Hendee, J. C., Stankey, G. H. and Lucas, R. C. (1978) *Wilderness Management*, Washington, DC: United States Department of Agriculture.

Hinch, T. and Butler, R. W. (1988) 'The rejuvenation of a tourism centre: Port Stanley, Ontario', *Ontario Geography* 32: 29–52.

Innskeep, E. (1987) 'Environmental planning for tourism', *Annals of Tourism Research* 14, 1, 118–35.

Jim, C. Y. (1989) 'Visitor management in recreation areas', *Environmental Conservation* 16, 1: 19–40.

Kenchington, R. A. (1989) 'Tourism in the Galapagos Islands: the dilemma of conservation', *Environmental Conservation* 16, 3, 227–36.

Lang, R. and Armour, A. (1981) *The Assessment and Review of Social Impacts*, Ottawa: FEARO.

Macfarlane, R. (1979) 'Social impacts of tourism: resident attitudes in Stratford, Ontario', unpublished M.A. thesis, University of Western Ontario.

Mathieson, A. and Wall, G. (1982) *Tourism – Economic, Social and Physical Impacts*, New York: Longman.

Meredith, T. (1991) 'Environmental impact assessment and monitoring', in B. Mitchell (ed.) *Resource Management and Development*, Oxford: Oxford University Press: 224–45.

Milman, A. and Pizam, A. (1988) 'Social impacts of tourism on Central Florida', *Annals of Tourism Research* 15, 2: 191–204.

Mings, R. C. (1978) 'The importance of more research on the impacts of tourism', *Annals of Tourism Research* 5, 3: 340–4.

Morris, A. and Dickinson, G. (1987) 'Tourist development in Spain: growth versus conservation on the Costa Brava', *Geography* 72: 16–25.

NEPA (1969) *National Environmental Policy Act*, Washington, DC: National Environmental Protection Agency.

OECD (1981) *The Impact of Tourism on the Environment*. Paris: OECD.

Pearce, D. (1989) *Tourist Development*, 2nd ed., Harlow: Longman and New York: Wiley.

Préau, P. (1983) 'Le changement social dans une commune touristique de montagne: Saint-Bon-Tarentaise (Savoie)', *Revue de Géographie Alpine* 71, 4: 407–29 and 72, 2–4: 411–37.

Sadler, B. (1989) 'Sustaining tomorrow and endless summer: on linking tourism and environment in the Caribbean', in F. Edwards (ed.) *Environmentally Sound Tourism Development in the Caribbean*, Calgary: University of Calgary Press: ix–xxiii.

Smith, L. G., Given, G. and Cafarella, P. (1988) 'An evaluation of Canadian impact assessment practice', *Ontario Geography* 32: 1–8.

SOTEAG (1987) *Environmental Monitoring Annual Report*, Lerwick: Sullom Oil Terminal Environmental Advisory Group.

Stankey, G. H. (1982) 'Recreational carrying capacity research review', *Ontario Geography* 19: 57–72.

Tourism Canada (1989) *Tourism on the Threshold*, Ottawa: Ministry of Supply and Services.

Wall, G. (1992) 'Tourism alternatives in an era of climatic change', in V. Smith and W. Eadington (eds) *Tourism Alternatives: Potentials and Problems in the Development of Tourism*, Philadelphia: University of Pennsylvania Press (in press).

Wall, G. and Wright, C. (1977) *The Environmental Impacts of Recreation*, Waterloo: University of Waterloo.

WATC (1989) *An Administrative Guide to Environmental Requirements for Tourism Developments in Western Australia*, Perth: Western Australia Tourism Commission.

Zinder, H. (1969) *The Future of Tourism in the Caribbean*, Washington, DC: Zinder & Associates.

Chapter 9

Planning for tourism in rural areas

Bridging the policy implementation gap

John J. Pigram

INTRODUCTION

Some fifteen years ago, Ingolf Vogeler (1976) deplored the lack of studies in rural recreation, the limited substantive results obtained, and the absence of any theoretical framework. Vogeler was referring specifically to income-producing rural recreation enterprises. However, the criticisms hold more generally for research in rural recreation and tourism which has attracted only spasmodic interest. Moreover, there has been a generally reactive tone to much of the research undertaken, with the emphasis often on justifying and defending competing claims on the rural resource base. Tourism and recreation are seen as a challenge and even a threat to established modes of productive resource use, and research interest is confined largely to addressing ensuing management or regulatory problems.

These circumstances reflect the absence of positive, proactive policies for the provision of opportunities for tourism and recreation in rural areas of the industrialized world. In many cases a policy vacuum exists in which resource management agencies either deny their responsibility for planning or relegate that responsibility to a low order of priority. The private sector, too, has often been hesitant to become involved in rural recreation and tourism enterprises. Agritourism activity, for example, is ephemeral and opportunistic, often surfacing only in response to crises in more conventional forms of rural land use, and then struggling to survive in a limited market characterized by rising operating and travel costs, and poorly developed entrepreneurial skills.

The response from planning agencies has also tended to be reactive and to focus on contemporary issues, particularly the spatial and social processes of tourism, impact assessment and economic assessment. However, as more and more tourists look beyond the cities, unwelcome changes to the rural environment and competition with other resource uses are likely to emerge. This makes even more urgent the development of policies for the planning and management of rural resources for tourism.

Policy development is given added emphasis by the perceived role of tourism in alleviating depressed rural economies (Messerli 1990). In both developed and developing countries, tourism is frequently put forward as a useful means of raising the level of economic activity in regions not otherwise well endowed with resource potential. Direct and indirect impacts of visitor expenditures, coupled with multiplier effects, have the potential to offset social and economic deprivation. Tourism can also bring cultural benefits to isolated communities through social interaction with visitors (Phillips and Williams 1984). Potentially negative impacts of tourism, arising from conflicts with residents and displacement of conventional resource uses, can be managed and benefits maximized if the appropriate policies are in place.

Given that pressures on the rural resource base exist and are likely to increase, the important policy considerations in expanding tourism opportunities in rural areas relate to: allocation of rural resources to tourism; institutional frameworks and the role of resource management agencies; and integration of tourism policy into rural resource planning.

Proactive policies are needed to address these interrelated issues if the demand for tourism is to be satisfied within the capacity of the rural environment to meet that demand. The development of policies for rural tourism is the focus of this chapter. Attention is drawn to the need to expand the spectrum of opportunities for tourism in rural areas and encourage the participation of a wide range of key providers in the process. Prospects for the development of such policies, their integration with other forms of rural resource use, and the constraints on the task of policy formulation and implementation, are also considered. Reference is made, by way of example, to the State of New South Wales, but the observations apply more generally to other parts of Australia and to comparable countries abroad.

RURAL TOURISM

The appeal of rural areas for recreation and tourism is well documented and the reasons are not hard to find. Whereas the greater part of leisure time in the industrialized world must be spent in an urban setting (much of it in and around the home), visits to the countryside are increasingly perceived as an extension of life in the city. Urban dwellers have an expectation that the natural attractions of the rural environment are part of their recreation space – an extension of life in the city. According to Cracknell (1967: 13), 'it is the garden for children to play in, a vista people can enjoy from their mobile room – their car. . . . For every city dweller it has become an integral part of . . . living space. In part this perception is an outcome of the urbanization process itself.' Janiskee (1976) explained the appeal of extra-urban environments in the context of a push-pull model of motivation. Periodically, environmentally undernourished urbanites are pushed from the city because of stresses imposed by their life style. At the same time, they are pulled into the more natural hinterland by the opportunity to experience compensatory alternative surroundings and activities.

This striving for self-renewal in a different, specifically outdoor setting is mirrored in the strength of the attraction which rural landscapes have for tourists – both day visitors and vacationers. For many city-based tourists, rural environments appear to support a serene, idyllic existence synonymous with an indefinable notion of the 'good life' (Middleton 1982). Whatever the reality of this idealized vision, it remains a powerful motivating force, driving the growing numbers of tourists seeking a rural experience.

In Britain, for example, informal trips to the countryside are one of the most widely appreciated forms of tourism for all ages and all kinds of people. Surveys by the Countryside Commission (1987) show that 84 per cent of the population of England and Wales visited rural areas as tourists at some time during the year. The English countryside also acts as a magnet for many visitors from abroad.

A decade ago, Middleton (1982) predicted that the massive consumption of rural areas of Britain by visitors on holidays or excursions would escalate with rising living standards and increasing car ownership. Moreover, the British countryside was seen to be the setting and resource for new attractions, both natural and managed, and for significant additions to the stock of tourist-orientated accommodation and transport facilities. The extent to which these predictions have been realized can perhaps be gauged from the gloomy, though humorous, lament of an English columnist. Writing in the *Daily Telegraph* (16 September 1991), Auberon Waugh deplored the use of Beatrix Potter's character Peter Rabbit as part of the British Tourist Authority's promotion of the Lake District to the Japanese. The question Waugh asks is 'whether . . . we really want vast numbers of foreigners coming over here, for whatever reason'. He goes on to suggest that the purpose of the British Tourist Authority should be to *discourage* tourism, for example, by publishing figures on serious crime in Somerset or infectious diseases in Cornwall!

In Canada, Butler (1991) documents the changing face of rural tourism from the time of European settlement to the present. A dominant feature has been the emergence of the private cottage as a focus for rural-based leisure pursuits, although some might argue whether such use can be categorized as tourism, or merely an alternative form of residential development. Water is a key element, the preference for a shoreline location supporting the view that the rural areas of Canada are, at best, a backdrop for tourism and recreation. However, the 1980s have seen more aggressive forms of alienation of the rural environment in the name of tourism. This, in turn, has led to some concern for the integrity of rural areas and prompted belated interest and reaction from provincial legislators.

Rural America with its natural and cultural diversity offers a range of touristic opportunities. Rural tourism spans the spectrum from low impact, seasonal, small country town festivals to year-round destination areas featuring scenic resources and developed attractions (Messerli 1990). In common with rural areas of many industrialized countries, the economy of rural America has been disadvantaged by structural change and economic dislocation, particularly during the 1980s. These problems, coupled with widening recognition of the potential contribution of tourism to rural economic development through the generation of off-farm employment opportunities, prompted a national study of rural tourism (Economics Research Associates 1989). The outcome offers a compelling insight into the need for and role of a federal policy regarding rural tourism. The findings and the implications for comparable economies are discussed further in this chapter.

In rural Australia, similar tourist interest has been demonstrated in experiences beyond the city. Table 9.1 reveals the most popular focuses for a holiday among the Australian interstate and intrastate mass markets. Although recurring energy crises and concerns over inflation may have caused intermittent fluctuations and a short-term slowing in growth of tourism, rural activities continue to figure prominently. The social, institutional and technological forces responsible for increasing opportunities to participate in tourism, generally, have been well documented and account for much of this trend and for the appeal of the countryside.

Similar interest in the attractions of rural Australia is apparent among visitors from abroad. However, some concern has been expressed that the Australian tourist industry is excessively geared to big city

Table 9.1 Popular focuses for a holiday

	Interstate %	Intrastate %
Outback visits	61	68
Camping	52	55
Weekend/midweek retreats	50	59
Beach	48	44
Farm holidays	41	53
River cruising	41	40
Snow skiing	33	42

Source: New South Wales Tourism Commission, 1989a, 2
Note: Visits to national parks, scenery based holidays, fishing and bushwalking were also popular focuses for a holiday

destinations and itineraries which 'fail to include the real traits of the country' (Ormonde 1991). A recent meeting of the Japan–Australia Business Co-operation Committee was told that most tours are directed towards Sydney, the Gold Coast, Melbourne and other large cities. Moreover, there was inadequate provision of high grade tourist facilities outside the metropolitan areas.

Tourism beyond the city takes many forms, although not all are inherently rural in character. Messerli offers the following operational definition of rural tourism:

Tourism which provides diverse opportunities for visitors to experience novel attractions and hospitality services through activities and services which are centered around a real or perceived nonurban way of life: occurring through the travel to a specific nonurban area or attraction, or travel through a nonurban area as part of an itinerary between other destination points.

(Messerli 1990, 36)

Given this broad perspective, the potential of rural tourism is limited only by the willingness of a host community to be creative and innovative.

To some, aspects of tourism in rural areas are best categorized under cultural tourism, with the emphasis on understanding contrasting ways of life and the interchange of knowledge and ideas. In this sense, rural tourism attracts those seeking personal contact and interaction with different cultures, environments and groups of people. Other manifestations of rural tourism could include:

1 recreation tourism, with the emphasis on physical involvement and environmentally-related activity, e.g. hiking or alpine pursuits;
2 environmental tourism, with the emphasis on nature and contrasting landscapes, e.g. national park visits;
3 heritage tourism, focusing on historical places or events, often with an educational purpose.

For some types of tourism, especially informal activities, the distinction between rural and urban relates more to distance travelled from the place of residence than to the rural context. As Patmore (1983) points out, a pleasant stroll in the town and a walk in the country differ in degree rather than in kind. However, for other activities, the important element *is* the rural setting and the opportunities and satisfactions that it provides which the urban environment cannot. Undoubtedly, for many urban dwellers, it is the rural ambience and the countryside experience which are the main considerations.

TOURISM AND THE RURAL RESOURCE BASE

It could be argued that the characteristics of rural tourism more closely reflect the French derivation – *tour* – meaning a circular movement and – *tourner* – to go around. Rural tourism may very well involve journeying from place to place in sequential fashion, in contrast to urban tourism, where the emphasis is on the urban destination as the focus for city-based touristic activities.

Given the extent of non-urban space in some industrialized countries, the adequacy of the resource base to support such itinerant tourism would seem assured. Yet the reality is that tourism in the countryside is concentrated in space, and in time; the focus is on certain 'corridors of movement' leading to a limited number of nodes or sites (Patmore 1983). Problems arise when these selected areas and zones of travel are not set aside exclusively for rural tourism, but must share the space and function with other forms of resource use.

This multifunctional character of rural land and water represents both a constraint and an opportunity for tourism potential. In the first place, the activities of tourists and the attitudes of other resource users can generate conflict. To some, the countryside is valued primarily for its agricultural, forestry and mineral products, or represents suitable space for urban expansion. To others, it is the tourism potential which is most important. For these people, the economic functions of rural land should give way to its amenity function for visitors. Such claims can cause conflict with more conventional users. Even in rural areas set aside for public use, for example, national parks, conflict can occur because of differing perceptions of their primary purpose and the priority which should be given to tourism and recreation.

In many countries, it is the landscape and distinctive architecture associated with agricultural land use which underpin much tourist interest. The farm structures of midwest USA, the Amish and Mennonite heartlands of Pennsylvania and Ontario, and the rambling homesteads and stations of outback Australia are examples. In Britain, Middleton (1982) warns of the serious implications for rural tourism of any significant alteration to such traditional scenic qualities. The demands of intensive modern farming can be a threat to the hedgerows, wetlands and wildlife of rural Britain. Middleton cites Shoard (1980) as stating that 'the English Landscape is under the sentence of death'. Clearly, rural environments cannot be regarded as unchanging, but the pace and irrevocability of change, and the environmental degradation sometimes associated with large scale agribusiness, represent a threat to landscape quality and, in turn, to the resource base for rural tourism.

Such concerns are not confined to Britain. In Canada, the 1980s saw 'vastly increased numbers of visitors to rural areas, some en route to other destinations, others . . . on day outings or . . . at cottages and resorts (Butler 1991: 9). Two major concerns have arisen as a result. First, the loss or alienation of land, especially shorelines, from the traditional agricultural sector to non-residents; second, the problems of trespass and landowner liability which improved mobility and accessibility to rural areas have brought with them.

Conflict has also occurred through increased access to the countryside in Australia. Once again, the basis for conflict rests on the multiplicity of functions seen for rural land. Tourists seeking closer contact with the rural environment are frustrated by the exclusivist attitude of landholders who fear, with some justification, negligence or vandalism by visitors. The lines are clearly drawn between town and country and the concept of inviolate rights of property ownership is widespread and generally accepted. The consequence is that, for many Australians, opportunities for rural tourism remain restricted, often confined to viewing from a moving vehicle.

Such confrontation is regrettable because the diverse attributes of the rural environment provide considerable scope for multipurpose resource use incorporating compatible forms of tourism. It is this capacity for compatibility which offers much potential for broadening the spectrum of opportunities for rural tourism in harmony with other resource users.

THE TOURISM OPPORTUNITY SPECTRUM

The quality and diversity of opportunities offered to tourists in rural areas reflect the particular kinds of environmental settings offered. Clarke and Stankey (1990) demonstrated the value of developing a spectrum of recreation opportunities to maximize visitor satisfaction within acceptable constraints. In such a model the dimensions and attributes of the Recreation Opportunity Spectrum, and the degree to which they can match and satisfy the experiences sought, are a function of the range of environmental settings available to participants. These settings are not inherent or spontaneous but are the outcome of manipulation of site characteristics by management.

In the same way, tourist settings and experiences do not occur spontaneously, but call for the development of a *Tourism* Opportunity Spectrum to meet the multiple demands of tourists (Butler and Waldbrook, 1991). Creation of an appropriate range of settings for rural tourism requires the deliberate selection and manipulation of features of the rural landscape to accommodate different types and styles of visitor use. The mere existence of suitable environmental attributes is only one dimension of the tourism potential of the rural resource base. To paraphrase Clawson and Knetsch:

> There is nothing in the physical landscape, or features of any particular piece of land or water, that makes it a . . . resource [for tourism]: it is the combination of the natural qualities and the ability and desire of man to use them that makes a resource out of what might otherwise be a more or less meaningless combination of rocks, soil and trees.
>
> (Clawson and Knetsch 1966: 7)

The concern, then, is not merely with supply but with opportunity, which, in turn, is dependent upon the extent to which available resources can function effectively to satisfy visitor demands. Factors which are seen to impinge upon the type, amount, range and quality of opportunities for rural tourism include the location and ownership of resources, accessibility, and management practices. Endorsing the process of recreation resource creation and incorporating these factors into meaningful policy initiatives is the challenge confronting resource management agencies in both the public and private sector.

POLICY INITIATIVES

The development of policies for rural resources management appears to be a complex and confusing challenge to all levels of the public sector. Moreover, conflict can emerge between regulatory agencies and private interests engaged in related areas of resource use. Such conflict occurs more readily in the absence of consensus on objectives for overall management of the rural environment. This situation only adds to the problems of development of appropriate policies for rural tourism. However, recent initiatives undertaken in North America represent a promising change in direction.

In Canada, for example, the involvement of the public sector in rural tourism has been intermittent and generally reactive to perceived exploitation of the natural environment by private interests (Butler 1991). Although federal and provincial governments have been active in park development, the emphasis has been mainly on environmental protection. Whereas there has been some recognition of the role of parks in regional economic development, until recently attempts to develop an integrated approach to the provision of opportunities for rural tourism have received little attention. Butler (1991) notes the absence of clear policies relating to tourism in rural areas and the 'formidable and confusing maze' of delivery systems. This is changing, at least at the federal level, with the publication in 1990 of the first tourism policy for Canada (Tourism Canada 1990). Whereas there is no specific reference to rural tourism in the document, the policy has scope for application to rural areas where it can be shown that the attraction of tourists might prove an effective stimulus for depressed rural economies (Butler 1991).

Recognition of the potential of tourism as a tool for rural economic development forms part of the explanation for the National Policy Study on Rural Tourism and Small Businesses undertaken in 1989 in America, and noted earlier (Messerli 1990). The study, directed by the United States Travel and Tourism Administration, identified a specific need for a federal policy on rural tourism. Four major reasons supported this conclusion:

1   the federal government already has a major presence in rural tourism;

2 tourism should play an important contributing role in the national agenda for rural economic development;
3 there are no explicit federal policies or programs that focus on rural tourism;
4 there is an apparent broad based interest in the creation of a federal rural tourism policy.

(Economics Research Associates 1989, ix–4)

The study went on to recommend that the US Congress:

1 specifically recognize tourism as a legitimate and important element of rural economic development by referencing 'growth and development of travel and tourism' in all policies and programs relating to rural development;
2 specifically recognize rural travel and tourism as a legitimate and important element of domestic travel and tourism policies by revising the language, where appropriate, of the National Tourism Policy Act of 1981, to include 'growth, development, and promotion of travel and tourism in rural areas';
3 specifically instruct appropriate federal agencies to accord due importance in their programs that target small business/economic development and foster the travel and tourism industry.

(Economics Research Associates 1989, ix–5)

The study led to the establishment of an interagency Federal Task Force on Tourism and the suggestion that rural tourism potential be developed through the concept of Tourism Enterprise Zones (Messerli 1990).

These policy initiatives represent a meaningful federal commitment to the fostering of rural tourism in America. Other industrialized nations would do well to observe closely the progress of the measures put in place and the extent to which the federal lead can promote effective interfacing between different levels of government, disparate resource management agencies, and the private sector. In particular, the performance of community-supported, tourism-specific rural enterprise zones as the platform for tourism development merits serious consideration.

PLANNING FOR TOURISM IN AUSTRALIA

In Australia, policy initiatives for the tourism industry are inhibited by fragmentation and overlap between decision-making bodies, and confusion regarding the responsibilities of respective government sectors and agencies. Referring to the closely-related area of outdoor recreation planning, Pitts argues:

> The management of outdoor recreation resources and facilities in Australia is characterised by a myriad of government departments, authorities and agencies operating in apparent isolation of each other. Outdoor recreation has rarely been recognised, on its own, as a legitimate function of government in this country. Rather it has been allowed to develop as a secondary function associated with more traditional government activities such as forestry, conservation, water supply and town planning. This approach has inevitably led to problems of co-ordination, conflicts in connection with overlapping responsibilities and doubts about the effectiveness of the whole delivery system in meeting community needs.
>
> (Pitts 1983: 7)

These comments could equally be directed towards tourism policy making, especially in rural Australia (Davis *et al.* 1988). Moreover, there is considerable competition between the many public agencies and private bodies interested in attracting people for the tourist dollar. In the absence of any clear aims and objectives on a local or regional scale, this creates problems for the development of adequate and appropriate policy for rural tourism.

In the state of New South Wales, by way of example, government instrumentalities have been generally slow and inflexible in responding to the needs of a society which has exhibited increasing interest in rural tourism. The end result is that there is no *formally* developed rural tourism policy in the state. A *Tourism Development Strategy* published by the State Government in 1988, for example, makes no specific reference to tourism beyond the capital city of Sydney, which is clearly seen as the major tourist destination (New South Wales Government 1988). The more recent strategy announced in 1990 devotes just one page (out of 173) to tourism in 'country regions' (New South Wales Tourism Commission 1990). In 1989, the Commission did produce a paper on Tourism Planning and Local Government which impinges on rural issues (New South Wales Tourism Commission 1989b). Subsequently, a cultural Tourism Strategy was developed as part of the 1990 report and placed stress on the opportunities for regional and local tourism, including the promotion of Aboriginal and Australian culture (New South Wales Tourism Commission 1991). However, it remains to be seen whether the coordinated planning mechanisms envisaged for implementation of the strategy can overcome the entrenched resistance to shared responsibility manifest to date in the various agencies involved.

Despite an impressive array of providers, with a wide range of services and facilities, there remains a need for coordination and mutual support to integrate the tourism functions of public and private sector organizations and voluntary services in the rural sphere. Among the largely independent agencies involved in the formulation and implementation of tourism policies in New South Wales are the Tourism Commission, the National Parks and Wildlife Service, and the Department of Planning. A number of peripheral bodies such as local government and voluntary organizations also have a share of the responsibility. In such a situation, involvement is disjointed and reactive rather than proactive. Rarely has policy moved in the direction of encouraging and providing for rural tourism, mostly it has merely tolerated it. The *ad hoc* and complex nature of the policy process complicates the task of identifying just who has the right to participate in the tourism decision making process.

Tourism policies appear to have developed incrementally and individual government agencies are affected by conflict and uncertainty over the nature of policy objectives. Once again, planning for tourism in New South Wales is a case in point:

> while the NSW Tourism Commission is charged with the development and marketing of tourism in the State, it has no statutory authority to intervene in the planning process. Therefore, there is no authority charged with coordinating tourism development and dispelling the conflict and confusion on the part of local authorities in the tourism development process.
>
> (Hall 1991)

Some hesitant steps have been taken recently towards the coordination and integration of rural policies for tourism. Developments have taken place in administrative frameworks, the role of the private sector, the delivery and use of resources, deregulation, transfers of authority between agencies, and changing responsibilities at all levels of government. Nevertheless, the role of tourism is still ill-defined and coordination and integration of recreation policies between government departments and agencies, local councils and community groups, and the private sector, remain poor.

The Murray region

Efforts to develop a regional tourism plan in the Murray River region in the inland of southwest New South Wales give some indication of the magnitude of the task of achieving consensus between inter-departmental policy makers (Atkinson and Bochner 1988). Proposed improvements to intra- and interregional accessibility, for example, require cooperation between at least five state government departments. Added to this is the need for interstate coordination, and liaison with local government and community groups, to address such issues as: four-wheel-drive access to riparian lands; rationalization of recreational access for boating; management of road, rail and air transport services; encouragement of new forms of tourist accommodation and investment; wastes management; and maintenance of the integrity of environmentally sensitive areas.

The challenge in finding common ground between diverse interest groups in such a complex operational environment is daunting (Mitchell and Pigram 1987). Yet some progress is being made. The draft Strategic Tourism Plan drawn up for the Murray River region is aimed at increasing the use of existing attractions, facilities and services, and expanding the tourism resource base of the region. Improvements to transport links and the development of an effective regional marketing strategy are essential elements of the plan.

Of greater interest for this discussion, however, is the way in which the Draft Plan attempts to grapple with the inherently interdisciplinary nature of tourism planning and bridge the gap between the regulatory authorities and the private sector (Atkinson and Bochner 1988). Specifically, the Draft Plan is intended to:

- make public authorities, investors and developers aware of the economic potential and new tourism development in the region;
- encourage the preparation of environmental planning instruments that will encourage capital investment and growth in tourism in an environmentally sensitive manner;
- enhance cooperation and understanding between regulatory authorities and the private sector;
- promote the better utilisation of private and crown land in prime locations for tourism where appropriate;
- provide direction to government on the allocation of government resources for public works within the region, including setting aside land for future use as may be required; and
- ensure that in areas of high tourism value an adequate supply of

suitable land is set aside for commercial tourism development which is environmentally acceptable.

(Atkinson and Bochner 1988: 46)

It remains to be seen how effective interpretation and application of the plan will be at the sub-regional and local level. What is important is that for a large rural region with significant tourist potential a planning framework has been put in place to facilitate the implementation of policies for rural tourism seen to be environmentally, socially and economically appropriate.

It is encouraging to see efforts to undertake planning for tourism specifically, rather than merely as part of an overall environmental plan. Servicing tourism needs reflects an important stage in the evolution of an entirely new relationship between cities and surrounding rural areas and requires the recognition of a wider perspective in the planning process. Without such recognition across the full range of resource management agencies, tourism is likely to remain an insignificant and unappreciated form of land use in rural planning. Such an outcome becomes even more likely in the present economic climate where financial constraints are now one of the main concerns impinging upon public policy.

Tourism policy and the rural planning process

Some insights into the required planning process can be gained from the work of Mitchell (1987) in the field of water resources management. The key to effective planning is to identify common goals and objectives as well as the general direction judged to be desirable, and then to explore how individual organizations can contribute to them. In making these observations, Mitchell was indirectly drawing attention to the 'implementation gap' in public policy. Indeed,

> the criterion of good administration is not how many agencies are involved but how effective the coordinating mechanisms are. There are plenty of examples of agencies which have been merged but which merrily go about their old ways as if little had changed; similarly, there are plenty of examples of problems transcending agency boundaries, but being quite well handled because of good coordinating mechanisms.

(Kellow 1985, in Mitchell 1987: 7)

Whereas these comments were made with reference to water resources planning, reservations as to policy implementation are just as relevant to planning for rural tourism. Worthwhile policies may be developed and even formally adopted by resource management agencies, yet formidable barriers may be encountered when attempts are made to translate them into action. Shortcomings in the policy implementation process account, at least in part, for the lack of progress towards an appropriate spectrum of tourism opportunities in rural areas.

Some of the barriers which typically inhibit successful achievement of recreation policy objectives were identified in a recent study in Ontario, Canada. Three broad areas were characterized – structural, operational and financial (Reid 1989). Within these categories, a lack of adequate funding and deficiencies in staff expertise and skills were seen as paramount from the perspective of agency personnel and management. It is interesting that a significant number of respondents in that study considered their organization otherwise structurally and operationally adequate for the task of policy implementation. Whether this perception is shared by other groups involved in the process is a matter for conjecture.

It would be unfortunate if the existence of an implementation gap in tourism policy, whether in Canada or elsewhere, was also explained only with reference to funding or resources. The issue goes much deeper than the mechanics of money or personnel. Policy implementation, in all areas of public concern, is a tricky business. It calls for the meshing of political and social acceptability with economic and technical feasibility, and administrative reality. Conflicts and resistance can emerge at any stage of the process because of the nature and complexity of the policy in question, the manner in which it is perceived by target groups and implementing organizations, and the ambient conditions – physical, socio-cultural, political and economic – that prevail (Pigram 1991).

Implementing a policy for rural tourism, in particular, is made more complex because of the need to convince the various interests involved that such a policy deserves priority in rural resources decision making. Not only must the policy be perceived by management agencies as justified, conceptually robust and amenable to implementation, but the *communities affected* must see it as a constructive response to their needs. Put another way, a policy for rural tourism must first be argued in conceptual terms and then considered in the functional context necessary to facilitate implementation at an operational level.

Community input

For the process to succeed, it is essential that decision makers become and remain aware of community reaction to policy proposals, and of how best to balance public input against professional judgement. Emphasis on public participation forms a fundamental component of Murphy's (1985) ecological community model for tourism planning. Murphy presents persuasive evidence of the importance of participatory planning in balancing the physical and commercial orientation of much tourism development. One of the greatest challenges in bridging the implementation gap in recreation and tourism planning, as in other areas of public policy, is to accept the need to temper the prevailing 'top-down' approach to planning with informed input from the 'bottom-up'.

Much more than lip-service to public participation is required if community-oriented development is to emerge. Ideally, consultation should proceed to the point where communities feel they 'own' the development and are in a position to monitor its evolution closely. Certainly, local residents could be expected to have a better appreciation of the attractions and qualities of the environment in which they live. Their local knowledge and experience in being host to visiting friends and relatives should also place them in a good position to recognize features in the immediate surroundings of interest to tourists. Such attitudes of pride and awareness, coupled with a sense of caring, can give meaning to the slogan 'Ours to Share'.

Prior assessment of the services and facilities required to meet visitor needs is also fundamental, along with consideration of the net impact of tourism, in terms of the costs to the public sector weighed against the contribution to economic and social wellbeing. Without understanding by the various sections of the community of the objectives, safeguards and projected benefits of tourism proposals, useful policy initiatives could be compromised. In rural situations, in particular, the 'community' includes business leaders, organizations, and other influences on public opinion, as well as local residents. Community involvement in planning for rural tourism is not merely good public relations; it also plays a vital role in facilitating policy implementation.

CONCLUSIONS

The primary aim of rural tourism planning and management is to balance demand and capacity so that conflicts are minimized and the countryside is utilized to its full potential without deterioration of the resource base. To achieve this, attention should be given to the links between formulation and implementation of tourism policies. However, this alone will not lead to more efficient provision of appropriate opportunities for tourists. In many rural areas, research to provide improved empirical information, especially on the preferences and experiences of tourists, is also needed.

The range of agencies involved and the conflicts arising from the planning of rural tourism suggest that policies have not been compatible in their objectives. In fact they have occurred mostly in response to tourism proposals and not through the use of proactive policies. There is uncertainty and confusion concerning the need for and the nature of tourism policies. A prime example is the uncertainty regarding the roles of government in profit-making tourist activities and in the sanctioning of private concessions within or adjacent to areas such as national parks. The large number of agencies in tourism policy making has led to inefficiencies in policy formulation, and conflict and confusion in policy implementation. Research has to be directed towards the coordination of policy initiatives across the whole spectrum of public agencies with a responsibility for rural tourism.

The sources and consequences of conflict among resource management agencies concerning the formulation and implementation of tourism and recreation policies are currently being explored in research being undertaken in inland New South Wales. These studies should help provide a better understanding of the diversity of interests involved and the major issues concerning the actors and agencies. They should also expose the inherent biases and assumptions of key personnel and decision makers within agencies, and the complexity of the policy process and associated spatial implications. The subject of conflict resolution in tourism is clearly an avenue for further research.

As noted earlier, management of rural resources is subject to pressure from a wide range of interests, each of which seeks a share of the resource base for their preferred form of land and water use. Provision for tourism results in the reallocation of resources among activities, some of which may be incompatible with each other, or with conservation and preservation interests, especially in sensitive areas.

Planning for tourism would benefit from input from a wide range of groups and agencies including not only government bodies, but local and regional organizations, private industry and interest groups, and the general community. Enhanced public awareness and participation in the planning process have important roles to play in the formulation and implementation of effective and appropriate tourism policies. Broad public acceptance and endorsement are also crucial in achieving tourism policy objectives. At the same time, public resource management agencies should assume the lead role in promoting research, coordination and cooperation between the often conflicting objectives of agricultural interests, foresters, conservationists, developers and tourists.

REFERENCES

Atkinson, W. and Bochner, S. (1988) 'Planning for tourism at the regional and local levels', *Planner* 3, 5: 45–9.

Butler, R. (1991) 'Tourism in rural areas: marriage of necessity or convenience', conference paper, unpublished.

Butler, R. and Waldbrook, L. (1991) 'A new planning tool: the tourism opportunity spectrum', *Journal of Tourism Studies* 2, 1: 2–14.

Clarke, R. and Stankey, G. (1990) 'The recreation opportunity spectrum: a framework for planning management and research', in R. Graham (ed.) *Towards Serving Visitors and Managing Our Resources*, Ontario: University of Waterloo: 127–58.

Clawson, M. and Knetsch, J. (1966) *Economics of Outdoor Recreation*, Baltimore: Johns Hopkins University Press.

Countryside Commission (1987) *Enjoying the Countryside*, Cheltenham: Countryside Commission.

Cracknell, B. (1967) 'Accessibility to the countryside as a factor in planning for leisure', *Regional Studies* 1, 2: 147–61.

Davis, G., Wanna, J., Warhurst, J. and Weller, P. (1988) *Public Policy in Australia*, North Sydney: Allen & Unwin.

Economics Research Associates (1989) *The National Policy Study on Rural Tourism and Small Businesses*, Virginia.

Hall, C. M. (1991) *Introduction to Tourism in Australia: Impacts, Planning and Development*, South Melbourne: Longman Cheshire.

Janiskee, R. (1976) 'On the recreation appeals of extra-urban environments', paper presented to the 72nd Annual Meeting of Association of American Geographers, New York, April.

Messerli, H. (1990) 'Enterprise zones and rural tourism development', unpublished MA thesis, Washington, DC: George Washington University.

Middleton, V. (1982) 'Tourism in rural areas', *International Journal of Tourism Management* 3, 1: 52–8.

Mitchell, B. (1987) *A Comprehensive-Integrated Approach for Water and Land Management*, Occasional Paper no. 1, Armidale: Centre for Water Policy Research, University of New England.

Mitchell, B. and Pigram, J. (1987) *Integrated Catchment Management and the Hunter Valley, N.S.W.*, Occasional Paper no. 2, Armidale: Centre for Water Policy Research, University of New England.

Murphy, P. (1985) *Tourism: A Community Approach*, London: Methuen.

New South Wales Government (1988) *Tourism Development Strategy*, Sydney: New South Wales Government Printer.

New South Wales Tourism Commission (1989a) *The Domestic Holiday Market*, Sydney: New South Wales Tourism Commission.

New South Wales Tourism Commission (1989b) *Planning for Tourism and Major Tourism Developments: Issues Affecting Local Government*, Sydney: New South Wales Tourism Commission.

New South Wales Tourism Commission (1990) *New South Wales Tourism Development Strategy: A Plan for the Future*. Sydney: New South Wales Tourism Commission.

New South Wales Tourism Commission (1991) *A Cultural Tourism Strategy for the NSW Tourism Commission*, Sydney: New South Wales Tourism Commission.

Ormonde, T. (1991) 'Land of the rising sum of tourists', *Sydney Morning Herald*, October 11: 6.

Patmore, J. A. (1983) *Recreation and Resources*, Oxford: Basil Blackwell.

Phillips, D. and Williams, A. (1984) *Rural Britain. A Social Geography*, Oxford: Basil Blackwell.

Pigram, J. (1991) 'Tourism and sustainability – policy considerations', *Journal of Tourism Studies* 1, 2: 2–9.

Pitts, D. J. (1983) 'Opportunity shift: development and application of recreation opportunity spectrum concepts in park management', unpublished PhD thesis, Griffith University, Australia.

Reid, D. (1989) 'Implementing senior government policy at the local level: the case of the province of Ontario's recreation policy', *Journal of Applied Recreation Research* 15, 1: 3–13.

Shoard, M. (1980) *The Theft of the Countryside*, London: Temple Smith.

Tourism Canada (1990) *Tourism on the Threshold*, Ottawa: Ministry of Supply and Services.

Vogeler, I. (1976) 'A critique of studies in rural recreation', paper presented to Annual Meeting of Association of American Geographers, New York, April.

Chapter 10

Global assessment of tourism policy

A process model
Donald E. Hawkins

Tourism is now a worldwide phenomenon commanding the attention of public policy makers and private sector leaders. It is becoming increasingly clear that tourism in the 1990s and beyond will be substantially different from what we have known during the dramatic growth years since the Second World War.

On the positive side, the World Travel and Tourism Council (WTTC) reports that tourism may now be the world's largest industry, expected to employ 130 million people, or one in fourteen workers worldwide in 1992. The travel and tourism industry is expected to maintain its high rate of employment growth, 5.2 per cent, far exceeding the world employment growth rate of 2.45 per cent. The annual gross output of the travel and tourism industry was expected to total US $3 trillion for the first time in 1992. From 1989 to 1992, travel and tourism gross output was expected to grow at an annual rate of 8.7 per cent, exceeding both world and service sector GNP growth (WTTC 1991a).

On the negative side, we are experiencing the shock effects of the Gulf War aftermath, worldwide recession, the hotel real estate depression, shortage of investment capital, and continuing security problems – particularly in Yugoslavia and major international cities with high crime rates (Lima, Caracas, New York, Washington, DC, Paris, among others).

On a global scale, international tourism arrivals in 1990 totalled approximately 415 million. Though a thirty-year trend shows the growth pattern slowing, the fact remains that only once in four decades of record keeping has tourism come to a standstill in terms of international receipts. This was in 1982–3 during the worldwide recession (WTO, 1990). Compared to other industries which have experienced many more fluctuations and frequent sharp declines, tourism has seldom fallen into a serious long-term down-turn, making it one of the world's most dependable revenue generators.

Supporting this general tourism growth is the projected growth of air travel. With increases in income and a decline in travel costs, air travel is estimated to increase again 100 per cent over the next fifteen years (Boeing, 1991).

While there is general recognition of these realities, there is a need to define them more clearly as policy issues on a global level. Traditionally, the World Tourism Organization (WTO) has attempted to coordinate the international policy concerns of countries, particularly through its membership of national tourism administrations. More recently (9 April 1990), the WTTC was established as a global organization to represent the private sector of the travel and tourism industry. While the WTO and WTTC activities in global tourism assessment are important, there is a need to address more comprehensively a broad spectrum of tourism issues of major international concerns which are related to the fields of health, energy, transportation, technology, finance, resource conservation, historic preservation and education.

With this challenge in mind, the Tourism Policy Forum of The George Washington University held its First International Assembly of Tourism Policy Experts in November 1990. The broad orientation of the Forum was to chart a global course for a new millennium of human development, social progress and of peace through travel. Its more operational goal was to formulate an assessment framework for international tourism policy analysis. It was felt that such a framework would be helpful in assisting governmental, business and international organizations in conducting policy reviews, formulating policy statements and developing strategic plans. At present, the Tourism Policy Forum consists of a small staff and ninety senior associates, representing twenty-three disciplines and twenty-six countries. These experts are assisted by sponsoring organizations and founding members who are concerned with the process of sustainable tourism development. The Forum's location in Washington, DC makes it an ideal place for an international centre for tourism policy making.

This chapter outlines the phases involved in the development of a process model by the Tourism Policy Forum to assist in the global assessment of tourism policy. Nineteen major issues identified by the model are then presented, together with research questions which arise from them.

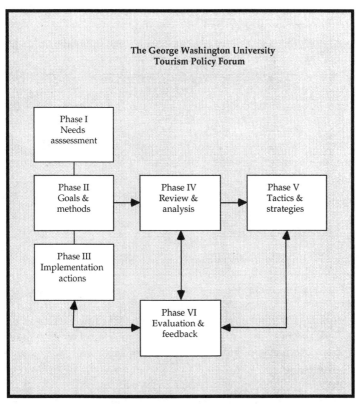

Figure 10.1 Global assessment of tourism: a process model
Source: The George Washington University

GLOBAL ASSESSMENT OF TOURISM POLICY: A PROCESS MODEL

The Tourism Policy Forum has developed a process model (Figure 10.1) consisting of six phases: needs assessment, determination of goals and methods, implementation actions, review and analysis, tactics and strategies, and evaluation and feedback. Specific criteria were used to ensure that the process model is responsive to global tourism policy assessment. The model attempts to:

1 provide broad international coverage including the concerns of: (a) developed, newly industrialized and developing countries; (b) regional variations related to geographic location, destination travel patterns, and originating markets;

2   relate to characteristics of the tourism industry, including concern
    for: (a) public, private and non-governmental organization roles
    and responsibilities; (b) the mission of specific multinational
    regional entities and international organizations;
3   apply to specific policy actions including: (a) public policy
    development and review; (b) strategic planning; (c) information
    and decision support strategies for the public and private sectors of
    the tourism industry.

In addition, the process model was adapted to the roles and
responsibilities of a higher education institution and its resource base. A
brief description of each phase and a description of the methodological
steps follow.

Phase I: Needs assessment

A review of the literature on general policy analysis and specific tourism
policy issues was conducted during the initial stages of the policy
forum's organization. Prior studies conducted at the end of the last
decade by The George Washington University, particularly the
International Symposium on Tourism and the Next Decade (Hawkins,
Shafer and Rovelstad 1980), were revisited to determine continuing
policy concerns that have prevailed up to the present time. The literature
on tourism policy analysis at the international level was also reviewed
(see Ascher and Edgell 1986, Richter 1989, OECD 1990). Except for
high visibility conferences (Manila, Acapulco and The Hague) and the
bi-annual General Assemblies conducted by the World Tourism
Organization, there was a surprising lack of attention given to global
tourism issues, particularly literature related to the policy concerns of
the private sector.

As stated previously, the recent formation of the World Travel and
Tourism Council (WTTC) has helped to fill this gap. The mission of
WTTC is:

> To marshal the resources of Chief Executive Officers and their
> companies from all sectors of the travel and tourism industry
> including transportation, accommodation, catering, recreation/
> cultural and travel service activities to: (a) convince governments of
> the enormous contribution of travel and tourism for both business and
> leisure purposes, to national and world economic development and
> ensure that policies appropriately reflect this fact; (b) promote the

expansion of travel and tourism markets; (c) eliminate barriers to growth of the industry.

(WTTC 1991b)

Due to the private sector gap identified in the needs assessment phase, the Forum gave priority to balancing the international policy concerns of government with those of the private sector. Based upon WTTC's analysis of global policy issues, their efforts are addressing the following priorities:

1 *Promoting tourism as the world's largest industry.* WTTC's goal is to convince governments to adopt policies which reflect the pre-eminent role of travel and tourism in world and national economic development and to seek clear identification of tourism in National Charts of Accounts.

2 *Building and expanding travel infrastructure.* The WTTC is highlighting transportation infrastructure, particularly airport and airways expansion, and is pressing for user fees to be directly applied to travel and tourism development.

3 *Liberalizing travel and tourism policies.* WTTC is supporting aviation liberalization, industry privatization and specifically supports the third phase of the European Community liberalization and expanded North American and Austral–Asian regional open skies arrangements.

4 *Ensuring environmentally compatible growth.* The WTTC promotes active cooperation between industry and government with particular emphasis on environmental impact assessments/ audits, the encouragement of environmental education, and monitoring the state of the tourism environment.

5 *Removing barriers to travel.* WTTC urges visa-free travel consistent with security requirements and challenges all forms of exit barriers.

6 *Resisting protectionism.* As regional markets develop in Europe, North America and the Asia–Pacific area, WTTC encourages governments to ensure that integration efforts do not result in limited access or protectionism.

7 *Supporting education and training.* WTTC encourages cross-sectoral education and training and the expansion of career opportunities for all employees. WTTC recognizes that this requires management vision and commitment, but states that the return on investment is long-lasting and adds substantial value to corporations and to staff.

In the future, there is much promise for cooperative efforts between the public and private sectors to conduct continuing needs assessment. The process model includes continuing provisions to review related literature and interview key people, develop global tourism policy assessment criteria, involve cooperating organizations, and develop funding sources for comprehensive information and decision support systems.

Phase II: Determination of goals and methods

After extensive analysis of relevant policy models, methods of the American Assembly, established over forty years ago at Columbia University, were adapted for use in the process model. The American Assembly is an educational institution that holds non-partisan assemblies and publishes authoritative books intended to focus on pertinent issues of concern to US policy makers. Also, the Delphi methodology utilized by The George Washington University in its previous trends analysis research (Hawkins, Shafer and Rovelstad 1980) was incorporated into the American Assembly methods, which focused principally on nominal group processes utilizing task oriented work groups.

Phase III: Implementation actions

The Assembly process was focused initially on the planning and convening of a group of tourism policy experts in Washington, DC, 30 October–2 November 1990, to present papers and to formulate an initial framework for policy analysis which involved the following steps:

1 Review and revise the methodology.
2 Develop instruments (Delphi survey, rounds one, two, and three):
    (a) establish instrument validity and reliability
    (b) pretest first round Delphi survey
3 Initiate International Assembly nominal group/Delphi survey processes:
    (a) develop background papers (invited and call for papers)
    (b) invite International Assembly participants
    (c) provide logistical support
    (d) convene the International Assembly
    (e) utilize invited speakers
    (f) conduct Delphi round one and present results

(g) conduct second round Delphi survey and present results
(h) execute four nominal group discussion sessions
(i) synthesize results of nominal group discussions
(j) prepare and present interim conclusions/recommendations report
(k) conclude International Assembly
4 Execute third round Delphi survey
(a) develop and pretest Delhi survey, round three
(b) conduct round three Delphi survey
(c) compilation of results

In summary, the International Assembly convened experts for the purpose of developing a framework for tourism policy analysis at the global level. The Assembly methodology was designed to ensure random group placement of participants in one of three parallel discussion groups in order to take advantage of the power of collective thinking, consensus building and group dynamics. Each of the discussion groups included participants who reflected broad geographic experience and represented industry, academic or governmental representation. The discussion topics included world events and impact-related, industry-specific and geopolitical issues. These issues were identified and prioritized by each of the panels involved in parallel discussion activity. The major outcome of these discussions was an elaboration of nineteen policy issues which were proposed as a strategic agenda for the 1990s. These are included later in this chapter.

The International Assembly discussion process was enhanced by the findings resulting from two rounds of a Delphi survey which identified world events influencing global tourism policy within the context of political, social, technological, economic, and physical environmental realities.

Round three of the Delphi survey included final judgements of the participant Delphi panel several months after the International Assembly concluded. As an example, Table 10.1 depicts events judged in terms of the combined likelihood of occurrence and importance in terms of the formulation of tourism policy.

Phase IV: Review and analysis

This phase of the process model is currently under way. In particular, the nineteen policy issues have been used by the Tourism Policy Forum and senior associates in highlighting global concerns for specific countries, industry sectors, and local destinations. As a means of facilitating this

Table 10.1 World events: combined judgement concerning likelihood of occurrence and the importance to tourism policy formulation

Rank	Mean*	Event
1	4.075	Political shift in the Eastern bloc countries to market economies
2	4.038	Escalation of terrorism and regional conflicts
3	3.925	International telecommunication systems and data banks worldwide
4	3.913	Infrastructure – roads, airports – fails to keep pace with technology
5	3.888	Airport facility limitations and air control problems reach crisis stage
6	3.850	Increasing degradation of physical environment of host countries
7	3.738	Deregulation of commercial transportation carriers becomes the norm in developed countries with market economies
7	3.738	Automated data retrieval interactive systems and data banks worldwide
9	3.688	Advanced transportation systems predominate
10	3.638	Global firms emerge and influence world economic policy
11	3.625	Infrastructure investments require public/private partnerships
12	3.588	Consolidation of the world's computer reservation systems – CRS
13	3.563	Greater awareness of history, culture and patrimony in destination areas
14	3.488	AIDS and related communicable diseases reach epidemic levels
14	3.488	Regional economic integration increases economic protectionism
16	3.363	Regional areas of the world establish programmes to reduce pollution
17	3.350	Two separate holiday periods dominant in developed countries
18	3.338	The public and private sectors work together
18	3.338	Vertical and horizontal consolidation of tourism industry components
20	3.332	Increased growth in special interest influence

21	3.288	Labour shortages and value shifts require organizational changes
22	3.238	Border formalities of most countries eliminated
22	3.238	Worldwide stock market crash recurrence
24	3.218	Public regulations over ecology discourage private investment
25	3.175	The four-day work week and annual month-long paid vacations characterize work patterns in most countries
26	3.125	Communications and fibre optic cable technology advantage
27	3.100	Increase in national and international peace movement
28	3.075	Visitors responsible for preserving ecological habitats of the host country
29	3.013	Non-traditional work lifestyles become common practice
30	2.975	Iraq–Mid East crisis results in stabilizing oil prices at US $40/barrel

Source: Tourism Policy Forum, Delphi survey, round 3, 1990.
Note: * Highest score = 5

process, an interim report summarizing this process model and including the elaboration of the nineteen issues has been distributed widely (Tourism Policy Forum 1991). In addition, a slide/narrative tape and script containing world and regional tourism statistics, trends and forecasts, and the policy issues have been made available in the English and Spanish languages. The Tourism Policy Forum staff and senior associates have used these materials for presentations.

Phase V: Tactics and strategies

Communication activities have been undertaken as each phase of the process model has been initiated. These activities included a review of the literature on international tourism policy issues, the development of background papers and subsequent publication by C.A.B. International as the first volume of the *World Travel and Tourism Review* (Hawkins and Ritchie 1991) and the broadcast of an international teleconference on tourism policy issues linking the United States with Venezuela through the US Information Agency's WorldNet. Dissemination of the International Assembly's outcomes in the form of press releases, speeches and other media has been initiated. The Tourism Policy Forum staff is currently developing a Speaker's Programme for Senior Associates and International Assembly participants to assist them in presenting the process model results to the widest possible audience. In order to respond to regional integration trends at the international level, the Forum is currently organizing affiliated regional tourism policy forums in Europe, the Americas, and the Asia–Pacific area.

Phase VI: Evaluation and feedback

This is an ongoing process designed to improve the overall performance of the process model's five phases. Evaluation and feedback procedures include validity and reliability checks on instrumentation, participant feedback on international assembly procedures and other process model activities, and third party monitoring of all phases of the process model. These results will be utilized by project staff and the steering committee to refine and improve the process model for future global tourism policy assessment applications. The results will also be essential in the development of strategic plans for the global tourism policy assessment activities of the Tourism Policy Forum.

MAJOR OUTCOMES

Nineteen major issues have emerged from the Process Model and these represent the major outcomes realized to date. In our view, these issues set the agenda for areas to be addressed by international tourism policy makers over the next decade. The Delphi questionnaire used in round three also asked respondents to rank the nineteen tourism policy issues and to formulate recommendations for three issues on which, in their judgement, they had specific expertise. Each respondent was asked to select ten policy issues considered to be most important in terms of shaping tourism policy at the global level. The listing of issues below is ranked in priority from the most important to the least important. Discussion of each of the following issues contains verbatim comments taken from the International Assembly Interim Report (Tourism Policy Forum 1991) prepared by Dr J. R. Brent Ritchie as rapporteur. To elaborate these comments, this author has formulated research questions based upon recommendations presented at the International Assembly and by the Delphi panel in the third round.

Issue 1: There is a recognition that there are finite limitations to tourism development, in terms of both physical and social carrying capacity of destinations

Comment: related to the concern for the environment is the broader recognition that tourism can potentially bring about a whole range of undesirable impacts. These impacts include increased crime, both to and by tourists, resulting in a growing anti-tourist sentiment, particularly in certain mature markets. The lack of an adequate transportation infrastructure has, in certain cases, led to a worldwide 'gridlock'. This problem is, perhaps, most pronounced with respect to air travel but also relates to automobile traffic in many countries – certainly during peak periods.

There are also very real social and cultural limitations to the levels of tourism development which are considered desirable. These limitations are in many cases ill understood and frequently neglected until they become unmanageable. Tourism policymakers cannot continue to ignore these limitations.

Research questions:

1 How can environmental issues be linked to tourism policy concerns?

2 What public and private partnership models can be applied to carrying capacity issues?

3 How can environmental impact assessments address both the social and physical carrying capacity limits for tourism development?

Issue 2: The physical environment is taking 'centre stage' in tourism development and management

Comment: clearly this concern reflects a much broader societal alarm about the degradation of our physical environment. Tourism, however, is perhaps even more sensitive and more dependent upon a high quality environment for its long-term success than are many other sectors.

All in all, it is recognized that there is a need to respect the environment. As such, well planned development and usage must be the goal. The attainment of this goal will require cooperation between all players in the tourism system.

In summary, it is acknowledged that as global, national and local political restructuring continues, policy makers must recognize that the economic, social, cultural and environmental significance of tourism is growing. Accordingly, they must see that it is incorporated into the planning and decision-making process in the public and private sector at all levels.

Research questions:

1 How can taxation policy reflect environmentally sensitive tourism development?

2 What can entrepreneurs and private companies do to develop tourism in an environmentally responsible manner?

3 How can broader support be developed from the cultural/ environmental communities for tourism facility and product development?

4 How can community tourism planning and development efforts achieve a balance among economic, social and environmental needs?

5 How can tourism facilities (most notably parks and reserves) that are facing increasing numbers of tourists (or would like to attract them) manage visitor impacts and avoid deterioration while generating necessary revenues and employment?

6 How can conflict resolution approaches be utilized to develop a consensus on 'tolerable limits of change' to the environment directly resulting from tourism development?

Issue 3: The growing demands of the high cost of capital for development of the tourism infrastructure and rising taxation/fees will maintain and increase financial pressures on the tourism industry

Comment: a broad range of economic factors appears to be acting in concert to maintain and even increase the current high cost of capital. Continued concern with the resolution of the Third World debt problems, the new and growing investment requirements of the former Eastern bloc countries, and continued high levels of inflation appear to indicate that the overall cost of capital will remain high in the 1990s. This fact, combined with the ongoing governmental deficits in many countries, means that tourism may be targeted as a new source of revenue. This implies rising taxes and fees from various tourism facilities and services – even to the point of discriminatory taxation concerning the tourism industry, which continues to be perceived as a 'leisure good' by many governments. In turn, a general overall higher level of taxation will mean less disposable income on the part of consumers who may be less willing or less able to travel.

Research questions:

1 What financial mechanisms will attract new investment to the tourism sector?

2 How can tourism gain direct access to a significant portion of tourism taxes and fees to support tourism promotion, education and training, destination/infrastructure development and natural resource protection?

3 At what point do rising taxation and user fees negatively effect the tourism sector?

4 What forms of bilateral and multilateral aid can be implemented to assist the tourism industry in developing countries – concessionary loans and credits, private foreign investment, joint ventures, local equity participation, employee ownership programmes, and similar measures?

Issue 4: Technological advances are giving rise to both opportunities and pressures for improved productivity, human resource development and restructuring of the tourism industry

Comment: the rate of technological innovation seems, at times, almost overwhelming – and tourism is not exempt from its effects. On the one hand – particularly in developed countries – technology is seen as a tool to greatly enhance performance and effectiveness. Computer reservations systems, video technology and air transport and traffic technology have been particularly significant in improving the ability of the travel industry to make new travel experiences available to a mass audience and to do so at prices which are affordable by much of the population.

On the other side of the coin, technological developments are frequently seen as 'job killers'. Both skilled and not so skilled individuals in the labour force may be replaced by various forms of technological substitutes. While some say that the increased use of capital/technology will require highly skilled labour, others argue that computer technology may, in fact, increase demand for a 'de-skilled' labour force.

Despite the above negative consequences, technology is a reality that needs to be managed. The real question becomes one of what technology should, rather than could, contribute to tourism development and how this can best be achieved. The positive aspects of technology (such as the development of cleaner fuels for environmentally less damaging travel) must be harnessed if tourism is to develop on a sustainable basis. Conversely, the potentially harmful impacts of technology must be understood and managed so that their introduction can balance economic efficiency and negative social impacts.

Research questions:

1   How can technology be directly related to improvement of tourism products and services?
2   How can computer reservation services and related telecommunications technologies be transferred to developing countries?

Issue 5: Tourism must strive to develop as a socially responsible industry; more specifically, it must move proactively rather than simply responding to various pressures as they arise

Comment: while tourism has done much to enhance economic development and encourage worldwide friendship and peace, the industry has not always been a willing nor proactive partner in the realization of these goals. While components of the industry have been oriented towards achieving socially desirable objectives, there is a general feeling that tourism has tended to be reactive to emerging global issues rather than providing leadership in their identification and resolution. This may have been acceptable in an era when tourism was relatively unimportant –it is no longer judged that this is the case.

Research questions:

1   To what extent can the tourism industry contribute to global restructuring by accepting responsibility for: (a) a more just distribution of resources on a global basis; (b) a more proactive position in the political process; (c) enhancing the understanding of the cultural and natural diversity of the world; (d) improving the natural and built environments; and (e) promoting and practising sustainable development?
2   What efforts need to be directed towards the removal, of all barriers to travel, including physical, economic, organizational, and legal constraints?

Issue 6: Continued regional conflicts and terrorist activities are impediments to the development and prosperity of tourism

Comment: the continuing escalation in armed and regional conflicts on a large scale is clearly a major deterrent to the development of tourism in the regions affected. In more general terms, the problems in the Middle East – during the past twenty years – and recently the Persian Gulf War and the uncertainty of political stability in parts of Asia have meant that tourism development in these regions has been substantially restrained and even curtailed.

In addition to the destabilizing effect of these regional and within-border conflicts, the associated escalation of terrorism has cast an even broader shadow over the travel industry. These realities have led to a heightened need to protect tourists from terrorists and other forms of political instability. Recognizing that the tourism industry can only thrive in a peaceful world, it is essential that it takes a pro-active role in collaborating with other organizations in promoting international understanding and goodwill at all levels.

Research questions:

1 How can local governments be prepared to identify and control sources of conflicts and reduce security problems in major tourism destination development areas?

2 What measures can be undertaken to prepare tourists to be more security conscious and to take necessary security precautions?

Issue 7: The political shift to market-driven economies is bringing about a global restructuring in which market forces rather than ideology are used to guide decisions and develop policy

Comment: since 1989 we have seen a rapid acceleration of a trend which started in the late 1970s and early 1980s. During the past decade, governments and individual ideologies have proven less and less able to develop and manage systems which satisfy the needs of the world's population. The initial movement in this regard was for deregulation of many markets – a movement which occurred largely in Western, capital-intensive countries. More recently, however, entire political systems have undergone dramatic changes in response to the pressure from their populations to provide the goods and services which they desire rather than those which are determined by the state.

For the moment, it appears that this trend is likely to continue and grow. While history warns that we must anticipate swings and counter-swings over time, it is probable that the next decade will see a continuation in the increasing role of market forces in determining the shape of the world economic activity in general, and tourism in particular.

Research questions:

1 What public and private partnerships will ensure tourism development which is economically viable yet socially responsible in countries undergoing radical economic conversions from planned to market economies?

2 How can new market-oriented economies develop a realistic understanding of the competitive forces operating in the global tourism market?

Issue 8: Resident responsive tourism is the watchword for tomorrow: community demands for active participation in the setting of the tourism agenda and its priorities for tourism development and management cannot be ignored

Comment: for too long, much of the concern related to tourism development has been focused on the needs of the consumer of the tourism service. While in a competitive world this concern will continue to be of substantial importance, there is a strong and growing recognition that a greater balance needs to be struck in weighing the desires of visitors against the well-being of their hosts.

In effect, these policy recommendations reflect a thematic need for consultation involving the local community in all forms of tourism development. In particular there is a sensitivity to the cultural disparities that may exist between the host region and visitors to this region. This results in the need to avoid the potential for social alienation on the part of host communities. There is genuine concern that if host communities do not benefit from tourism they will become alienated and reject tourism in all its forms. In this regard, there is particular concern with respect to Third World countries and the need to optimize economic benefits from tourism – a recognition that this has not always been the case in the past.

Research questions:

1 What measures can be taken to assure that tourism development is in harmony with the socio-cultural, ecological and heritage goals, values and aspirations of the host community?

2 What creative approaches foster host country citizen participation in the economic benefits resulting from tourism facilities and services?

3 How can we improve our understanding of resident perceptions, values and priorities regarding tourism's role in their community?

Issue 9: Despite recent progress, recognition by governments of the tourism industry and its importance to social and economic development and well-being of regions is still far from satisfactory: one part of the reason is a lack of credibility of tourism data

Comment: during the 1980s, tourism made substantial progress in gaining recognition as the important contributor to the social and economic well-being of countries that it is. Despite this, tourism is still viewed in many quarters as a marginal industry, largely due to the fact that its impacts are poorly documented and poorly understood. As such, there is a need for further effort to develop industry support for an integrated tourism lobby.

For this to occur, however, there is a very strong need to enhance the credibility of the tourism industry by promoting accepted international standards for data collection and dissemination so that the quality of data for policy-making can be improved and made more credible.

Research questions:

1 What standard definitions, nomenclatures, and methodologies can be utilized to assure data consistency and relevancy for tourism research purposes?
2 How can tourism data be effectively used for market intelligence, industry credibility, cost/benefit analysis and other purposes?

Issue 10: Demographic shifts are occurring which will dramatically influence the level and nature of tourism

Comment: in simplest terms, these demographic shifts are characterized as 'the developing country's boom – the developed country's bust'. In effect, what we are seeing is an ageing of the population in developed countries and the very real possibility that populations in these regions will not only stabilize, but may shrink if no action is taken to counter this trend. At the same time, the populations of the developing countries continue to undergo substantial increases with no apparent reversal in sight.

Research questions:

1 How can global demographic changes be taken into consideration in planning and decision making with respect to the design, development, delivery and utilization of tourism facilities and services?
2 What methodologies can be employed to evaluate the tourist

facility, product and service needs of the growing population of older persons worldwide?

3 To what extent do the functional aspects of travel need to be modified to reflect emerging demographic realities – most notably, health care requirements while travelling?

Issue 11: Patterns of tourism are being transformed by increasingly diverse life styles

Comment: a number of very fundamental changes appear to be occurring in the very nature of the travel experience itself. These changes reflect fundamental and broad based changes in the way people now live and work, particularly in the developed western world. As a result of these changes, the existing tourism facilities which were based on older values and lifestyles have now become obsolete in many cases. Consumers are now more educated, more demanding and more sophisticated with respect to both the kind of travel experience sought and the information they require in making decisions and travelling. In addition, there has been a broad scale 'democratization of travel'; a 'deprivilegization' of the travel experience. Travel is no longer reserved for the élite segments of the population or, perhaps, it is more accurate to say that the size of the élite population has become substantially larger.

Following from this are a number of visible changes in relation to tourism. Vacation is now seen as a 'lifestyle' – an integral part of a balanced way of living and thus, a critical part of household expenditures. Some would argue an even more extreme case where a vacation is seen as an entitlement or a right. Household structure and working patterns have led to shorter, more frequent vacations. . . . In parallel with these market based trends there are some broader societal ones. Tourism is slowly becoming a part of the total education system, thus enhancing the understanding of tourism as a social and economic phenomenon. Perhaps as a result, there is increased receptivity to the concept of 'responsible travelling'.

Research questions:

1 What measures can be taken to assist consumers in recognizing that they have an obligation to have some understanding of the places they are visiting and to respect the values and lifestyles of residents of the host region?

2 How can lifestyle changes be monitored and applied to tourism niche marketing and differentiated product development?

Issue 12: The human resource problem: there is a continuing and growing need to increase the supply of personnel and to enhance their professionalism

Comment: tourism is a labour-intensive, 'people-oriented', industry. As such, its success depends heavily on the availability of a high quality and committed work force. This issue has become even more important in recent years in developed countries as the number of younger persons – a traditional source of labour – has declined as a percentage of the population. Because of this, it has become even more important to develop strategies to enhance both the reality and the image of working conditions in tourism so as to more effectively attract and retain workers.

From a policy standpoint, there is a need to integrate labour demand planning in tourism into overall strategic planning of the work force efforts in both the public and private sector. More specifically, there is a need to redefine human resource 'costs' as 'human investment to improve productivity' in the tourism sector.

One of the more specific needs that must be specifically addressed is for an enhanced development of the human resource base in tourism through education and training.

Research questions:

1 How can greater priority be given to tourism education and training programmes at all levels?

2 What models encourage all sectors of the tourism industry to actively cooperate in the development of training and education programmes to ensure that training meets the needs of a diverse work place, particularly in relation to the special needs and areas of multi-culturalism, gender and age?

3 What curricular approaches enhance the integration of tourism subjects into the public sector education system on a worldwide basis?

4 To what extent can human resource development systems foster the training, education and placement of indigenous management and workers?

5 What mechanisms can be established to finance tourism education and training through greater public/private cooperation?

Issue 13: Cultural diversity should be recognized within the context of a global society

Comment: international trade, world travel and mass electronic communications have created tremendous pressures for a global homogenization of products, lifestyles, architecture, food and eating habits, entertainment and many forms of everyday behaviour. From a tourism perspective this creeping homogenization has led to some concern that one of the most fundamental motivations for travel – the desire to observe and be a part of a different environment for a short period of time – may be threatened.

At the same time, and perhaps as a counter-reaction to this homogenization process, there has been an increasing effort on the part of many societies and cultural groups consciously to undertake efforts to strengthen and develop clear cultures and their supporting value systems. Thus, what seems to be emerging is a rather paradoxical situation in which cultural diversity is thriving in a sea of homogenization. Perhaps most telling is that this phenomenon is being recognized and embraced at a worldwide level.

Research questions:

1 In the context of an emerging global society, how can we assure recognition of and support for the protection of cultural diversity and indigenous heritage resources, including their incorporation into tourism facilities, events and programmes?

2 To what extent can tourism development reflect new or existing cultural manifestations which strengthen local cultural identity?

3 What incentives can be provided to the private sector to protect and enhance human, cultural and natural resources both during product development and delivery?

Issue 14: The trend to market economies and shrinking government budgets is creating strong pressures for privatization and deregulation of tourism facilities and services

Comment: while the decade of the 1970s saw governments become increasingly involved in many areas of social and economic development, the realities of the 1990s are forcing a drastic retrenchment of government activity. The reality is that governments in many countries have found that they are unable to support the many programmes and initiatives that were put in place in earlier years. As a result of this reality, there is an overall tendency on the part of governments to cut back on subsidization, to reduce levels of regulation and to transfer responsibility for the management of many social and economic programmes to the private sector. Tourism, as one sector of the economy and society, will be directly affected.

One of the first indications of this was the process of liberalization and deregulation of airline and commercial transportation – first in the United States, and increasingly on a worldwide basis. Government subsidies to support tourism development are declining. Increasingly, fees are being imposed for the use of tourism facilities and services which were previously 'free'. Government investment in tourism facility development is also declining with increasing pressures for privatization of all forms of tourism development. This trend is causing a marked change in the structure of investment portfolios in tourism related projects. Finally, the trend to government decentralization of its structures and programmes is pushing responsibility for tourism planning and development to the regional and local level.

Research questions:

1 What alternative rationale can be used to support tourism development, in addition to historical justification, as a form of social development or as a mechanism for the redistribution of income and employment?

2 What privatization models utilized in developed economies can be adapted and applied to countries attempting to privatize state owned tourism facilities and services?

Issue 15: Health and security concerns could become a major deterrent to tourism travel

Comment: an emerging concern which could act as a major constraint to travel relates to the health and security of tourists. Specifically, it has been noted that the perceptions of the dangers associated with AIDS has greatly reduced tourism to such African countries as Kenya and The Gambia. Given this situation, it is essential that all components of the tourism industry be proactive in collaborating with international, national and local health organizations to ensure that food and water for travellers are safe and that medical supplies and services are effective and disease free. While tourists should not necessarily expect a level of medical services which is superior to that enjoyed by local populations, they should be made aware prior to travel of the quality of medical services that can be expected should they decide to travel in a given region.

Research questions:

1 How can health related policies affecting tourism be established, and mitigated as necessary, to promote optimum health and sanitation conditions for the tourist and the receiving country?

2 How can international organizations charged with tourism responsibilities (World Tourism Organization) and health responsibilities (World Health Organization) develop effective cooperative mechanisms with other international bodies, national governments and the private sector?

Issue 16: Regional political and economic integration/cooperation will predominate

Comment: the advent of the integration of the European economy and its formalization as of 1992 is perhaps the most visible manifestation of a worldwide trend towards the establishment of hemispheric trade blocs and, indeed, a movement towards world regional economic and political integration. It is anticipated that in the relatively near future the world may be characterized by three major trading blocs: Europe, the Asia–Pacific Region and the Americas.

While tourism is generally considered to be a 'free-trade industry', there is a strong realization that emergence of these new political/economic blocs may lead to increasing tensions as well as pressure to harmonize jurisdictional conditions across countries within each trading area. While such harmonization will encourage travel within the integrated regions, it could potentially lead to new barriers to travel across trading blocs.

Research questions:

1 How will international tourism be affected by regional integration in Europe? the Americas? Asia–Pacific?
2 How will GATT negotiations affect the regional integration efforts now under way?

Issue 17: The rise in influence of the global/transnational firm will accelerate

Comment: while slower to develop than in other industries, tourism has in recent years seen its ownership and management increasingly assumed by large multinational firms. While many of these firms were once viewed as corporations belonging to a single country (such as the United States or Germany), they are increasingly falling into the category of transnational, in that they do not identify with any one national entity. As one result of this process, we are seeing substantial shifts in the ownership of air transport companies throughout the world and a major re-alignment of air transport routes.

One of the greatest concerns with respect to transnational corporations is the risk of loss of host country control over tourism as the supra-national institutions increase their dominance of the industry. The financial and marketing strength of these corporations is leading to a widening gap between the transnational firms and the smaller industry players. Furthermore, the access which these firms have to technology (and in particular computerized reservation systems) provides them with a tremendous international competitive advantage. In addition, these corporations are very adept at forming global strategic alliances with other key players – a fact which only serves to further strengthen their competitive advantage and their hold on the industry.

Research questions:

1   How can transnational corporations demonstrate sensitivity to the impact of their operations on host countries and communities?

2   To what extent can transnational firms influence investment decisions in support of the tourism sector as a priority?

Issue 18: The widening gap between the North/South (developed/developing) nations continues to cause frictions and to be a constant source of concern for harmonious tourism development

Comment: while again part of a much larger issue, the increasing rich/poor gap between developed nations in the northern hemisphere and developing nations in the southern hemisphere is leading to growing hostility between the populations of these regions. This North/South disparity occurs across a broad range of areas including economic well-being, the quality of health care and access to technology and information. This disparity is reflected in massive unemployment in the lesser developed countries and a deteriorating quality of life in growing populations which are sharing decreased resources. There is a recognition that if the North/South dialogue does not succeed, certain parts of the globe will be increasingly less attractive to visit.

While, as implied above, this issue needs to be addressed on a very broad scale by all sectors of the economy, tourism must also do its part. In this regard, it is seen that there is a growing demand for specialized tourism research capabilities particularly focussed on developing countries. In addition, there is a need for increased protection of, and the provision of greater assistance to, Third World tourism enterprises.

Research questions:

1 How can developing countries utilize technology and human resource development programmes to enhance their international competitiveness?

2 What economic policies can be developed to minimize the leakage from tourism development so as to ensure a fair and equitable return from tourism development to the host nations?

3 How can inter-governmental agencies expand training and technical assistance activities to developing countries to enhance their competitiveness in the global tourism marketplace?

Issue 19: Growing dissatisfaction with current governing systems and process may lead to a new framework (paradigm) for tourism

Comment: the broad scale political transformations which have occurred throughout the world since 1989 may, in effect, be precursors of a much broader and sweeping rethinking of the government process. While this trend has been classified as an emerging, rather than established one, it does appear that the peoples of the world, as they become more educated and more informed, are seeking to put in place new processes of government which are more directly responsive to the wishes of the population in question. There is increasingly a negative reaction towards economic development and wealth distribution policies which are put in place often without representation by those being affected. What is more, the collective wisdom of the people seems to be recognizing the need for a switch from short-term to long-term planning in such areas as economic, social and environmental planning.

Research questions:

1 What tourism decision-making systems can be applied to tourism planning and development in order to reflect more accurately the wishes of host populations?

2 What political measures can be undertaken to encourage an expanded concept of tourism policy in which tourism development is more thoroughly integrated with the overall economic and social policy of a country, region or locality?

CONCLUSION

This chapter has presented a process model for tourism policy assessment at the global level. It could also be adapted to other levels, for example, rural policy issue assessment as discussed by Pigram in the previous chapter. The basic strength of the model is that it draws upon the collective wisdom of the public and private sectors in order to provide generic guidance for tourism development from an international perspective. It is not a didactic or prescriptive set of guidelines. It can be adapted to different situations. The major limitation of this process model is that its Delphi and nominal group process approaches have drawn upon limited sources of expertise, due to cost and time limitations. Since it is not based upon quantitative data, it may be unduly influenced by the dominance of the major ideological trends of the times – for example, the uncritical acceptance of airline liberalization/ deregulation. The process model may be naive in that it assumes that persons in positions of power can be persuaded to take the proper course of action, which may be in conflict with vested interests and political realities.

The process model described here is in an early development stage. It is not presented as an alternative to more traditional master planning, market research, and cost–benefit analysis approaches which are essential to tourism policy formulation. It does present, however, a practical and cost-effective method of bringing public and private sector concerns together to identify needs, formulate clear statements of policy issues and identify research questions as the basis for formulating policy recommendations and implementation. Other aspects of developing such research questions further are dealt with by Ritchie in the following chapter.

REFERENCES

Ascher, B. and Edgell, D. L. (1986) 'Barriers to international travel: removing restrictions to trade in service and tourism', *Travel and Tourism Analyst*, October.

Boeing (1991), *Current Market Outlook: World Market Demand and Airplane Supply Requirements*, Seattle: Boeing Commercial Airplane Group.

Hawkins, D. E. and Ritchie, J. R. (eds) (1991) *World Travel and Tourism Review: Indicators, Trends and Forecasts, Vol. I 1991*, Wallingford, Oxon: C.A.B. International.

Hawkins, D. E., Shafer, E. and Rovelstad, J. (1980) *Summary and Recommendations: International Symposium on Tourism and the Next Decade*, Washington, DC: The George Washington University.

OECD (1990) *Tourism Policy and International Tourism OECD Member Countries*, Washington, DC: OECD.

Richter, L. K. (1989) *The Politics of Tourism in Asia*, Honolulu: University of Hawaii Press.

Tourism Policy Forum (1991) *Interim Report: Global Assessment of Tourism Policy*, Washington, DC: The George Washington University.

WTO (1990) *Tourism to the Year 2000: Qualitative Aspects Affecting Global Growth*, Madrid: World Tourism Organization.

WTTC (1991a) *The WTTC Report: Travel and Tourism in the World Economy*, Brussels: World Travel and Tourism Council.

WTTC (1991b) *WTTC Mission and Policy Summaries*, Brussels: World Travel and Tourism Council.

Chapter 11

Tourism research

Policy and managerial priorities for the 1990s and beyond

J. R. Brent Ritchie

As has become abundantly clear over the past several years, the period of the 1990s and beyond is showing itself to be radically different from the three previous decades. While technological change has been with us for some time, it continues to accelerate and its impacts increasingly reverberate throughout society. Added to this, the dramatic political changes that have occurred in recent years are only manifestations of more deep-seated social and cultural transformations which reflect changes in human priorities concerning the way the populations of the world wish to live. Tourism, as a phenomenon, is clearly affected as much and perhaps more by these changes as any other sector. The result is forcing a constant and ongoing reassessment as to the directions which future tourism development should take and the policies which are appropriate to support these new directions.

One recent attempt to identify the major policy issues which will face the tourism industry as we move through the 1990s and beyond was that carried out by the international Tourism Policy Forum (Chapter 10). While the issues which emanated from this forum vary, in terms of their significance, they do provide a very clear agenda of what needs to be addressed by tourism policy makers at the international, national and local levels if tourism is to continue to grow and prosper in the coming years.

In order to address these policy issues in a meaningful and effective manner, it will be necessary to provide information on which to base policies to deal with them in an effective and timely manner. It follows that research will play an important role in assembling that information. Towards this end, it becomes imperative to establish a research agenda which defines the specific kinds of research which need to be carried out and to assign some kind of priority to the implementation of the overall research agenda. It is in this light that this chapter has been prepared. Its goal is threefold:

1 To select those policy issues which are most significant and which lend themselves to better resolution through research information.
2 To provide examples of the specific kinds of research projects that need to be undertaken in relation to each of the priority research areas.
3 To discuss a mechanism whereby academics may contribute to providing some of the required research.

SOME PARAMETERS OF THE PROPOSED RESEARCH PROCESS

Just as the policy environment for the 1990s and beyond is different from that of the three previous decades, so too are the parameters or conditions under which research should be conducted if it is to be truly effective. While perhaps idealistic in nature, the parameters described below provide some insight into the desired nature of the research programme which will be required as we move towards the year 2000.

A genuine effort to provide a multidisciplinary perspective

All of us in the tourism field know that the tourism phenomenon is truly a multidisciplinary one and that to achieve a meaningful understanding of the major issues it faces, it is essential that we bring to bear as many disciplinary skills, methodologies, concepts and energies as possible. This needs to be done in an integrated manner in which there is meaningful sharing of ideas and values among researchers and their supporting disciplines. Indeed, at some point it is hoped that a holistic multifaceted approach to the study of tourism will emerge. Under this scenario, tourism would be seen both as a field of study in itself and one which can be related to the many other fields of study and sectors of the economy with which tourism interfaces on a continuing basis.

The globalization of world activities needs to be reflected in tourism research

While those involved with tourism should perhaps have taken the lead in recognizing and reacting to the globalization which has occurred in recent years, such has not been the case. Indeed, while many countries seek to attract visitors from different parts of the world, the development, organization and delivery of tourism facilities and services has tended to retain a very national or local perspective, particularly in

North America. This reflects the accepted truism that for the majority of destinations, the tourism market is relatively local. At the same time, it denies the ability of a destination to compete effectively in international markets where expectations concerning the types and quality of services/facilities which they demand are highly varied and often different from those demanded by the local marketplace. In any event, as the tourism industry moves increasingly towards putting more emphasis on international markets, as transnational corporations play a greater and greater role in the development of local tourism facilities, and as world cultures continue to intermingle, it will be increasingly essential to develop a research agenda which places a greater emphasis on international and cross-cultural comparisons.

The rigour and credibility of tourism research needs to be constantly enhanced

Traditional tourism research has always had a number of special characteristics which pose somewhat unique challenges to the researcher (Ritchie 1975; Ritchie and Goeldner 1987). The great majority of these concerns have reflected some very real problems associated with the gathering and interpretation of reliable data in a timely manner. These issues remain far from being resolved. In addition, as tourism has become recognized as a leading industry, its visibility has attracted much more attention and criticism than has previously been the case. As a consequence, the statistics which are used to describe the industry, and the reports which delineate its impacts, have come under greater scrutiny and more detailed evaluation. Many of these statistics and reports have not stood up to this more demanding scrutiny. As a result, the industry has very appropriately recognized the need to enhance the credibility of its data and its research (TTRA 1991). This concern will only grow in importance in the coming decade and must be the constant concern of every responsible researcher.

ROLES OF RESEARCH IN TOURISM MANAGEMENT

Before launching into a detailed formulation of the research agenda for the 1990s and beyond, it is essential to address the ambiguities related to the term 'research' itself. This term is one which describes a broad range of processes designed to provide policy makers and managers with information which is as objective, reliable and reproducible as possible. This said, it must be recognized that there are many different kinds of tourism research and an even greater number of research methods and techniques. This may cause difficulties for the research professional, create confusion among managers as to the true nature of research and frequently leads to inappropriate research approaches being used in a given decision-making situation. In order to be effective, research strategies must correspond to the nature and level of the issue being addressed.

One attempt to clarify the nature of management research as it relates to tourism identifies five distinctly different kinds of research approaches: policy, managerial, operational, action and evaluation (Ritchie 1987). These research approaches vary with the stage of the management process (analysis, planning, execution and control) as well as the level of management activity (strategic, managerial/tactical, or operational). Figure 11.1 relates these five types of research to these two major dimensions as well as to various functional areas of management activity (coordination, finance, marketing, production, control, personnel).

As seen in Figure 11.1, each of the five research approaches has some very distinct characteristics which are appropriate to the needs of different management processes. At one end of the spectrum, policy research attempts to analyse the overall organizational situation with a view to formulating major policy proposals and establishing their priorities. This research approach is seen to be most relevant for dealing with the major policy issues discussed in Chapter 10. Specifically, policy research is designed to address strategic questions, and to do so from a pre-action perspective. That is, it encompasses the analysis and planning stages of the management process.

However, each major issue facing the tourism sector will eventually need to be researched using all five approaches if tourism programmes are to be designed, developed and implemented effectively. It is with this in mind that the framework for developing an overall research agenda for the tourism sector has been developed. Accordingly, the approach followed in the remainder of this paper has been based on two main elements:

1   A limited set of policy issues which are considered of highest priority have been retained for detailed analysis from the standpoint of developing a research agenda.
2   For each of these priority areas in tourism, an attempt has been made to identify a research agenda in which suggestions are made concerning the kinds of research projects that exemplify each of the five major research approaches.

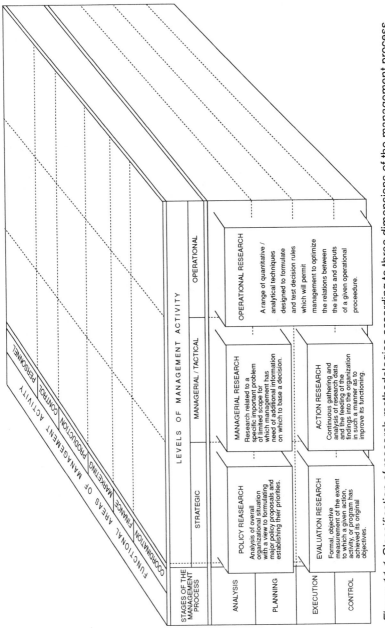

Figure 11.1 Classification of research methodologies according to three dimensions of the management process

A RESEARCH AGENDA FOR TOURISM

Based on the foregoing discussion, an attempt has been made to develop a framework within which a research agenda for tourism for the 1990s and beyond might be formulated. This framework is presented in Tables 11.1 to 11.7. As can be seen, selected examples of the kinds of research relevant to seven major policy areas are explicitly identified and classified in accordance with the roles of the research framework in Figure 11.1. It should be emphasized that the specific research needs identified within each of the categories are by no means considered exhaustive. However, they are considered to be representative of the kinds of research which are required in each of these areas, as well as being substantive in their own right. It is hoped that the overall framework, as well as the specific examples, will provide a basis for identifying additional critical research areas and for providing suggestions for comparative research in different countries and destinations.

THE ACADEMIC COMMUNITY AS A SIGNIFICANT PLAYER IN FULFILLING THE RESEARCH AGENDA

It is felt that it would not be appropriate to conclude this discussion of a research agenda for tourism for the 1990s and beyond without seriously addressing how some of the research contained in this agenda might be carried out. Clearly, the operational research needs that are identified will be of interest primarily to those organizations and/or individuals whose success is most directly affected by the operational issues involved. The managerial and action research type projects which are outlined will also be of primary interest to a particular firm or operator. However, they may also be of interest to a broader audience such as the members of a destination management organization (for example, a convention and visitor bureau). Certain of these issues may also be of interest to policy makers and some members of the academic community. Finally, the studies which fall into the category of strategic research are obviously of most direct interest to policy makers and academics. Policy makers will tend to focus on research which addresses a strategic issue of immediate concern. While academics may also wish to focus their efforts on such topics, they have an interest in more fundamental or basic research addressing major issues with medium- to long-term implications. Academics may also be prepared to attack more complex issues involving greater ambiguity and the need to interpret nuances.

Table 11.1 A research agenda for tourism and the environment on centre stage (selected examples)

Research type	Research
Strategic	
Policy research	Value research – identifying and measuring the values which drive/should drive tourism development
	Assessment of alternative planning methods for reaching workable/acceptable consensus concerning directions for tourism development
	Measuring and balancing environmental and development impacts
	Measuring and managing cultural and social 'pollution'
	How to best develop educational programmes which provide a balanced perspective on the environment and the economy
Evaluation research	Assessment of the effectiveness of programmes designed to protect the environment in the face of tourism development (e.g. Canadian Government's 'Green Plan')
Managerial	
Managerial research	Assessment of environmental impact of alternative Olympic sites with a view to choice of best location
	Assessment of architectural designs of a resort to maximize compatibility with the local ecology
Action research	Monitoring of changes in tourism profiles and behaviour patterns as protected areas are opened up to visitors
	Tracking of changes in wildlife behaviour and reproductive patterns during the establishment of new recreation areas
Operational	
Operational research	Determining the most appropriate location and design of an information programme to explain proper use of protected areas
	Assessing the effectiveness of a new interpretive centre in encouraging more responsible behaviour by visitors to a sensitive areas

Table 11.2 A research agenda to encourage and facilitate resident responsive tourism (selected examples)

Research type	Research needs
Strategic	
Policy research	Methodologies for improving public participation/input into tourism development priorities and directions
	Establishing the role, impact and acceptability of non-resident ownership of tourism facilities/services
	Formulation of a local vision for tourism development
Evaluation research	Assessing the impact of a programme to enhance public participation in tourism planning and development
	Determing the impacts of foreign ownership on resident support for tourism
Managerial	
Managerial research	Determining the best location and design for a major new convention centre so as to provide the best mix of market appeal and local benefits
	Design of a cost effective programme to provide information to the community concerning tourism impacts and issues
Action research	Assessment of the on-going implementation of a programme to enhance resident reception of visitors
	Assessment of the effectiveness of promotion programmes to attract visitors seeking experiences comparable to those offered by the region
Operational	
Operational research	Determining which kind of traffic signage meets the needs of both residents and visitors
	Determining where to locate city-related information so as to benefit both residents and visitors

Table 11.3 A research agenda related to tourism and changing global
demographics and lifestyles (selected examples)

Research type	*Research needs*
Strategic	
Policy research	Understanding the nature and distribution of global demographic trends and their implications for tourism
	Identifying a destination's competitive advantages/weaknesses in relation to the ageing populations of tourism generating countries
Evaluation research	Assessing the effectiveness/impacts of major promotion programmes aimed at specific demographic segments of the market
	Assessing how well service/facility modifications to meet the needs of an ageing clientele are being implemented and received
Managerial	
Managerial research	Determining how the ideal or desired travel experience for a particular destination varies across different demographic segments of the market
	Understanding how older, experienced travellers modify their choice and travel behaviour over an extended period of time and how these changes should be addressed
Action research	Monitoring the implementation of a programme to attract seniors back into the ski market
	Monitoring the adaptation of travel programmes desired to educate different age groups over a period of time (e.g. language, cultural, educational travel)
Operational	
Operational research	Determining the special travel needs of the growing female segment of the business market
	Identifying the specialized convention needs of associations focused on the interests of seniors

Table 11.4 A research agenda for tourism to better understand the impact of the trend to market driven economies, deregulation and privatization (selected examples)

Research type	Research needs
Strategic	
Policy research	Identifying those aspects of the tourism facilities and services infrastructure which are likely to be favoured or neglected by the trend towards privatization brought about by a market economy emphasis
	Determining the impact which alternative national policies re airline ownership might have on the nature and extent of tourism development of a country or region.
Evaluation research	Assessing which approaches to tourism development are most appropriate for countries/destinations making major shifts from a centrally administered to a market driven economy
	Assessing the extent to which the shift from public funding to user fees for the use of various tourism facilities and services impacts on different segments of the population
Managerial	
Managerial research	Determining how best to privatize a tourism facility or resource which is currently owned by the public sector
	Identifying the most effective ways to antici-pate and deal with complaints that are likely to arise from the privatization of facilities and services which were previously publicly owned
Action research	Implementation of a programme to modify personnel hiring and training practices as a result of privatization
	Monitoring the acceptance by residents of a transnational corporation which establishes a new resort in a destination
Operational	
Operational research	Determining appropriate admission charges to a privatized facility which was previously free of charge
	Determining the market viability of various types of services which were previously provided free or at low cost

Table 11.5 A research agenda for tourism related to the North–South gap and the resulting frictions (selected examples)

Research type	Research needs
Strategic	
Policy research	Identification of the major sources of tourism friction between developed and developing countries with a view to establishing their seriousness, generalizability and possibility of resolution
	Identification of the kinds of bilateral/multilateral cooperation/collaboration that are most likely to contribute to successful tourism development in emerging countries
Evaluation research	Assessment of the effectiveness of alternative approaches which have been tried for enhancing tourism development in Third World countries
Managerial	
Managerial research	Identifying the appropriate travel experiences which can/should be offered by a developing country
	Identifying the target markets most likely to be attracted to the appropriate travel experiences offered by a developing country
Action research	Assessment of the implementation of tourism education and training programmes to develop managers and staff in a particular country or region
	Assessing the implementation of programmes to introduce appropriate technology within the tourism sector in emerging destinations
Operational	
Operational research	Determining minimal acceptable standards for sanitation and health services provided to visitors from developed to developing countries and how to operationalize these minimums
	Determining how best to facilitate tourist entry/exit without compromising national integrity

Table 11.6 A research agenda for tourism and its human resource needs
(selected examples)

Research type	Research needs
Strategic	
Policy research	Determination of the short-, medium- and long-term human resource needs of the tourism sector both in terms of management and staff
	Determination of the most appropriate/ effective education and training approaches for each type of career path
	Determination of what constitutes true quality of service for different market segments
Evaluation research	Assessing the effectiveness/impact of standards and certification programmes designed to upgrade/enhance quality of service
	Assessing the impact of improved staff qualifications on profitability in the industry
Managerial	
Managerial research	Determination of the most effective content and delivery methods for advanced programmes for senior executives in tourism
	Determination of appropriate course content for high school courses to introduce tourism at the secondary school level
Action research	Implementation of a cooperative education programme – identifying the determinants of success
Operational	
Operational research	Determining the specific skills which need to be included in occupational standards leading to certification

Table 11.7 A research agenda for tourism concerning the impact of technology on tourism (selected examples)

Research type	Research needs
Strategic	
Policy research	Analysis of major emerging technologies and their potential for impact on the tourism sector
	Identification of the major barriers to greater use of technology within different areas of tourism
Evaluation research	Analysis of the impact which various technologies have had on the competitive position and profitability of various tourism destinations and firms
	Assessment of the impact of programmes to encourage the adoption of specific technologies by the tourism industry
Managerial	
Managerial research	Determination of which computer reservation system is most appropriate for a given firm
	Assessment of the potential value/impact of teleconferencing on a proposed convention/meeting facility
Action research	Monitoring the impacts of implementation of a new electronic mail system among partners in a tourism destination
	Monitoring the establishment of a new video information service for visitors
Operational	
Operational research	Determination of the most effective approach to automated hotel check-out
	Determination of optimal design and location of a new high speed ski lift

In any event, from the perspective of the author, it is argued that tourism academics have a major obligation to contribute to the development of knowledge in the field. It is assumed that in the main they will focus on those kinds of research which are of interest to them and where they are best equipped to contribute. As indicated above, this largely pertains to the study of fundamental issues having long-term consequences. Unfortunately, such projects often require a major commitment of time, energy and resources. While the time and energy are often available, resources are frequently in short supply in the academic community. Therefore, if academics are to make the contributions of which they are capable, it will be necessary to identify highly cost effective research approaches to the study of large scale problems which are often international in scope. To date, the academic community has not been very successful in this type of research. Rather, it has tended to focus its energies on more narrowly defined issues where data can be collected locally and therefore inexpensively.

What is needed in these circumstances is the creation of a significant new organizational network which will enable academics to build on their major strength (that is, highly focused local competence), while minimizing one of the greatest barriers to research on meaningful topics (that is, limited financial resources). Specifically, modern technology might be utilized to create what will be termed a Global Tourism Research Network (GTRN). In essence, the proposed network would be a voluntary arrangement whereby committed centres in various parts of the world would agree to participate in research as members of an ongoing network. While varying degrees of commitment to a research programme for such a network are possible, it is believed that even a minimal commitment would be a good starting point. As an example, preliminary terms of reference for such a possible network are presented in Table 11.8.

Three possible levels of commitment might be considered in establishing this network:

1   An agreement to simply collect data for one another on a reciprocal basis. In such a case, the data collection instruments would be developed at a given centre and administrated cooperatively throughout the network.
2   At a second level of commitment, it might be possible to identify common research priorities and conduct joint research. This could be carried out by all members of the network or simply by a subset.

Table 11.8 A proposed terms of reference for a global tourism research network

---

Overall structure and purpose

The Global Tourism Reseach Network is a consortium of academic research institutions which have entered into a voluntary agreement to cooperate and assist each other in the design, execution and reporting of research intended to advance our understanding of the field of tourism.

Roles of the network

1   To provide a vehicle for identifying priority areas of research as defined by the interests of the members of the network.

2   To provide a vehicle for assisting members of the network to collect research data for the global/international level at significantly lower costs than would otherwise be possible.

Functioning of the network

1   It is intended that members of the network will communicate primarily via electronic means. As such, members should be a member of or have ready access to the BITNET electronic mail communication network and/or its equivalent in other countries.

2   The underlying philosophy is that bureaucracy and the cost associated with the operation of the network should be kept to a minimum; to the greatest extent possible, any expenditures incurred should be related to the collection of data and the dissemination of research findings.

3   Membership in the network is voluntary; however, members of the network who do not collaborate on a regular, dependable and reciprocal basis should not expect to continue to benefit from membership in the network.

4   The University of Calgary is prepared to act as coordinator of the network. However, it is expected that individual members of the network should and will take the initiative in making suggestions concerning research projects and/or other appropriate activities for network members.

---

3   As a third and perhaps ultimate level of commitment, it might be feasible to develop a common research programme and a joint publication vehicle within which the results of common research could be disseminated.

Perhaps the greatest strength of the above approach is that it provides a very cost-effective means for the generation of data on a global basis by people who truly understand the local situation and who have recognized expertise in the area of tourism research.

CONCLUSION

In summary, for reasons of need, and as a consequence of the means made available by modern technology, it is felt that the time has come for the creation of some mechanism such as the Global Tourism Research Network. Through the creation of such a network, the development of the research agenda proposed in this chapter becomes more than an academic exercise. Indeed, it is believed that by means of the network, academics would have in their grasp a unique mechanism for providing true research leadership for the global tourism industry of the future.

Finally, the questions raised here, together with those of earlier chapters, underline the challenges facing researchers today, provide direction for future efforts in this field and demonstrate the contribution of research to tourism management, planning, policy and development.

REFERENCES

Ritchie, J. R. B. (1975) 'Some critical aspects of measurement theory and practice in travel research', *Journal of Travel Research* 13, 1.

Ritchie, J. R. B. (1987) 'Roles of research in tourism management', in J. R. B. Ritchie and C. R. Goeldner (eds) *Travel, Tourism and Hospitality Research*, New York: Wiley.

Ritchie, J. R. B. and Goeldner, C. R. (eds) (1987) *Travel, Tourism and Hospitality Research: a Handbook for Managers and Researchers*, New York: Wiley.

TTRA (1991) *Tourism: Building Credibility for a Credible Industry*, Proceedings of the 1991 Annual Conference of the Travel and Tourism Research Association, Salt Lake City: University of Utah.

Index

Thailand; Third World; United
Kingdom; United States
touristologue 84–6
trading blocs 196
training 179, 193; Third World
promoters 73–7
transferability 24–5
transnational corporations 78, 97–8,
182, 196–7
transport *see* airlines; infrastructure
travel 11; career tapestry 124–32; *see
also* tourism
Travis, A. 27, 30, 31
Triandis, H. 91
Trinidad 100
Trip Index 28
Turks and Caicos Islands 143
Turner, V.W. 42
Twain, M. 119
typologies *see* classifications and
typologies

unavoidable, development seen as
145
United Kingdom and tourism 23, 24,
30, 91, 94, 100; impact assessment
140, 147, 150; rural areas 158–9,
162, 164–5; tourists from 91, 92,
95, 96
United States and tourism 22–3, 24,
93, 99, 100, 183; accountability
research 4; deregulation 195;
impact assessment 147, 150;
national parks 25; perceptions of
Indians 59, 62; rural areas 159,
162, 164–5; security problems
175; tourists from 90–1, 92, 95,
96, 104, 105; transnationals 197
USSR, former 98
Uysal, M. 28

Valentine, E.R. 121
values 116
van den Berghe, P.L. 37, 103
Var, T. 93
variables, independent 21–2, 30, 31;
see also 'nationality' and 'country

of residence'
Vassiliou, V. 91
Venezuela, tourism in 175, 183
Vienna, tourism in 29
Vienne, B. 59
Virgin Islands, tourism in 90
Vogeler, I. 156
Vroom, V.H. 122

Waldbrook, L. 163
Wales, tourism in 94
Walker, M.B. 2
Wall, G. 91, 105, 136, 138, 140, 143,
145
Warwick, D.P. 21, 30
Washington (DC) 175
water resources management 169–70
Waugh, A. 158–9
Weber, S. 3
Weiner, B. 116
West, S.J. 27, 32
Wetherell, M. 117
Wheatcroft, S. 24
White, K.J. 2
White, R.W. 116
Williams, A. 21, 157
Wilson, T.D. 128
world *see* global; globalization
World Health Organization 196
World Tourism Organization 175–6,
178, 196
World Travel and Tourism Council
175–6, 178–9
Wright, C. 140
WTCC *see* World Travel and
Tourism Council
WTO *see* World Tourism
Organization
Wynegar, D. 4

Ya'ari, E. 53
Young, G. 53, 119
Yuan, S. 91
Yugoslavia 98; tourism in 30, 94, 175

Ziff-Levine, W. 4
Zinder, H. 137